YALE CLASSICAL STUDIES

Adam Parry, Yale University

Frontispiece

YALE CLASSICAL STUDIES

EDITED FOR THE DEPARTMENT OF CLASSICS

by

DONALD KAGAN

VOLUME XXIV
STUDIES IN
THE GREEK HISTORIANS

IN MEMORY OF
ADAM PARRY

CAMBRIDGE UNIVERSITY PRESS

CAMBRIDGE

LONDON · NEW YORK · MELBOURNE

Published by the Syndics of the Cambridge University Press
The Pitt Building, Trumpington Street, Cambridge CB2 1RP
Bentley House, 200 Euston Road, London NW1 2DB
32 East 57th Street, New York, NY 10022, USA
296 Beaconsfield Parade, Middle Park, Melbourne 3206, Australia

Library of Congress catalogue card number: 74–12982

ISBN 0 521 20587 5

First published 1975

Printed in Great Britain
at the University Printing House, Cambridge
(Euan Phillips, University Printer)

Contents

Adam Parry Yale University,   *frontispiece*

Preface   *page* vii

In Memoriam Adam and Anne Parry   E. A. Havelock   ix

Learning through suffering? Croesus' conversations
in the history of Herodotus
     Hans-Peter Stahl   I

An Athenian generation gap
     W. G. Forrest   37

Thucydides' judgment of Periclean strategy
     George Cawkwell   53

The speeches in Thucydides and the Mytilene debate
     Donald Kagan   71

Xenophon, Diodorus and the year 379/378 B.C.
Reconstruction and reappraisal
     David G. Rice   95

Aristotle's *Athenaion Politeia* and the establishment of
the Thirty Tyrants
     W. James McCoy   131

Nearchus the Cretan
     E. Badian   147

Myth and *archaeologia* in Italy and Sicily – Timaeus
and his predecessors
     Lionel Pearson   171

Symploke: its role in Polybius' Histories
     F. W. Walbank   197

Plutarch and the Megarian decree
     Charles Fornara   213

Herodian and Elagabalus
     G. W. Bowersock   229

Preface

THE PLAN for this volume was conceived by Christopher M.
Dawson, who took the first steps in soliciting contributions to it.
His death on 27 April 1972 left the task of completing the under-
taking to the present editor. The subject seems a fitting memorial
to Adam Parry, for his most important and original work was on
Thucydides, and he was always fascinated by the relationship
between history and literature. The present volume tries to present
an unusually broad panorama of the varieties of Greek historical
writing. Chronologically, the historians treated range from the
father of history in the fifth century B.C. to Herodian, who lived
into the third century of the Christian era, and almost every
century in between is represented. Geographically, they came
from as far west as Sicily and as far east as Syria. They had in
common the Greek language and the tradition of historical writing
which is a distinguishing feature of Greek culture.

Not all the authors treated are historians, strictly speaking.
Plutarch is a biographer, the 'Old Oligarch' wrote a political
treatise, Aristophanes is a comedian and Aristotle a philosopher.
But all are important historical sources. Plutarch, moreover, is at
least a quasi-historian while Aristotle's treatise on the Athenian
Constitution is in part an attempt at history. They all deserve
discussion in a volume on the Greek historians.

Finally, the contributors to this volume examine their subjects
from different points of view. Some consider their value as historical
sources. Others deal with problems of historical method. Still
others treat ideas that arise from the works of the historian. This
variety of treatment is in keeping with the volume's intention to
see the Greek historian in the broadest context.

New Haven   *January 1974*

[vii]

Adam and Anne Parry

Ob. June 1971

ADAM PARRY was born in Paris forty-three years ago and although he was to spend most of his life in the United States it is fair to say that his personal style always had in it a faint flavour of France and French culture. His father at that time was attending the Sorbonne where he published the thesis, heralding a new era in Homeric scholarship, to which his son, forty years later, was to pay signal tribute. The elder Parry, himself, was a graduate of Berkeley, but on his appointment to the Harvard faculty in the department of Classics the family moved to Cambridge, Massachusetts. Their travels were not ended. It was with the aid of a grant from the university that Adam's father was enabled to pursue those studies in the oral poetry of Southern Yugoslavia which were to confirm the thesis that the Homeric poems were orally composed. He took his family to Yugoslavia with him. One of Adam's earliest memories was a recollection of the great blue pot of goat's milk simmering on the stove. There at an impressionable age he encountered hardy men and strenuous conditions of living, while his eyes rested on the rugged mountains of the Balkan peninsula, a Homeric landscape haunted by memories of latter-day heroes. Soon after their return to the United States the father's life by tragic accident was ended before it had scarcely begun, and Adam's mother took the family with her back to California. It was at Berkeley that Adam, like his father, achieved his initial mastery over the Greek tongue. He owed a debt to some great teachers there, not least to Ivan Linforth and Harold Cherniss, names honored in our profession and whom he honored himself as I have heard him testify, for he was a man who had a nice understanding of those pieties which are proper to the scholar's vocation, and on occasional visits to Berkeley in later years he was glad to seize the opportunity of calling on Professor Linforth in his retirement.

From Berkeley he came to Harvard and to the scholars of Harvard – let me mention in particular John Finley his father's colleague and friend, and Cedric Whitman his near contemporary – in whose classrooms and company he encountered those influences which at once enlarged the humanity of his interests and sharpened his critical intelligence. The years of graduate study were interrupted by a year's return to France as a Fulbright scholar at the Sorbonne, where his father had studied twenty-five years before. And then in the spring of 1952 he confronted his examiners – I happened to be one of them – in the preliminaries to the Harvard Ph.D. In academic circles it is not usual to commemorate the examinations we may have passed in the course of gaining our professional standing. They involve experiences which most of us, I am sure, would, for ourselves, prefer to forget. But never shall I forget the brilliance of that oral confrontation in which the examiners instead of controlling the candidate cheerfully surrendered control to him as he led us through a critical review of the literatures of Greece and Rome. Here, it was clear, was a man who in his own time might leave a stamp upon Greek and Latin scholarship.

However, the completion of the thesis did not follow automatically. He had to earn a living for himself and his family. Always versatile as well as vigorous, he had partly supported himself at Berkeley by serving as a seaman on the Seattle run, and in fact held a union card. As a graduate student at Harvard he did not hesitate to supplement the meager earnings of a graduate fellowship by becoming a taxi driver. The streets of Boston provide a test of driving skill second to none in America. His instructors can remember him showing up for classes and conferences still attired in his taxi-driver's uniform. So now he accepted an appointment as instructor at Amherst College. It was characteristic of his enterprise and his ability to respond to students and student needs that while there in his spare time he offered a voluntary class in elementary Russian. It was at the height of the cold-war frenzy, and it is perhaps a reflection on the Amherst of those days that this small contribution to the cause of education when it became known did not do him much good. Now, in retrospect, we can salute his courage, and also his intuition of what was to become a pressing need in the area of language instruction in this country in years to come. At Amherst he encountered fresh scholarly company in the persons of John Moore, Wendell Clausen and Thomas Gould. If I have named names among his friends, it is because part of Adam's quality and his contribution to humane letters in this country and abroad lay in the conversations and the intellectual exchanges which he shared with colleagues in our profession. Where others may have preferred to give their professional best to their books he gave much of his to the minds of those whom he encountered in the voyage of life. That is one reason why his departure means such an irreparable loss. Aristotle long ago pointed out the relationship between friendship and a special kind of rational consciousness, and though I am sure that Adam would wish me to say that Aristotle was not his favorite author, his own life-style was a living exposition of certain doctrines which one encounters towards the conclusion of the ninth book of the *Nicomachean Ethics*.

After three years at Amherst, Professor Frank Brown on behalf of the Yale department invited him to come down to New Haven, and here for five years he served his Yale apprenticeship, first as instructor and then as Assistant Professor. It was during these early years, and before attaining the doctorate, that his first published works appeared in book form, both of them translations. In the first, he united his talents with those of Barbara Parry to translate from the French the Sather lectures delivered by Professor Festugière, *Personal Religion Among the Greeks*, and this was followed by a translation from the modern Greek of a chapter in a volume published in Leiden dealing with the imagery of the Igor Tale. Already he was showing that the range of his linguistic abilities and literary interests extended beyond the classical tongues.

In the spring of 1957 he completed his Harvard dissertation, '*Logos* and *Ergon* in Thucydides'. Its direction, carried on mainly by correspondence, became a dialogue for which I shall always be grateful. This unpublished work began to assume an importance, in the eyes of those who read it, not usually accorded to a doctoral thesis. At Oxford the informal suggestion was heard that it be published virtually as it stood. But Adam rejected an opportunity which he considered premature and which a scholar of less integrity might have jumped at. The completion of the book on *The Mind of Thucydides* was the project to which, had his life been spared, he was preparing to devote his immediate energies. It is possible to predict that in this work he would have exposed to view some new perspectives in classical scholarship which are made possible by applying the concepts and methods of intellectual history.

He next received a Morse fellowship from Yale, and spent a year in England as a Research Associate at University College, London. This second period of study abroad, during which he lectured at various institutions, provided opportunity for an enlargement of his professional circle to include many friends and admirers in the English university and classical community. A year later the Harvard department invited him, as it had invited his father before him, to accept an Assistant Professorship, but his stay at Harvard was cut short when Amherst in the succeeding year and perhaps in repentant mood invited him to return on tenure appointment. Short as was his tour of duty at Harvard, his colleagues of that year can recall how much he put into it, how unsparingly he gave his leisure to his tutorials and students, and what energy he threw into the task, a thankless one at times, of directing the Greek play, the *Ajax* of Sophocles, in which, suitably equipped with tunic, spear and greaves, he took the lead role, supported by his younger son.

Amherst in turn had to yield him up to Yale, where he returned as Associate Professor in 1962. Six years later found him as full Professor and Chairman of the department. It was just after he had accepted, with some reluctance, reappointment for an extra fourth year that his life was cut short.

In April of 1966 he had married Anne Reinberg Amory who herself at that time was a visiting lecturer in the Yale department, and it is fitting that we remember her with an equal affection and an equal sense of professional as well as personal loss. Anne like him had from her early years known what it is to be a traveler in distant places and venturesome surroundings. She had frequently been her father's companion in the course of his visits to South America and to the mining towns of Peru. Vassar College where she took her B.A. remembers her academic brilliance and her vigorous leadership in student activities. At Harvard she presented her thesis, on the topic of the treatment of 'Dreams in Homer's Odyssey', in the same spring of that year in which Adam presented his, a fortuitous coincidence. It is perhaps permissible here on this last occasion devoted to her memory that I record, as a personal recollection of my own, the fact that the Harvard department at that time would have given serious consideration to her appointment as an instructor, if her plans had not called for her to follow her first husband to California. This was some years before the Women's Liberation movement had begun to make such appointments more fashionable than they once were.

She began teaching at Berkeley that same fall and after an interlude of part-time teaching at Mills College she was appointed a lecturer and then Assistant Professor in the Berkeley Classics department, a post she left in 1965 to join the Yale faculty. Her marriage to Adam terminated her tour of duty in the Yale Classics department, but she accepted a post at the Connecticut College for Women, and in 1970 was appointed Associate Professor of Classics at the University of Massachusetts in Amherst.

As a career woman devoting her life to teaching and scholarship, and possessed of a social charm which could equal her husband's, she was united with him not only in a marriage of minds but in a partnership of hospitality. Entering their door, one was likely to encounter conversation lively or learned, amusing or serious, in the company of friends not only of the Yale community, but of that larger fraternity of scholarship which extends across America and reaches into Europe. Despite her domestic preoccupations, Anne found time for authorship. With Professor Mason Hammond she collaborated in the composition of a Latin Reader published by the Harvard Press and contributed a chapter on the *Odyssey* edited by the provost of this University. Readers of her article on Lucretius, 'Science and Poetry in *De Rerum Natura*', which appeared in the twenty-first volume of *Yale Classical Studies*, will recognize that she was a sensitive critic of Latin literature no less than Greek. Posthumously the house of Brill in Holland will publish a monograph of hers on Homeric formulaic verse, and she was at the time of her death already planning a wise and witty book on the role of *Women in Antiquity*. Those who had been privileged to hear excerpts of this work from her own lips realize how much better equipped she was for such a task than certain male authors who have been unwise enough to attempt it.

Our memorial, in its close, returns to her husband from whom in death she was not divided. Of his own publications it has been said that a page from Parry was often worth a chapter from somebody else. He was the kind of writer whom people often like to cite or quote and also to reprint. Students of the scholarship surrounding Homer will be aware how often an essay of his of only seven pages on the 'Language of Achilles' is now cited by writers in this field, as well as having been reprinted in a work of standard reference, *The Language and Background of Homer*, published by the Cambridge University Press. With that same press, a day or two before he died, he had completed a contract to act as an American editor of the forthcoming *Cambridge History of Classical Literature*, but in the conduct of this magisterial enterprise his influence and judgment will now be absent.

He shared with Anne that fundamental training in Classics which enabled him to move as easily in the field of Latin studies as Greek. His memorable essay on 'The Two Voices of Virgil's *Aeneid*', which when it first appeared in *Arion* broke new critical ground, was promptly reprinted in the volume of Virgil which is included in the series *Twentieth Century Views*. By the time of his death he had completed and published two books. One, written some years ago in collaboration with Robert Fagles, supplied an English version and commentary for the Greek dithyrambic poet Bacchylides. This contribution of his to scholarship, even if not a major achievement, will always remind us how he combined to a unique degree philological accuracy with literary acumen. The book by which he will be most remembered, and which indeed may become a famous book of its sort, is that which at last emerged from the Clarendon Press a few months before his death. *The Making of Homeric Verse* is at once a memorial to his father's genius and to his own, notable not less for the masterly editing of his father's life-work than for the comprehensive survey of the Homeric Problem which the son wrote by way of introduction, and in which he not only traced the course of its evolution from its beginnings to the solutions achieved by Milman Parry, but did not hesitate to forecast certain steps which may still have to be taken before the final formulation is achieved. Of what these might be he had already given some indication in the twentieth volume of *Yale Classical Studies*, in his article 'Have We Homer's Iliad?'

On the Thursday after the accident in France which took both lives there appeared a letter in the London *Times* from which I will be permitted to quote a few sentences:

'By their premature deaths classical scholarship has suffered a devastating blow. Parry was a brilliant Greek scholar, one of the very best of his generation. He was one of the very few, can there be more than three or four others, who could apply to Greek and Latin poetry the kind of discrimination that is sometimes directed to modern literatures. His wife's qualities too were unusual ones and complemented those of her husband's. She too had a keen interest in Homer and ranged over Latin poetry as well. Both of them were warm delightful people who might have been formidable but were not, both had the gift of civilized hospitality and friendship. There are many in Europe and America who will not forget them.'

The letter carried the initials GSK, HLl-J and DLP, the signatures of the professors of Greek respectively at Bristol, Oxford and Cambridge Universities, all of whom, as colleagues or visitors in in the Department of Classics, had shared Adam and Anne's company and know their work during the Yale years.

E. A. HAVELOCK

This obituary was read at a memorial service held in Battell Chapel in Yale University on October 6, 1971.

Learning through suffering?
Croesus' conversations in the
history of Herodotus

HANS-PETER STAHL

I. The national and the human theme

HERODOTUS has organized the vast material of his work in a way which allows him to accentuate two major themes:

I. The long fight between Greeks and non-Greeks, including the question of war guilt.

This subject is so important to the historian that it overrides even a major structural principle of his, i.e. the chronological succession of Persian kings. By starting his work with the Lydian king Croesus, the first man he 'knows' to have harmed the Greeks (τὸν δὲ οἶδα αὐτὸς πρῶτον ὑπάρξαντα ἀδίκων ἔργων ἐς τοὺς ῞Ελληνας, I. 5. 3),[1] Herodotus is forced to break up the continuum of Persian history at a later point of his work:[2] having related Croesus' defeat at the hands of the Persian King Cyrus II, in 547/6 B.C., he must make a digression to inform his reader about the earlier Median–Persian history in general and Cyrus' personal career specifically,[3] before resuming his narrative which from now on will generally follow the chronology of Persian kings (although digressions are not banned).[4]

II. The general instability of human conditions.

This theme is not referred to in the work's opening sentence

---

1. Cf. 6. 2 πρῶτος τῶν ἡμεῖς ἴδμεν, and see also the proem's words δι' ἣν αἰτίην ἐπολέμησαν ἀλλήλοισι.

2. Cf. H. R. Immerwahr, *Form and Thought in Herodotus* (Cleveland 1966), pp. 40f.

3. I. 95–130; note the acknowledgment of reversed time order in 130. 3: Κῦρος...Κροῖσον ὕστερον τούτων...κατεστρέψατο ὡς εἴρηταί μοι πρότερον; cf. ὀπίσω, 75. I.

4. The latest account (given by a historian) of Herodotus' apparent *Verstoss* against his own *Schema* may be found in A. Heuss' thoughtful article 'Motive von Herodots lydischem Logos' (*Hermes* 101 (1973), 387ff.). From a literary reading, I am not able to confirm Heuss' initial charges (pp. 387ff.), that Herodotus contradicts his own evidence as early as I. 5–14.

[I]

which invites readers to expect conventional aspects of writing as they are expressed in the poetic tradition deriving from Homer: a writer saves human achievements from oblivion. But the theme is mentioned as soon as Herodotus, áfter dismissing some untrustworthy mythical constructions about war guilt (1. 1–5. 2), returns to the description of his own interests (ἐγὼ δὲ...5. 3). Here he surprises his reader by the paradox that he will treat large and small states of men on an equal basis (because 'large' and 'small' prove to be no lasting predicates in history). He can do so because he 'knows' that human welfare is never stable, τὴν ἀνθρωπηίην ὦν ἐπιστάμενος εὐδαιμονίην οὐδαμὰ ἐν τὠυτῷ μένουσαν (5. 4). What lasts in history is change, we are to understand from the introduction's last sentence.

While theme I influences the order of facts as recorded in Herodotus' work, theme II concerns the meaning of the facts recorded. And, as theme I is important enough to demand an occasional deviation from the principle of chronological succession, theme II may occasionally have priority even over the facts themselves. As I have argued elsewhere,[5] Herodotus has not generally achieved the high qualities of a Thucydides whose literary art can create a homogeneous unity of facts and of meaning so that the facts themselves become symbolic. The kind of discrepancy between facts and meaning found in Herodotus may be illustrated from the account he gives of how Croesus' ancestor Gyges came to seize the throne of Lydia (1. 8–13). According to his narrative, Gyges, being a loyal advisor of ill-fated King Candaules, was forced by Candaules' wife, against his own will, to become a usurper (...με ἀναγκάζεις δεσπότεα τὸν ἐμὸν κτείνειν οὐκ ἐθέλοντα, 11. 4) – a truly tragic situation. Herodotus has carried the theme of human instability, which here stresses despair and humiliation, so far that in the end he fails to reconcile his own account with the given historical fact that there existed partisans willing to fight for Gyges' cause (οἱ τοῦ Γύγεω στασιῶται, 13. 1) against the party of assassinated King Candaules. How can a loyal advisor and involuntary usurper have political followers?

If, for the sake of theme I, Herodotus is willing to disregard the major structural principle of his work in order to present the story of Croesus first, we are encouraged to ask how much of theme II

5. See 'Herodots Gyges-Tragödie', *Hermes* 96 (1968), 385ff., 400.

he has incorporated into the same opening story of his work. Now any reader of Book I will confirm that King Croesus' rule contains the exposition of the human theme as well as introducing us to the fight of Greeks and Barbarians. And we also know that, for instance, its most famous part, the conversation between Solon the wise and Croesus the blind, is not historical (because, at the supposed time of the meeting, Solon was already dead). Therefore we may feel tempted to postulate that, wherever Herodotus' narrative transcends historical facts known to him, he wishes to tell us something about the meaning of his historiography. However, we have no general certainty about when he departs from the facts or when he stays within their limits, and therefore, alas, we must drop our methodical postulate the moment we envisage it. What we can do is to trace carefully the literary presentation of human instability (theme II) throughout the narrative about Croesus. In doing so, I wish to take the position that literary composition starts even before and extends as far as Croesus appears as an agent in the work, but does not stop e.g. with Croesus being rescued from the pyre by Apollo. In other words: if for Croesus, i.e. the first of the Greeks' enemies, Herodotus is willing to break up the order suggested by Persian history (which would demand Media-Persia and Cyrus to be treated before Lydia and Croesus), we should ask whether the historian does not make use of his peculiar arrangement of facts also and even more on the second level (i.e. that of meaning). Precisely formulated, our question should be: Does Herodotus, by giving literary precedence to Croesus' fortune and fall, influence our understanding of his ensuing report on Cyrus' success and failure? My answer, of course, will be yes.

II. King Croesus' blindness and fall

Naturally, my thesis, although leading up to Croesus' role in the fate of Cyrus, presupposes a correct understanding of Croesus' own story as told in Herodotus' literary categories. Therefore I shall first give a short paraphrase of chapters 5–92 of Book I, centering on those features that point forward to events narrated later. And although my narrative will move over a field well ploughed by scholarship, I shall for the sake of brevity refrain from listing agreements and discrepancies with the accounts given by others.[6]

A fairly reliable guide to key sections of Herodotus' narrative, beside comments in his own voice, is his use of direct discourse or even dialogue as well as questions put to, and answers given by, oracles (after all, a sort of dialogue, too). The first section thus marked is Gyges' tragic rise to power (9–13). Gyges' story is part of Herodotus' account of Croesus, because, among other reasons, Gyges, first ruler of the Mermnad dynasty, by his act of usurpation determines the fate of Croesus, his fourth successor and the last ruler of the Mermnad family. According to a Delphic oracle, revenge will come four generations later. According to Herodotus, however, the Mermnadae (Croesus included) did not pay any attention to the oracle – at least not before it was fulfilled (13. 2). By telling us this much in advance, Herodotus grants his reader an insight which goes beyond his Croesus' viewpoint. We readers know that – after Ardys, Alyattes, Sadyattes – Croesus represents the fourth generation down from Gyges, and therefore we see his success against the background of his expected doom, and all his smart reasoning appears to us as the cleverness of the ignorant, if not worse: of the forgetful, who could know better but belongs to those who do not pay attention. Through his ancestor Gyges, the story of Croesus' life has begun long before he is actually born and ascended the throne, in two respects: (a) he will have to pay for the past, and (b) he does not know what can and should be known.

From the beginning, Croesus' problem as presented by Herodotus is a lack of knowledge. Can the information gap that should not exist be closed by help from outside? Although a first approach may suggest a positive answer (Croesus does listen to advice and, accepting wise Bias' warning, refrains from waging naval war against the superior Greek islanders, 27), the reaction of Croesus, by now at the peak of his power, to the considerations of Solon the

6. Of the interpretations known to me, I feel closest to Walter Marg's '"Selbstsicherheit" bei Herodot', *Studies presented to D. M. Robinson on his 70th Birthday* (St. Louis, Miss. 1953), vol. II, pp. 1103ff. = *Herodot. Eine Auswahl aus der Neueren Forschung.* Herausgegeben von Walter Marg, 2nd ed. (Darmstadt 1965), pp. 290ff. Although his notion of 'self-reliance' proves very fruitful, I must for my own purposes rather stress systematically elements of the intellectual process and of literary organization.

sage makes clear that nothing blinds more and preserves ignorance better than success itself. Without going into Herodotus' Solonic topic that satiety creates arrogance and hybris, I here merely draw the lines from Solon's paradigms to Croesus' own situation: upon Croesus' rhetorical question, who is the happiest of men, Solon does not give the desired answer 'Croesus', but names some rather obscure people and states his reasons for naming them: (1) Tellus of Athens (30. 2) was happy because (a) his country was in flourishing condition, (b) his offspring became honorable men and they all had offspring all of whom stayed alive, (c) he lived in relatively easy circumstances, (d) his life's end was praiseworthy. (2) Cleobis and Biton (31. 1), two young men, were happy because (a) they were citizens of Argos (a powerful city, we understand), (b) were in good health and, so, in great honor so that even their mother was called happy, (c) they lived in sufficient circumstances, (d) the gods granted their lives the most beautiful ending. When Croesus demands the prize of happiness (εὐδαιμονίη, 32. 1) for himself, Solon refers to his 'knowledge' (ἐπιστάμενον) of divine jealousy and destruction and – like another Herodotus (cf. 1. 5. 4) – answers the question ἀνθρωπηίων πρηγμάτων πέρι by embarking on a speech about the general instability of man's condition, which may be subject to change on any of the thousands of days a man sees in his lifetime: man is totally accident, πᾶν ἐστι ἄνθρωπος συμφορή (32. 4). Concerning Croesus' personal situation, Solon expressly acknowledges Croesus' exceedingly wealthy circumstances as well as his political power (32. 5: this acknowledgment corresponds to sections (c) and (a) in the two foregoing examples), but refuses to call Croesus happy before he has seen the way in which he will end (corresponding to section (d) of the examples). Solon does not directly analyze Croesus' situation with regard to section (b) of his earlier paradigms, which located part of man's happiness within his well-thriving family. Only indirectly does Solon hint that wealth, although helping to fulfil desires and protect against calamity, cannot compensate for the advantages which a fortunate man of modest means may enjoy, viz. health and the blessing of children (32. 6).

Croesus himself fails to fill in that section (b) which Solon has left blank, although the king – he has a son who is deaf and dumb (34. 2)! – might have reason enough to start pondering about his

alleged happiness from what his guest said. Instead he dismisses his
guest as foolish (ἀμαθέα), because Solon ranks the future ending
higher than the present good (33). Thus it turns out that Croesus
personally takes the warning of the wise in exactly the same way
as his family as a whole has taken the Delphic oracle once given to
Gyges: he pays no attention. My earlier question, if outside help
can make Croesus aware of his dangerous situation, must now be
answered in the negative. That Herodotus had this same sort of
question in mind, may be seen from the way he connects the
ensuing events (1. 34. 1) with Solon's warnings: 'after Solon's
departure' (μετὰ δε Σόλωνα οἰχόμενον), Croesus is punished by
god for – as Herodotus conjectures (ὡς εἰκάσαι) – 'considering
himself the happiest of all men'. This connection raises Solon's
visit and warnings to the rank of a last chance granted to Croesus
to recognize his true situation. But he has rejected it, thus personally, but unwittingly endorsing the Delphic oracle (13. 2) which
his family as a whole has neglected.

It may be worth while to pause here for a moment and consider
in which way Herodotus has led us to see Croesus' almost
Aeschylean condition.[7] He has, to state it flatly, made use of the
poet–audience relationship of contemporary tragedy:[8] the far-
seeing god of the πρόλογος is replaced by Herodotus himself
telling his reader of the Delphic oracle (13. 2), which predicts
Croesus' doom. Within the 'play' proper, knowledge of the oracle
does not exist, so that we, the readers or onlookers, know more
about Croesus than he himself does. This creates a situation of
'tragic irony', when Croesus insists that he is happy and calls wise
Solon 'ignorant' or 'unlearned' (ἀμαθής) – just as e.g. the
Sophoclean Oedipus abuses the seer Teiresias as intellectually
blind as well as physically.[9] The predicates 'wise' and 'foolish'
are applied contrariwise by open-eyed reader and blind main
character. In this way, too, the Lydian king is close to King
Oedipus (and other rulers in tragedy), in that he is given clues by
his warner, from which he could diagnose his true condition: apart

7. 'Αλλ' ὅταν σπεύδῃ τις αὐτός, χὠ θεὸς συνάπτεται, Aesch. *Pers.* 742.
Properly speaking, Croesus is here the one who συνάπτεται.
8. Influence of contemporary drama is generally acknowledged: Immerwahr,
Herodotus, p. 70; John F. Myres, *Herodotus: Father of History* (Chicago 1971),
pp. 137f.; Heuss, 'Motive', *passim*.
9. τυφλὸς τά τ' ὦτα τόν τε νοῦν τά τ' ὄμματ' εἶ, *Oed. Tyr.* 371.

from unwisely boasting of the wrong achievements, he is not as happy in his children as Tellus of Athens or as the mother of Cleobis and Biton. What is different in Herodotus' pattern, if compared with tragedy, is the intellectual equipment of the warner: while a seer like Teiresias presages the actual truth of what is and what will happen, Solon, although knowing of divine jealousy and disturbance, is not granted any divine enlightenment of the present or presentiment of the future. His specific concerns are derived from his empirical knowledge about the general instability of man's condition. Clearly, he is the author's spokesman because he elaborates and expands what knowledge Herodotus himself has claimed in a programmatic section of his introduction (1. 5. 4): τὴν ἀνθρωπηίην...εὐδαιμονίην οὐδαμὰ ἐν τὠυτῷ μένουσαν. Thus, in order to understand Herodotus' composition, we must recognize that he adapts drama's possibility of having more than one dimension of speech at the same time and of presenting contradicting views on wisdom and foolishness. But he also would wish us to recognize his point of departure: the wise man of Herodotus' own making is not defined any longer by supranatural information and inspired prediction (Herodotus is too much aware of his mortal shortcomings anyway to claim any certainty of his own *in theologicis*), but by a modest assumption of probability, which is established by empirical knowledge of man's condition.[10]

It is important that we see the dramatic pattern and the changes Herodotus built into it for his own purposes, for only so do we fully appreciate the consistency of what follows upon the meeting of Solon and Croesus. Croesus has boasted of his excellent circumstances (= Solon's arguments (c) and (a)), has not given thought to happiness of health and family (argument (b)), declared as foolish the regard for life's ending (argument (d)). It appears only consistent within Herodotus' arrangement that Croesus must first relearn, where he has disregarded one existing clue already, viz. in the field of argument (b). Of his two sons, one is deaf and dumb, the other is healthy and promising in every way (τῶν ἡλίκων

10. Although agreeing with Heuss ('Motive', p. 394) about 'die funktionale Gleichordnung der beiden Komplexe Solon und Delphi', I do not agree with subordinating Solon to Delphi ('Motive', p. 408): both have become elements in Herodotus' own new context.

μακρῷ τὰ πάντα πρῶτος). After Solon's departure, the healthy one – the only one recognized by Croesus, 38. 2 – is killed in a most unglorious manner, which can in no way be likened to the beautiful death of Cleobis and Biton and the honor they bestowed on their mother or to Tellus' well-reputed offspring. There is even one further parallel (and contrast): by her prayers to the gods, the mother of Cleobis and Biton obtains and causes an early and beautiful death for her sons. Croesus, by employing an unlucky man and involuntary murderer for his son's protection, himself causes his own son's wretched death. The whole passage (1. 34–45) is organized into a series of well-composed scenes and marked by several dialogues – a clearly dramatic setting,[11] which corresponds to the composition of the Gyges story.

Croesus is thrown into deepest mourning (46. 1). But, although he sees his son's death as a god's deed rather than his mortal murderer's (whom he forgives, 45. 2), he is not able to put two and two together, i.e. to understand the sad fate which by now has struck both his sons as an intensified verification within the framework which Solon had outlined to him. Consequently, he fails to see his private unhappiness (the often repeated key term is συμφορή) as an early indicator of his political downfall. Thus, when his brother-in-law is deposed by Cyrus of Persia and the prospect of revenge and political expansion knocks at his door, he gives up his grief (Solon's area (b)) and turns to self-confident activity (in Solon's area (a)).

His blindness is brought out in the manner in which he tries to achieve divine support for his military campaign (according to Solon's 'knowledge', the divine is rather φθονερόν and ταραχῶδες, but cannot be pinned down! 32. 1). He first tests the existing oracles by a fake question in order to pick out the best (46ff.); then he sends gifts to the winner (Apollo at Delphi) and asks another question: if he should go to war against Persia. The ambiguous answer, that, if he attacks, he will destroy a great empire, fills him with excessive joy (ὑπερήσθη 54. 1) and the strong expectation (πάγχυ...ἐλπίσας) that he will destroy Cyrus' monarchy. His growing confidence is expressed in a third question addressed to

---

11. For details, see *Hermes* 96 (1968), 397f. As in the story of Gyges, so here the involuntary murderer Atys becomes the main character, and his part almost outweighs the exemplificatory function of the whole passage.

Apollo, which concerns the longevity of his own rule. The answer, warning him of a mule on Persia's throne, leads him to the final climax of his blind joy (πολλόν τι μάλιστα πάντων ἥσθη, 56. 1) – blind in so far as he fails to understand the oracle. (Cf. ἁμαρτὼν τοῦ χρησμοῦ, 71. 1. He should, Herodotus tells us later – 91. 5 – apply the image of the mule, offspring of different parents, to Cyrus, son of Median mother and Persian father.) However, Croesus' conclusion from the oracle is: his and his family's rule will NEVER cease (56. 1).

Such an expectation is not only against Solon's and Herodotus' words about the average instability of human affairs, but directly contradicts the forgotten oracle given to Croesus' forefather Gyges by *the same* Delphic Apollo, who then predicted doom to come in Croesus' generation! Again we must state that there is tragic irony when we, the informed onlookers, watch Croesus' climactic joy before the background of his destiny.[12] And if we are willing to take Croesus' repeated inquiries and Apollo's answers as a sort of dialogue, then we appreciate in area (a) (= politics) the same literary borrowings from tragedy, which we have named in area (b) (= happiness of health and family) before. The resulting unification of Herodotus' concept also heightens our appreciation of its lucidity. I wish to stress this issue of unity and logical exposition because it secures for Herodotus the long-range design which readers who were bewildered by his many 'short novels' have sometimes wrongly denied him.

Before Croesus begins his campaign against Cyrus and Persia, he is given a final warning through wise Sandanis (chapter 71), who in vain tells him that, in case of a victory over poverty-stricken Persia, nothing will be gained, but, in case of a defeat, all will be lost, because the indigent Persians will never give up rich Lydia again. Croesus' own idea of a preventive strike against Persia (46. 1) is thus seen to contain the danger of provoking a Persian invasion, to which so far the Persians have – 'I personally am thanking the gods', says Sandanis (71. 4) – not been inspired. The parallel to Adrestus' death seems obvious to me: in both fields, private (b) and political (a), Croesus himself, by his course of

12. If indeed the oracle of the mule was originally invented by Delphi *ex eventu* in self-apology (as Heuss, 'Motive', p. 406 suggests), we must state that Herodotus has fully integrated it into his own conception of Croesus.

action, involuntarily triggers the chain of events which he wishes
to prevent. His political plans, however, now go far beyond the
original concern (46. 1) for self-protection. Now, in the final
enumeration of impulses, Herodotus lists first 'desire for expansion' (γῆς ἱμέρῳ), second 'reliance on the oracle' (μάλιστα τῷ
χρηστηρίῳ πίσυνος ἐών), and in the third place only (the enumeration is an anticlimax) the original occasion which by now has
become no more than a pretext: revenge for his deposed brother-
in-law (73. 1; cf. 75. 1). Thus the attack upon Persia in Herodotus'
accounts turns largely into a symptom of Croesus' hybris, and his
first act after crossing the river Halys (the borderline between his
empire and that of Cyrus) is one of excessive injustice: he devas-
tates the country of the Syrians and enslaves the inhabitants, who
'were not guilty in any respect' (76. 2). Clearly the reader is
supposed to feel that this king is ripe for punishment in the
political sphere as he had appeared in the private sector before (cf.
34. 1). His blindness in both spheres can be seen as parallel, too:
Croesus' complete misjudgment of his military situation is
elaborated in detail: after a not successful battle, he still believes
himself to be his own (and the war's) master; he even disbands his
troops for this year and, making idle plans, summons all his allies
for the spring of next year (77. 1–4), not at all realizing that the
tragic 'too late!' might apply to himself and his vain actions. Thus
Cyrus' invasion of Lydia – fulfillment of Sandanis' warning! –
takes him by surprise: οἱ παρὰ δόξαν ἔσχε τὰ πρήγματα ἢ ὡς
αὐτὸς κατεδόκεε (79. 2). The discrepancy between reality and
Croesus' concept of it is reaching its peak. Even when he is already
surrounded in his own city, he still counts on having much time
for sitting it out and waiting for relief (81). But after only fourteen
days (84. 1; 86. 1) Sardis is taken. Thus we may state that throughout the whole narrative about Croesus' campaign so far as we have
reviewed it Herodotus continuously envisages the theme of
subjective (and wishful) thinking versus the objective (but un-
recognized) truth of the facts. Accordingly, the final disaster, by
removing all possibilities of wishfully interpreting reality, must
serve as an eye-opener to blind Croesus, showing him the truth of
his own situation as well as of Solon's words and of the oracles.

The first feature that meets the reader's eye in Herodotus'
report (84–91), is that the fall of Croesus is accompanied by a

large number of fulfilled oracles (which I shall merely enumerate in passing). A second indicator of the passage's importance is the renewed occurrence of dialogue (Cyrus–Croesus, Croesus' envoys –Apollo) as well as the fact that we meet another set of well-composed scenes (1. 85–91). They concentrate on Croesus himself, who, having so far been Herodotus' main character, naturally receives more attention than his country.[13]

The capture of the city is connected with an oracle (= no. 1)[14] insofar as it bears out the negligence of a former king, who had been warned by the prophets of Telmessos (84). Croesus himself receives a tragic confirmation (= fulfillment no. 2), when his dumb son, seeing his father's life threatened, all of a sudden opens his mouth and speaks. In happier days Delphi had warned Croesus that his son would 'speak for the first time on the day of unhappiness' (αὐδήσει γὰρ ἐν ἤματι πρῶτον ἀνόλβῳ, 85. 2). Now Croesus' συμφορή (85. 3) has made him so indifferent (παρημε-λήκεε, *ibid.*) that he does not even pay attention to his attacker. Herodotus connects the event with the false happiness which Croesus boasted of at the time of Solon's visit, in three ways: by contrasting the present calamity (συμφορῆς 85. 3) with the former well-being (ἐν τῇ...παρελθούσῃ εὐεστοῖ 85. 1), by quoting the Delphic prophecy in full (85. 2), and by expressly identifying this dumb son (85. 1) as the one mentioned in the context of his brother Atys' death and the punishment of Croesus' hybris (cf. 34. 1ff.). The tie between the two passages appears even stronger if we recall our interpretation that the crippled son could have served as a clue to Croesus for understanding Solon's warning and as an indicator of his true situation. Now everything is out in the open, but it is too late for making amends.[15]

Herodotus' literary architecture is revealed even more lucidly in what follows. By stating (86. 1) that Croesus has, 'in accordance with the oracle' (= no. 3), destroyed 'a great empire (viz. his own), he refers his reader back not only to the unjustified confi-

13. Cf. the way he is singled out: καὶ αὐτὸν Κροῖσον 86. 1, κατ᾽ αὐτὸν δὲ Κροῖσον τάδε ἐγίνετο, 85. 1.

14. Not counting the snake-oracle of 1. 78, the essence of which expresses a tragic 'too late': πρὶν γὰρ ἢ ὀπίσω σφέας ἀναπλῶσαι ἐς τὰς Σάρδις ἥλω ὁ Κροῖσος.

15. One may pointedly say that a 'Delphic' element (the oracle about the son) has been incorporated into Herodotus' 'Solonic' argument.

dence which Croesus derived from Delphi's (and Amphiaraos')
prophecy (cf. 53. 2–3), but even further to the warning of Solon,
who had also included political power in his considerations (32. 5;
labeled as category (a) by us). As two more of Solon's categories
((b): happiness of health and family; (c): wealthy circumstances)
can easily be seen to have become relevant already in Croesus' change
of life, any reader, who has paid attention to Herodotus' systematic
exposition, may now expect to be informed about how Croesus
will fare in Solon's last and main category, (d), which concerns
the ending of a person's life (we recall the praiseworthy death of
Tellus as well as of the pair Cleobis and Biton). In other words:
Herodotus' literary concept demands that he now insert a scene
which shows Croesus' miserable death – as his painting of 'Croesus
on the pyre' actually seems to confirm. But – and this is the point
which my paper wishes to bring out – if the historian intends that
Croesus' personal experience has some bearing on the ensuing
story of Cyrus, i.e. that the figure of Croesus guides our view and
understanding of Cyrus' career (at least from a certain point
onwards), then Croesus must survive that dreadful final situation
and live on – as he does in Herodotus' version: rescued from the
burning pyre by Apollo, and permanently accepted into Cyrus'
retinue so as to follow him (almost) everywhere. I do not discuss
here the possibly uncertain historicity of Croesus' travels with
Cyrus. I am only pointing out how the version adopted and
developed by Herodotus in this prominent passage fits in with the
long-range design of his literary architecture.

III. From Croesus to Cyrus:
Solon's wisdom established

If my hypothesis is correct, that Herodotus' narrative of Croesus
is fully understood only when seen to include the larger context of
Cyrus' career, then Croesus' ruin must also be reviewed with
regard to the effect it has on the mind of Cyrus. Now it is interesting to see that Herodotus lets his Cyrus display a certain curiosity
in Croesus' person: after listing two possible conventional motives
Cyrus may have had for burning Croesus, Herodotus dwells in
detail on a third: 'or, having heard about Croesus being pious, he
made him climb the pyre because he wanted to know if a god

would rescue him from being burned alive' (86. 2). I have no doubt that Cyrus is here made to ask a question which the reader, too, who has followed Herodotus' report so far is expected to ask: 'Will the many gifts which Croesus sent to Delphi on many occasions influence his fate or not?' In this way, Cyrus is introduced as a human character who thinks in Herodotean categories.

As for Croesus himself, we are told that in spite of his predicament[16] Solon's message that nobody alive is happy comes to his mind and Solon, it now appears to him, has spoken under divine influence (ὡς οἱ εἴη σὺν θεῷ εἰρημένον, 86. 3). This, of course, means that Solon has proven to be right also in his fourth category, ((d): Croesus' situation is actually that of a dying man), and the phrase 'εἰρημένον σὺν θεῷ' raises his warning to the rank of a prophecy (so we may justly here register fulfillment no. 4 within the context of our passage). Croesus' insight into Solon's rightness is the first step (of two)[17] in coming to his senses and losing his blindness. His enigmatic utterance (ἄσημα, 86. 4) that he would greatly appreciate it if *all* rulers could have a conversation with Solon (τὸν ἂν ἐγὼ πᾶσι τυράννοισι προετίμησα μεγάλων χρημάτων ἐς λόγους ἐλθεῖν, 86. 4) is a break-through which interpreters of Herodotus have underrated: by extending the applicability of Solon's warnings beyond his own person and by expressing the desire that Solon's wisdom be spread and communicated to all rulers, Croesus potentially becomes a 'Solon' himself.[18] He undergoes a change, a human conversion, as becomes even more apparent from what he is about to say about Solon. All[19] things have turned out for him the way Solon has predicted (ὡς τε αὐτῷ πάντα ἀποβεβήκοι τῇ περ ἐκεῖνος εἶπε = fulfillment no. 4), although Solon had not spoken with special regard to Croesus, but 'with regard to all that is human (ἐς ἅπαν τὸ ἀνθρώπινον), and most to those who seem happy in their own eyes' (86. 5).

---

16. καίπερ ἐν κακῷ ἐόντι τοσούτῳ, 86. 3. Croesus' ability of lifting himself above his personal worries is stressed elsewhere, too: καίπερ ἐὼν ἐν κακῷ οἰκηΐῳ τοσούτῳ after Atys' death, he actually feels pity for his son's murderer: τόν τε Ἄδρηστον κατοικτίρει (45. 2).

17. The first concerns man's general insecurity, the second Croesus' specific situation and own vain actions.

18. 'Kroisos ist zum Weisen geworden.' Marg, '"Selbstsicherheit"', p. 294.

19. I take πάντα to mean 'events in all four of Solon's categories'.

Indeed, the final disaster serves, as I said earlier, as an eye-opener
to Croesus, overthrowing all earlier standards of thinking: a Solon
moves, in Croesus' estimation, from foolish (ἀμαθέα, 33: because
he ranked the ending always higher than the present-day goods)
to a wise man. The fact that Croesus points away from himself
(οὐδέν τι μᾶλλον ἐς ἑωυτόν, 86. 5), and stresses the general
applicability of Solon's truth to all mankind, must be seen from
two aspects: (1) Croesus realizes that he had excepted himself from
the *condition humaine*, and now ruefully accepts a more modest
standpoint. (2) In doing so, he qualifies for presenting to the reader
(and to Cyrus) Herodotus' own message about man's insecurity.

In a rare moment, humanity may appear contagious: when
Cyrus is informed about Croesus' words, he changes his mind
(μεταγνόντα, 86. 6, cf. μετάγνωσιν, 87. 1) and – in vain – orders
the fire extinguished, motivated by three considerations: (1) 'that
he, being himself a human being, hands over another human
being (who had known no lesser happiness than he himself) alive
to the fire' – a surprising humility: a man recognizes his very own
existence in the reflecting mirror of another man's fate; (2) in
addition, he is afraid of retribution (τίσις – we recall what
Herodotus conjectured about νέμεσις coming to confident Croesus,
34. 1); (3) he thinks over 'that none of the conditions among
human beings is stable' – i.e. he has accepted Solon's message
(which, we recall, is one of Herodotus' major themes) immediately
upon hearing it from his interpreters! The story of Cyrus' moral
and human conversion appears almost too unrealistic to be true,
we may feel. I do not think our impression is very far off Herodotus' own track. However, as his interpreters, we will have to look
out for his reasons for presenting an ideal scene of human sympathy
and enlightened humility. For now, we can definitely state that
Herodotus indeed utilizes his sequence of treating Croesus before
Cyrus for literary purposes as well. When the reader meets the
Persian King Cyrus, this Cyrus' mind is influenced and shaken by
the fate of the Lydian King Croesus. And we may also state that
in the sequence of scenes discussed by us at present (1. 85–90), the
author's interest and his literary emphasis begins to expand from
Croesus to Cyrus. This may be seen from the viewpoint from
which the miracle of Croesus' rescue (a sudden rainstorm extin-
guishes the fire) is told. Although the pyre is the last gruesome

disillusionment for Croesus to experience, which makes him call and appeal to Apollo, we are made to view the result through the eyes of Cyrus (who, we recall from 86. 2, wishes to find out if a god would save pious Croesus!): it is Cyrus who 'thus learned (i.e. received the answer to his former question) that Croesus was dear to the gods and a good man' (87. 2).

The following conversation between the two humble kings is opened by Cyrus' question: which man caused Croesus to attack him and 'become my enemy instead of my friend' (πολέμιον ἀντὶ φίλου ἐμοὶ καταστῆναι)? The question would appear almost sarcastic for one who deposed Croesus' brother-in-law (46. 1; 75. 1)! But instead of accusing Herodotus of contradicting his own earlier narrative, I prefer to suggest that the historian here again speaks on his highest literary level, on which, for the sake of his human subject (= theme II), he feels free to take leave of the 'facts' for some time. As for corroborating evidence in general, I point once more to the discrepancy of facts and of meaning in the opening narrative about Gyges, and to the unhistorical conversation between Solon and Croesus. As for our specific context, I refer my reader back to 73. 1, where Herodotus, in an anti-climactic enumeration, gave precedence to the human motivation over the political (and the historical) *casus belli*. I also would like to stress that, from the moment when Herodotus had conjectured a special human motive for Cyrus to burn Croesus on the pyre (86. 2), his report has been given in indirect discourse, as if what he tells us here is not warranted by historical evidence. This in itself goes together with our earlier observation that the picture of a sympathetic Cyrus appears unrealistic and idealized: wishful thinking rather than historical fact. Thus, of Cyrus' question why Croesus became his enemy, it is sufficient to say that it is asked on the literary and human, but not on the historical (in the narrow sense of this word), level of Herodotus' work. I venture the hypothesis that Herodotus trusted his reader to distinguish between the two levels from the indications he gave him. As for Croesus' answer, it is influenced by his newly acquired sense of humility: no human (he now says) would be so foolish as to choose war for peace, for in peace sons bury their fathers, in war fathers their sons. Croesus has achieved a new, truly wise standard of what is 'foolish' (ἀνόητος), a standard from which he cannot under-

stand his own former actions. Therefore he (wrongly, as we shall
see) now holds Apollo (ὁ ῾Ελλήνων θεός, 87. 3) and his oracle
responsible for his unlucky campaign against Cyrus. Croesus'
hybris clearly is gone. The end of this remarkable scene (88. 1)
shows us the two wise kings sitting in silence side by side, united in
their common recognition of what man is and how a man should
act. Croesus has been freed from his fetters and is meditating;
Cyrus and his entourage are feeling admiration for him. The
result of our story so far is as humanly attractive as it appears
unexpected and even improbable: Croesus has learned wisdom
through suffering; Cyrus has been converted by watching Croesus'
experience. Is it then Herodotus' belief that man does learn from
his own mistakes, or that he can learn from seeing his fellow-man
suffer the consequences of earlier mistakes? We have seen how, all
through the story of Croesus, Herodotus pointed to the problem
of blindness and knowledge. Can it be solved, however late?

In the next scene, it looks as if in fact Herodotus answers this
question in the positive. When Cyrus tells Croesus that his city is
now being pillaged, Croesus corrects him: your city, not mine any
longer (88. 3). Croesus expressly acknowledges that his famous
riches are gone (= category (c) of Solon's analysis)! But he goes
beyond that, addressing Cyrus thus: 'As the gods gave me to you
as your servant, I think it is right, in case I see something more
than you, to point it out to you' (89. 1). In these words we see
Croesus assume a new role and take on a new responsibility. By
becoming an advisor or warner to Cyrus, he is himself what Solon
was to him: the new Solon is born, i.e. – as we shall see – the
second circle of history's merry-go-round is beginning, after the
first is completed. I have no doubt that Croesus' offer here is
meant to be sincere: for the advice he gives is good and helpful to
Cyrus. What is perhaps even more surprising is that it is based on
Croesus' new state of wisdom. For his counsel (Cyrus ought not to
let his poverty-stricken Persian soldiers become rich from the
pillage of Sardes, because the new taste of luxuries would nourish
a usurper against his throne), is *mutatis mutandis* the same which
Sandanis gave to Croesus himself, and which he, to his own
disadvantage, neglected (71): that the poor Persians would never
again give up rich Lydia, once they had tested its luxuries. Cyrus'
joyful consent (ὑπερήδετο) to the apparently good counsel (οἱ

ἐδόκεε εὖ ὑποτίθεσθαι,[20] 90. 1) may confirm the harmony between the two men who share the same views. Cyrus listens to Croesus' advice as Croesus did once, at an early point of his career, to Bias.[21]

Herodotus seems almost ready to embark on the narrative of Cyrus' career (with Croesus being only a subordinate character from now on), except for one issue: a clarification of Croesus' relationship to Delphi and Apollo, whom Croesus blames for having misled him. With Cyrus' friendly permission (cf. γελάσας εἶπε etc., 90. 3), he sends envoys to Delphi and asks two questions: (1) Does Apollo not feel shame about having, by his oracle, aroused Croesus to wage war against Cyrus with the prospect of victory? (2) Is it a custom of Greek gods to be ungrateful? (90. 4).

The Pythia is said to have made a statement of principle before answering: 'Even for a god it is impossible to avoid the decreed fate' (τὴν πεπρωμένην μοῖραν ἀδύνατά ἐστι ἀποφυγεῖν καὶ θεῷ, 91. 1). To explain the statement, she revealed that Croesus had paid for the fault of his fourth ancestor, Gyges the usurper. In this way we see Croesus being acquainted with the forgotten oracle once received by Gyges (1. 13. 2), which Herodotus' reader has known all the time (we may here register oracular fulfillment no. 5 within our context), but which, although being an essential condition to Croesus' life, has been unknown to the last Mermnad King. The involuntary crime and its late vengeance form the immovable foundation that limits the architect's freedom, or, one may say, they are the skeleton which bears the living flesh of Herodotus' story.

Before this ever-valid background, Apollo's answers are given, first to the second question:

(2)

(a) The only concession Apollo could win from the Fates has been a delay of three years in Croesus' fall.

(b) It was Apollo who rescued Croesus by extinguishing the pyre. This does away with the charge of ungratefulness (ἐχαρίσατο 91. 3; ἀχαρίστοισι, 90. 4).

20. For ὑποτίθεσθαι meaning 'advise, counsel' see chapter 1 of my 'Interpretationen zu Platons Hypothesisverfahren' (Diss. Kiel 1956), pp. 3f.
21. 1. 27, see above, p. 4.

(1) As to the oracle, Croesus is not justified in blaming Apollo:

(a) Croesus should have asked whether the great empire he was about to destroy was Cyrus' or rather his own (= fulfillment no. 2, cf. 86. 1). He should declare himself responsible: ἑωυτὸν αἴτιον ἀποφαινέτω (91. 4).

(b) Croesus also failed to see that the mule mentioned in the final oracle (55. 2) pointed to Cyrus, son of different parents (91. 5–6, = fulfillment no. 6).

So far Delphi's answers are given in the same systematic manner in which the questions had arisen from Croesus' experience as told by Herodotus. What is left now is to see Croesus' reaction upon receiving the answers: his reaction forms the second and final step of his enlightenment. First he saw that his behaviour did not befit a human being (87. 4). Now he learns that this does not mean it had been 'caused by the Greek god' (αἴτιος δὲ ἐγένετο ὁ Ἑλλήνων θεός, 87. 3), but rather by his own misleading desires: 'he became aware that the fault was his own and not the god's' (συνέγνω ἑωυτοῦ εἶναι τὴν ἁμαρτάδα καὶ οὐ τοῦ θεοῦ, 91. 6).

Thus, in the end, things seem to fall in place on all three levels: (1) Fate's long-range calendar is fulfilled. Candaules, ill-fated last king of the Heraclid dynasty (χρῆν γὰρ Κανδαύλῃ γενέσθαι κακῶς, 1. 8. 2), was killed by usurper Gyges of the Mermnad family. Four generations later Gyges' descendant Croesus pays the penalty for the crime as predicted. (2) Within the unchangeable pattern of destiny, Apollo has tried to help his worshipper Croesus, acknowledging what acts of piety Croesus performed. (3) Croesus himself, not knowing of his destiny all the time, has, by his very own behavior, fulfilled it and justified it.

What is important for us to understand is that all acts and motives of level (3), although fulfilling the conditions of destiny (and, as much as possible, of historical or semi-historical traditions Herodotus may have encountered), do not depend on any supranatural impulses and causations, but can be accounted for by empirical psychology alone. And it is this dimension, as we have seen, to which Herodotus dedicates his skills of literary composition. The group of scenes that develops the fatal triangular relationship of King Candaules, the queen, and royal advisor (1. 8–13), is based exclusively on the psychology and different viewpoints of the three persons involved.²² Solon's advice to Croesus (29–33) is expressly founded on average (today we would say statistical) human expectations. Atys' and Croesus' futile attempts to cheat the oracle (34–45) are not different from the usual human habit of trying to eliminate objective obstacles by wishful thinking. The same can be said about Croesus' optimism concerning his Persian campaign (46ff.). In this case, Herodotus takes great pains (by adding two special chapters, 1. 90–1) to show that the erring king finally himself became aware of and expressly acknowledged his impulses and motivations as exclusively human and as his own! Almost as with Sophocles' King Oedipus, Croesus' process of learning leads to human self-discovery – with one significant difference. Oedipus finally brings out into the open the dreadful conditions of his existence, while Croesus beyond that must realize that his motives justify his destiny: συνέγνω ἑωυτοῦ εἶναι τὴν ἁμαρτάδα καὶ οὐ τοῦ θεοῦ (91. 6).

The last set of scenes to be mentioned in the present context are those around Croesus' fall and the communications of Croesus and Cyrus (85–91). They, as I need not repeat, are built on the fundamental idea that Solon's empirical knowledge of man's insecurity can or should be spread. To summarize: what Herodotus as a writer emphasizes by his literary art is man's live experience of himself before a background of traditional forces. In the case of Croesus, the process appears to be moving from blindness to insight, from haughtiness to humility.

IV. King Cyrus and his advisor Croesus: from wisdom back to blindness

With Croesus having understood not only the wrongness of his opinions (= step I) but also his own responsibility (= step II), Herodotus can (except for the report on some local Lydian specialties, 93f.) close the books on his empire and the harm he did to the Greeks of Ionia: κατὰ μὲν δὴ τὴν Κροίσου τε ἀρχὴν καὶ Ἰωνίης τὴν πρώτην καταστροφὴν ἔσχε οὕτω (92. 1). These words refer back to the opening words of 1. 6. 1f. about Croesus, the first man known to have harmed the Greeks (πρῶτος τῶν ἡμεῖς ἴδμεν τοὺς μὲν κατεστρέψατο Ἑλλήνων) and subjected the Ionians and

22. See *Hermes* 96 (1968), pp. 385ff.

others (κατεστρέψατο μὲν "Ιωνάς τε καὶ...). In other words: as far as major theme I, the long fight of Greeks and barbarians, is concerned, Croesus' part is over: the next in line to have harmed the Greeks is Cyrus, who has defeated Croesus.

Herodotus' overall composition (Croesus' story told first, Cyrus' next) is dictated by the chronological order in which these kings were encountered by the Greeks (= theme I). I hope, however, that I have established that Herodotus utilizes this compositional order also for theme II (man's unstable conditions): the reader meets Cyrus at a time when the Persian king stands under the influence of, and is shaken by the fate of, his enemy the Lydian king. A line of communication is opened between the two, which points to a beginning, not an ending: by assuming towards Cyrus the role which Solon (and Bias) had played in his own life, Croesus, at least for the time being, becomes the new Solon, i.e. the spokesman for the author's human theme – which transcends the national theme of Greeks versus barbarians. If the connection I have just outlined is valid, and the human theme is passed on from Solon to Croesus, from Croesus to Cyrus, then it should be (from the aspect of theme II also) easy to understand and unobjectionable even to the most sceptical critic of Herodotus why the earlier life of Cyrus and the history of his country down to 546 B.C. are treated in a sort of parenthesis or even postscript: 'Now my account goes on to inquire who this Cyrus was who destroyed Croesus' empire, and in which way the Persians had become the lords of Asia' (95. 1). This procedure seems appropriate, the more so as the story of Cyrus ascending the throne, humanly interesting as it is, is not so much the result of Cyrus' own action (we do not yet see the full-grown man of power), but rather of personal revenge taken by a maltreated Mede named Harpagus who uses young Cyrus as a tool for his personal satisfaction (123. 1ff.). For the continuity of major theme II Cyrus' early years are not of interest and therefore may be subsumed and summarized as follows: 'In this way Cyrus was born and raised and became king and, after that, subjugated Croesus who had started injustice – as I have narrated before' (130. 3). Even the following years of Cyrus' rule, e.g. his conquest of Greek Asia Minor through General Harpagus (163–71), or his victories in Inner Asia, do not revive the literary categories of his encounter with Croesus (except for a short and limited interlude, in which Croesus gives a piece of advice that helps Cyrus and at the same time saves the rebellious city of Sardes from destruction, 155f.). The goals Herodotus pursues in using his highest literary level can best be seen by comparing his presentation of Cyrus' last two campaigns, against Babylon (178–200) and against the Massagetae (201–16), both supposedly representing the ones 'which gave him greatest trouble and are worthiest to be reported' (177). While the earlier does not grant us any look into Cyrus' heart (except perhaps once, when he angrily 'punishes' the River Gyndes for having drowned one of his sacred horses, 189f.), the latter characterizes his state of mind in the first sentence: (having defeated Babylon, too) 'he conceived the additional *desire* of subjugating the Massagetae' (201). Even in the broadest outline of Cyrus' plans (153. 4), which include a campaign against far-away Egypt, no 'desire' was mentioned. We must go back as far as Croesus' hope and desire (73. 1; 75. 1) to pick up the thread again. In addition, the fact alone that Croesus himself (whom we had last seen together with Cyrus on their way to Agbatana from Sardes (155. 1ff.) and who has not been mentioned at all during Cyrus' Babylonian campaign) is said to accompany Cyrus to the Massagetae and is again shown to converse with him in dialogue is a clear compositional symptom for us that Herodotus continues his second major theme. The occasion, we may state in advance, appears worthy of the effort: after Croesus' fall it is now King Cyrus' ruin we readers will witness: a degree of parallelism seems indicated. From a slightly different viewpoint we may say: Cyrus' rule as narrated by Herodotus is set in two conversations he has with Croesus.

Of the strong *stimuli* that work in Cyrus at the time he plans to go against the Massagetae, Herodotus specifies two: (1) his birth, which has led him to believe that he is 'something more than a human being' (τὸ δοκέειν πλέον τι εἶναι ἀνθρώπου), and (2) his military fortune (ἡ εὐτυχίη ἡ κατὰ τοὺς πολέμους γενομένη), which so far has not allowed a single nation he attacked to escape him (204. 2). Clearly, as far as (1) is concerned, we are asked to realize that this Cyrus has completely moved away from the Cyrus we met before, who, in humble acknowledgment of his own human condition, spared his fellow-man's life (ἐννώσαντα, ὅτι καὶ αὐτὸς ἄνθρωπος ἐὼν ἄλλον ἄνθρωπον...ζῶντα πυρὶ διδοίη, 86. 6).

Point (2) can easily be paralleled in Croesus' career: to be convinced of one's invincibility and military εὐτυχίη as a lasting
quality is as unwise as was Croesus' claiming the prize of
εὐδαιμονίη for himself: both attitudes neglect Solon's warning
(communicated to Cyrus through Croesus, 86. 5–6). However –
as we said earlier – [23] nothing blinds more and preserves ignorance
better than success itself. What is new in the picture Herodotus
paints of Cyrus, if we compare it with that of Croesus, is this: there
is not only a development from blindness and *hybris* to insight and
humility, but the opposite is apparently possible, too: although
one may possess and start out with a humble awareness of man's
basic insecurity (and feel a moral appeal originating from it), this
possession can nevertheless be lost or may yield to those instincts
one had decided to avoid. In the light of Cyrus' later career, that
earlier scene, which showed his conversion (μεταγνόντα, 86. 6, cf.
μετάγνωσιν, 87. 1) in the face of Croesus' suffering, must now
appear as an empty lie, a beautiful idealization which does not
stand up to the reality of human behavior. That this is what
Herodotus had in mind when he composed Book 1 will become
clear immediately. Already we may sense a note of deep pessimism, if we watch Cyrus' development which runs counter to
what we read of Croesus'. Our impression will be enhanced when
we see even Croesus unwittingly joining his advisee instead of
trying to keep him back.

After an attempt to win the country of the Massagetae by
trickery (Cyrus ingenuously proposed to their Queen Tomyris)
has failed, Cyrus energetically turns to crossing the River Araxes
by force with his army (comparable to Croesus' crossing the Halys,
75). While still building and fortifying his bridge, he is surprised
by a tempting offer made by Tomyris: she invites him to come
over safely and unharassed by her troops and then do battle in her
country, or, alternatively, to grant her the same occasion on his
side of the Araxes. Cyrus takes counsel with his chiefs and accepts
their unanimous vote to have Tomyris and her army come over to
the Persian side. Apparently, the general warning[24] undertones of
her message have been lost on the Persian king: she had first asked

23. See p. 5.
24. Already here Tomyris' words have the rank of an oracle, which Heuss
('Motive', p. 395, n. 10) rightly sees in her later speech (1. 212ff.).

him to stop his enterprise, stay within his present boundaries, and 'endure' seeing her ruling in hers (ἡμέας ἀνέχευ ὁρέων ἄρχοντας τῶν περ ἄρχομεν, 206. 1). At the same time, she had indicated that she did not expect him to accept her advice: οὐκ ἂν ἐθελήσεις ὑποθήκῃσι[25] τῇσίδε χρᾶσθαι, ἀλλὰ πάντως μᾶλλον ἢ δι' ἡσυχίης εἶναι (206. 2), i.e. she is seen vainly to confront Cyrus with his lust of expansion which Herodotus himself ascribes to the Persian king at this stage of his career.

How does Croesus, 'who was present' (παρεών, 207. 1), fit in here, when he contradicts Cyrus' and the chiefs' decision? From his earlier role as the new Solon, we would expect him to exercise a restraining effect, the more so as he expressly wishes his present advice to be seen in line with what 'I said to you before' (εἶπον μὲν καὶ πρότερόν τοι), viz. that, once given into Cyrus' hands, he will, as much as he can, stave off ruin from Cyrus' house (207. 1 = 89. 1). Croesus goes out of his way to restate what Herodotus' reader understood to be the essence of that earlier scene when the two kings met for the first time and acquired their humble attitudes (1. 86ff.): 'My sufferings, by their bitterness, have taught me', τὰ δέ μοι παθήματα ἐόντα ἀχάριτα μαθήματα γέγονε. We cannot help feeling the anachronism that the deposed Lydian king appears to have sat among the audience of Aeschylus, who makes Zeus, while leading men to wisdom, validate the law of πάθει μάθος, 'learning through suffering' (*Ag.* 177). However, what are we to think if we are taken beyond Aeschylus and see Croesus' newly acquired wisdom turn back into foolishness? If the advice based on the new wisdom is wrong and faulty, what are we to think about those lofty μαθήματα? Must we not conclude that Aeschylus' ode is too optimistic with regard to man's learning capacity? The most striking feature in Croesus' latest activity is that he still believes he has not left the ground of that humility which befits a mortal being: if Cyrus should consider himself immortal, ἀθάνατος, Croesus says (207. 2), then any advice will be wasted on him. The reader already knows that Cyrus indeed now does consider himself 'more than man' (τὸ δοκέειν πλέον τι εἶναι ἀνθρώπου, 204. 2), and that therefore, from Croesus' viewpoint, any advice should indeed be idle. However, things do not work out along these lines. Croesus proceeds to explain the alternative

25. See note 20 above.

to what he has said: 'On the other hand, if you have recognized
that you, too, are a human being..., then learn this first: that
there is a wheel of human affairs and further that, by turning, it
does not let the same men always be fortunate.' This is the fifth
time (and probably in the most aphoristic way) that the theory
about man's unstable conditions has been mentioned so far: first
by Herodotus himself (5. 4), then by Solon towards Croesus (32f.),
in the third place by Croesus in his soliloquy on the pyre (86. 5),
fourth in Cyrus' thoughts when he realized that he was a human
being, and therefore changed his mind (86. 6). The fundamental
idea, originally endorsed by the historian himself, must still be
correct. If unsound advice is now derived from it, the fault must be
Croesus', the advisor's – almost in the way that the fault was
Croesus' when he misunderstood the oracles. My assumption that
Herodotus presents his Croesus as being unknowingly back again
on the path of error is in harmony with the self-contradicting
picture of Cyrus, who, in spite of considering himself more than
human, is willing to accept human advice. There is no contradiction if Cyrus, himself blind to man's limitations, gives his ear to
an advisor who is likewise blind when applying a fundamental
truth to a given situation. (We should note the strong emphasis
Croesus places on distinguishing the next logical step, which
supposedly takes him from the generic to the specific to be subsumed under and warranted by it: 'Consequently, I at this point
(= secondly) am entertaining an opinion contrary to those (*sc.*
chiefs of yours) concerning the matter we have before us here',
ἤδη ὦν ἔχω γνώμην περὶ τοῦ προκειμένου πρήγματος τὰ ἔμπαλιν
ἢ οὗτοι.) I would like to ask my reader to follow me on the
hypothesis that in Herodotus' account not only Cyrus has lost his
former sense of modesty and given in to blind greed, but that
Croesus, too, does not any longer act on the principles which he
professes to have learned from his bitter experience. Both men have
lost again that deep sense of humanity which Herodotus so
unrealistically ascribed to them as the alleged result of their first
meeting (a conversation no more historical than that of Solon and
Croesus).

I foresee one objection to my interpretation, which I should take
seriously: if Croesus' counsel turns out to be fatal for the recipient,
can it not be that Croesus acted on purpose? If we picture Croesus

as a man who slyly takes revenge on his victorious enemy by
sending him on a dangerous mission suggested by Cyrus' own
inner drive, is such a sly fox not covered by the law of 'learning
from suffering'?

My answer requires a digression. First, I would say that so far
no doubt has been cast on Croesus' self-chosen devotion to Cyrus.
On the contrary, the first advice he gave in his new role was
expressly acknowledged as good and helpful by Cyrus himself (οἱ
ἐδόκεε εὖ ὑποτίθεσθαι, 90. 1). Secondly, and from another angle,
Croesus' later loyalty in dealing with Cyrus' son and successor,
Cambyses, is mentioned by Herodotus himself: it was εὐνοίην
φαίνων (3. 36. 2) that Croesus, in compliance with Cyrus' last will,
gave moderating counsel ('it is good to have forethoughts, and
caution is something wise') to Cambyses. But Cambyses by then
had already fallen into madness (cf. πανταχῇ ὦν μοι δῆλά ἐστι
ὅτι ἐμάνη μεγάλως ὁ Καμβύσης, 3. 38. 1). The context of Book 3
also shows that Croesus' warning there is doubtless in place and
truly wise again – but this time not accepted by the advisee. It
takes considerable time until Cambyses too, if we may say so, will
'learn through suffering' – emotional and physical suffering –
and return from madness to humility (ἐσωφρόνησε, 3. 64. 5).
However late, Cambyses too, as once Croesus had, will realize that
'it was not contained in the nature of man to stave off the future'
'ἐν τῇ γὰρ ἀνθρωπηίῃ φύσι οὐκ ἐνῆν ἄρα τὸ μέλλον γίνεσθαι
ἀποτρέπειν, 3. 65. 3). But before that, and especially at the time
of his conversation with Croesus, he possesses no such insight into
the limitations of the human mind. Therefore he turns the tables
on Croesus and declares him not qualified to give advice to others,
because his advice produces disastrous consequences: 'You ruined
yourself by ruling over your own country badly, you ruined Cyrus
who followed your advice.' In sarcastic words he ridicules Croesus'
advice itself (as distinguished from its consequences): 'You dare
advise me too, – you who *profitably* guided your own country; you
who *well* advised my father by bidding him cross the river Araxes
and then go against the Massagetae – while those were willing to
come over into our country!' (3. 36. 3).

Like Herodotus himself, Cambyses does not express doubts
about Croesus' loyalty (he ranks Croesus' and Cyrus' defeats
parallel, two sides of the same coin, so to speak (μὲν... δέ), as both

having happened against Croesus' will). What he scornfully
doubts is that Croesus' well-meaning counsel can ever have
beneficial results for the advisee. We here watch Solon's problem
of how to close Croesus' knowledge gap, being revived on a new
level. After all, Cambyses' suspicion itself would not seem so 'mad'
to us. Rather, his caution towards the voluntary advisor could be
seen as 'learning through suffering', i.e. the sufferings of Croesus
and Cyrus. How could he be supposed to know that this time
Croesus' advice (viz. to stop killing people at random lest he should
provoke a revolt against himself) is sound? Moreover, he cannot
know of its soundness, because to himself his own ability to kill (for
instance to shoot Prexaspes' son right through the heart with his
first shot, 3. 35) is a proof of his own sanity! But if mad Cambyses
is convinced that he is right, then his censurer Croesus must appear
wrong to him. Therefore he tries to shoot this obtrusive warner
too. It is Croesus' tragic experience that Cambyses the son does not
follow his good advice, but Cyrus the father did follow his bad
advice. Is there no certain basis at all for well-meaning human
advice and no chance of avoiding calamity by good counsel in
history? Is this the result we learn from Croesus' conversations?[26]
At least Cambyses, the fratricide, ἀδελφεοκτόνος, as we have seen
(3. 65. 3f.), will later arrive at such a conclusion. But by then it
will of course be too late – once again. Croesus' last appearance in
Herodotus' work, then, amounts to nothing: it confirms his previous
ineffectiveness.

One result I hope to have established by the above digression:
although Croesus' advice to Cyrus turned out to be wrong, it was
not malicious or insidious by intention, not even in the eye of

26. My account does not include Croesus' *bon mot* on Cambyses in 3. 34,
because Herodotus does not, as in the other cases, tie it in with his long-range
composition by an explicit reference.

On the other hand, an occasion where Croesus does not speak but is said to
have burst into tears may well be cited as typical: when a messenger explains
the immeasurable sorrows which Cambyses has brought over his enemy
Psammenitus, Cambyses himself follows Croesus in being touched with pity
and releases his enemy's son from execution – in a similar way Cyrus had once
felt pity for his prisoner Croesus. That Croesus is introduced to carry the human
theme once more may be concluded from the fact that his presence in Egypt
is not mentioned before this event: 'For he, too, happened to follow Cambyses
to Egypt', 3. 14. 11.

Cyrus' son Cambyses. Herodotus himself credits him even with εὐνοίη towards Cyrus' son. Our result excludes one side of the alternative we considered earlier and throws us back on the other: we must now assume that Croesus, although subjectively believing himself still to possess the wisdom he gained from his bitter sufferings, objectively leads Cyrus further on the path of error. The tragic irony consists in the fact that the loyal Solonic warner actually turns into a risk-prone seducer, and, in this function, involuntarily brings about a repeat and almost a copy of his own ill-fated past – that past which allegedly taught him to be wiser! Can man try to be open-eyed and nevertheless commit the same mistake twice? Herodotus' answer is, apparently, 'Yes'.

As Croesus (a) warns of the 'wheel of human affairs', and (b) is well-meaning towards Cyrus, we should grant him that, by his lonely counter-advice, he wishes to save Cyrus from danger supposedly not envisaged by his chiefs (cf. 207. 2). To make himself clear, he expounds the facets of the alternative (207. 3ff.) as follows:

(1) Tomyris' army is allowed over to the Persian side of the river.

(a) Cyrus is defeated (ἑσσωθεὶς μὲν...). In this case he will lose not only the battle but also his empire because the victorious Massagetae will push on.

(b) Cyrus is victorious. (νικῶν δὲ...). In this case he will be prevented from exploiting his victory, because the Araxes will stop him from immediately invading Tomyris' country.

(2) Cyrus and his army cross the river and the battle is joined on Tomyris' territory.

(a) Cyrus is victorious. He will be able to pursue the fleeing Massagetae right into the center of their empire (ἰθὺ τῆς ἀρχῆς τῆς Τομύριος).

Herewith Croesus' analysis ends, short of – as can easily be seen – alternative 2 (b), viz. that Cyrus may be defeated on Tomyris' territory (the alternative that will actually become true in the later course of events). Why does Croesus not mention 2 (b)? It has been suggested that he was reluctant to mention a possibility, enunciation of which might have sounded like an ill omen. I do not believe that a Solon-like warner would withhold a gloomy

alternative (he does not withhold 1 (a), for instance). Rather, I am
inclined to assume that Croesus is truly blind regarding instance
2 (b). To understand his thinking, we must see that it is pro-
grammed as well as limited by his own experience: (1) he has learned
his lesson of the 'wheel of human affairs': success and military
fortune do not last forever. Therefore he expressly confronts Cyrus
with the possibility of defeat (ἑσσωθείς, 207. 3); (2) he himself has
lost his empire to an invader. Therefore he wishes to protect
Cyrus against Tomyris' invasion by keeping the Araxes between
Tomyris and the Persian empire. However, although intended to
be protective, his thinking is blind to dangerous (and not unforeseeable) aspects contained in his advice: (a) even on the far side of the
river Cyrus may lose his empire, viz. by being killed in or after the
battle (this will actually happen, and being killed almost happened
to Croesus himself on the pyre);[27] (b) crossing the river may be a
sign of hybris and of greed for expansion unbecoming a mortal
(Croesus himself once, at the beginning of his self-ruining campaign, crossed the Halys!).[28]

Croesus' renewed blindness appears the more unbelievable when
we see him, instead of rationally completing section (b) of alternative 2, having recourse to emotional appeal: in spite of his desire
to protect Cyrus (cf. σφάλμα...κατὰ δύναμιν ἀποτρέψειν, 207. 1)
and to keep him from running any risk (cf. ὅδε τοι ἐν αὐτῷ
κίνδυνος ἔνι, 207. 3), he actually urges him to reverse his former
decision and talks him into aggressive action by provoking his male
pride: 'And apart from what I have expounded, it is shameful and
intolerable that Cyrus the son of Cambyses should yield his ground
by withdrawing before a woman!' (207. 5). How powerful this
argument was considered in Herodotus' own time may be seen
from Sophocles' insecure Creon who repeatedly shrinks away from
taking a softer stand towards his niece Antigone, because this could
be at the same time misunderstood as a defeat he, man and ruler,
suffered from the hands of a woman: ἦ νῦν ἐγὼ μὲν οὐκ ἀνήρ, αὕτη
δ' ἀνήρ.[29]

27. For an opposite view, cf. Immerwahr, *Herodotus*, p. 75 with note 81.
28. Croesus' own 'learning' had covered precisely the field of his unbecoming greed for expansion, γῆς ἵμερος (73. 1), so that we would expect a warning
rather than an encouragement from the new Solon.
29. Soph. *Antig.* 484; cf. 525; 678; 680.

With his appeal to Cyrus' male pride, Croesus manifests that he has unwittingly switched roles: from restraining warner to encouraging seducer. His earlier insight and wholesale condemnation of war in which 'fathers bury their sons' instead of vice versa (1. 87. 4) appears forgotten. He does not confine his advice to stimulating Cyrus into crossing the river and doing battle in Tomyris' country, but he also (which hardly betrays the spirit of humanity we may expect from Solon's disciple) comes up with a very tricky stratagem: Cyrus should pretend to withdraw from Tomyris' country, leaving behind his worst troops and a huge amount of fine food and wine. After slaughtering the inferior Persian troops, Croesus reasons, the Massagetae, unacquainted so far with Persian luxuries, will overly give themselves to eating and drinking and thus will be an easy prey to the returning Cyrus and the better part of his troops (207. 6f.).

Naturally the argument finds Cyrus' consent, for he had himself once made use of human appetite (when he induced the poverty-stricken Persians to revolt, he pointed out to them the attractive luxuries of the Medes, 1. 126). The potential danger inherent in the plan does not seem to occur to Croesus: in case of a Persian defeat, the Massagetae might, induced by their fresh acquaintance with Persian luxuries, find Persia an attractive objective of conquest (while in case of Cyrus' being victorious nothing much can be gained from the poor Massagetae). And yet this danger of provoking the attacked into a counter-invasion (together with its alternative of an empty victory over an impoverished enemy) had once been outlined by Sandanis to Croesus (1. 71). Then, to his later sorrow, Croesus would not listen and, by his attack, himself triggered the Persian invasion into Lydia. It is surprising that even now, after he allegedly 'learned through suffering', and after he himself earlier adjusted Sandanis' advice to Cyrus' situation (1. 89; see p. 16 above), he does not avoid a similar pattern again. I count this as another feature through which Herodotus points to man's narrow learning capacity.

If we summarize Croesus' position in the present conversation, we find that his returning blindness expresses itself in three steps.

(1) His knowledge of the 'wheel of human affairs', which does not grant continuous success to mortals, should make him try to dissuade Cyrus from any further conquests. But he fails to do so

(leaving this function to Cyrus' enemy Tomyris, 1. 206. 1f!).
Instead, he tries to manipulate the 'wheel of human affairs' himself: by letting the battle take place on Tomyris' side of the river,
he hopes to prevent the major disaster which the wheel may have
in stock for undefeated Cyrus and his empire, and, at the same
time, not to let slip a chance of expansion. The way in which he
manipulates a defensive aggression or a calculated risk definitely
repeats the scheme by which he tried to employ the Delphic
oracle for taking the risk out of his own campaign against Cyrus
and Persia. In both cases, he attempts to pressure a higher and
more general principle into serving a personal and limited purpose.

(2) The second step back to blindness occurs when he fails to
explain the possibility of Cyrus' disaster on Tomyris' side of the
Araxes (the uncompleted section 2 (b) in Croesus' analysis).
When, instead, he introduces an irrational urge for military action
by appealing to Cyrus' male pride, he positively advocates a course
of action the result of which he cannot overlook.

(3) His last step to blindness is the most concrete one: by
devising his dirty stratagem of using alcohol against the enemy's
army, he assumes the role of a military expert who guarantees
success on the ground of his superior knowledge. Croesus is not
aware that, the closer he becomes involved with the details of the
action he proposes, the more he exposes himself to chance. It
appears only consistent that Cyrus' disaster will originate from two
unexpected occurrences (only one third of the enemy's army goes
into the trap; among the prisoners is the widowed queen's son),
which not only wipe out Croesus' stratagem, but even turn it into
a cause for the enemy to show incomparably greater ferocity.

For the unconvinced among my readers, I would like to point to a
parallel in Herodotus' work, where likewise a supposedly prudent
advisor gives in to his advisee's overpowering drive for expansion,
and, by joining the advisee's urge, helps to ruin him. Artabanus, a
warner of Solonic stature ('φιλέει γὰρ ὁ θεὸς τὰ ὑπερέχοντα πάντα
κολούειν... οὐ γὰρ ἐᾷ φρονέειν μέγα ὁ θεὸς ἄλλον ἢ ἑωυτόν', 7. 10.
ε), at first resists Xerxes' plans for a campaign against Greece; his
caution is guided by experience, i.e. recollections of earlier campaigns with unhappy results, among them Cyrus' campaign
against the Massagetae (μεμνημένος μὲν τὸν ἐπὶ Μασσαγέτας Κύρου

οτόλον ὡς ἔπρηξε, 7. 18. 2). Even Xerxes' nightmarish dreams, which press for war against Greece, at first are prudently explained by Artabanus not as divine admonitions, but as natural reflections of Xerxes' present daytime concerns. For his warning against the war, Artabanus can refer to his implicit ability to distinguish a wise attitude (εὖ φρονέειν) from a hybris which always covets more (7. 16.α). For his explanation of the dreams, he can refer to the wisdom of his age as compared with Xerxes' youth (σε ἐγὼ διδάξω, ἔτεσι σεῦ πολλοῖσι πρεσβύτερος ἐών, 7. 16. β. 2). But *nevertheless* he changes his mind about the campaign as well as about the dream's nature (ἐγὼ μὲν καὶ αὐτὸς τράπομαι καὶ τὴν γνώμην μετατίθεμαι, 7. 18. 3), when he, dressed in Xerxes' clothes and sleeping in Xerxes' bed, experiences the same sort of nightmare as the young king: how much more would his own theory of dreams as reflecting daytime concerns fit his own situation! Of course I am convinced that Herodotus wishes his reader to see the stories of Croesus and of Artabanus, the two wise counselors who gave up their wisdom without realizing it, as related to each other (Artabanus' reference to Cyrus' campaign against the Massagetae and its unhappy result is enough to prove the connection). I must refrain here from drawing out all the lines that lead from Croesus/Cyrus to Artabanus/Xerxes and from explaining the meaning of recurrences in Herodotus' long-range composition for the understanding of his historiography. At present, I confine the role of Artabanus' change from wise to bad counselor to that of a parallel which supports my interpretation of Croesus losing his wisdom.

A position opposite to my interpretation would be to state that, since it is impossible for the wise warner to give bad counsel, we should abstain from any interpretation of Croesus' self-contradictory behaviour. This position has been energetically put forward by von Fritz,[30] whose approach to Herodotus' work may here exemplify the traditional type of *Quellen-Analyse*, which can easily be traced at least as far as F. Jacoby's article 'Herodotos' in Pauly–Wissowa's *Realenzyklopädie* of 1913. To von Fritz, Croesus' self-contradictory advice is just another discrepancy like, for instance, the different motives Herodotus supposedly gives for Croesus' campaign against Persia in 1. 46. 1 and 73. 1, cf. 75. 1

30. See his *Die Griechische Geschichtsschreibung*, Band 1 (Berlin 1967), pp. 237f.

(which I, as my reader will recall, interpreted as a change of priorities gradually taking place in Croesus' thinking).[31] The alleged discrepancies are then taken to be indicators of contradictions in Herodotus' sources on Croesus, which the ancient historian was not able to synthesize and amalgamate into one consistent story – but did not wish to drop from his work in spite of their incompatibility![32] In this way, von Fritz believes he has forced his foot into the door of Herodotus' workshop: the 'eklatanten Unvollkommenheiten' in Herodotus' report allow von Fritz 'einen tieferen und sichereren Einblick' into the 'Arbeitsweise Herodots und sein Verhältnis zu seinen "Quellen"'.[33]

Apparently the modern professor is in danger of seeing no more in Herodotus than an ancient colleague or student of his field. His expectations being predisposed by his attitude, he looks over Herodotus' shoulder, relentlessly pointing out any supposed unremoved blunders. What is so destructive about this and similar approaches to Herodotus, is that they do not grant the ancient historian even the capability of revealing man's self-contradictory behavior, of showing what is 'der Mensch in seinem Widerspruch'. In other words: above all we must *a priori* allow the ancient author to use his literary skills for literary purposes of his own. But even before that, we, his modern interpreters, must be prepared and willing to face the possibility that the ancient author surprises and exceeds us by the depth of his insight into man's situation. Otherwise, we might deprive ourselves of a chance of learning, by reducing, for instance, an author's human message to the theological or historical traditions and superhuman forces, which form his work's background and his point of departure,[34] but not his goal.

31. To the discrepancies, von Fritz makes involuntary contributions of his own by an incomplete translation of 1. 46. 1 (on p. 224) and by a misunderstanding of 1. 208. 1 (on p. 233; cf. his n. 72).

32. Here we face the powerful influence of Jacoby, according to whom Herodotus makes Solon tell 'stories' to Croesus, 'weil er (i.e. Herodotos) sie hübsch fand und sie sonst nicht unterbringen konnte' ('Herodotos', column 421).

33. Von Fritz, *Die Griechische Geschichtsschreibung*, p. 234.

34. Von Fritz' involvement in Hellmann's and Bischoff's considerations on a theodicy in Herodotus' account of Croesus may be contrasted with Marg's finding, 'wie hier vom Menschen aus und zu ihm hin gesehen werden soll, nicht vom Gott aus'. '"Selbstsicherheit"', p. 245.

Reviewing the last conversation of Croesus and Cyrus as a whole we may call its outcome striking: the king who considers himself more than a human being changes his mind and accepts the supposedly 'safe' advice of the man who claims to be aware of the limits set to human beings: Κῦρος δὲ μετεὶς τὴν προτέρην γνώμην, τὴν Κροίσου δὲ ἑλόμενος (208. 1). Herodotus leaves no doubt that Cyrus' decision to cross the Araxes and enter Tomyris' territory is solely and exclusively due to Croesus' influence. This statement itself would suffice to justify the blames uttered later by Cyrus' son as well as Cambyses' refusal to follow Croesus' advice (3. 36).

The scene does not end before being topped by another touch of tragic irony and blindness: it is Cyrus himself who unsuspectingly adds alternative 2 (b) to Croesus' incomplete considerations, 'in case the expedition across the river against the Massagetae should not be successful', ἢν ἡ διάβασις ἡ ἐπὶ Μασσαγέτας μὴ ὀρθωθῇ (208), Cyrus, before crossing the Araxes, sends his son and successor Cambyses safely home to Persia – and with him his advisor Croesus! Even more: Cambyses receives strict injunctions 'to honor him and do him well', τιμᾶν τε αὐτὸν καὶ εὖ ποιέειν. I cannot conceal my impression that Croesus' presence on the Persian bank of the Araxes is due to literary rather than historical reasons – as is his safe trip home to Agbatana, and his later journey to Egypt as a member of Cambyses' entourage. Herodotus wishes that Cyrus, when entering and when leaving his historical work, have conversations with Croesus. So Croesus must travel to the Araxes, no matter whether he historically did so or did not. And as Cyrus (unlike Croesus) did not live to learn the lesson from his own fate, Herodotus leaves it to the son to blame the father's unsuccessful advisor. Thus Croesus must travel to Egypt to have a vain dialogue with Cambyses, who has himself just recently embarked on the voyage of royal megalomania. All the time Croesus figures as the catalyst for theme II: man's unstable situation.

After crossing the river, Cyrus cannot escape his doom any more: in the first night he spends on Tomyris' territory, he dreams (as will his successor Cambyses) of a threat against the throne. Misunderstanding the prediction of his own death (210. 1) as an expression of divine care for his person (ἐμεῦ θεοὶ κήδονται καί μοι πάντα προδεικνύουσι τὰ ἐπιφερόμενα, 209. 4), he sends the suspected usurper's father (!) home to arrest the son and produce

him before Cyrus upon his return, for cross-examination. Thus
Dareius' father Hystaspes is allowed to cross the Araxes again, in
homeward direction: διαβὰς 'Αράξεα ἤιε ἐς Πέρσας. Another truly
symbolic crossing of the river.

Cyrus now gets to work and does 'what Croesus had proposed'
(ἐποίεε τὰς Κροίσου ὑποθήκας, 211. 1): Herodotus wants his reader
not to forget Croesus' responsibility. However, this still leaves room
for Cyrus' personal behaviour. Croesus' plan works out well – but
only in part: not more than one third of Tomyris' army attacks
the Persian camp and is defeated by the wine. Among the drunken
prisoners is Tomyris' son Spargapises. The widowed queen sends a
message to Cyrus (given in direct discourse by Herodotus), blaming
his guile and his use of alcohol against her army, but above
all granting the Persians safe withdrawal under the condition
that her son be returned. Otherwise, she threatens, she will quench
Cyrus' thirst for blood in her own way (212). The message takes
the place of a last warning to Cyrus, especially as Tomyris presents
herself as admonishing Cyrus well (εὖ παραινεούσης, 3). But Cyrus
does not listen (οὐδένα... ἐποιέετο λόγον) and thus misses his last
chance when young Spargapises, sober again from the unknown
experience of drunkenness, kills himself (from shame, as we easily
understand). As Cyrus would not listen, ὡς οἱ Κῦρος οὐκ ἐσήκουσε,
214. 1), Tomyris gives him battle, and Cyrus falls with the larger
part of his army – without having been granted a return from
megalomania to human consciousness and sanity. His departure
from Herodotus' work is narrated with remarkable brevity (214.
3), and instead of some final words of his we read of Tomyris'
triumphant gesture. After dipping the dead man's head into a skin
filled with human blood she addresses it thus (in direct discourse
again): 'Although I live and have defeated you in battle, you have
destroyed me when you caught my son through guile; but I shall,
exactly as I threatened, satiate you with blood' (214. 5).

Of the many reports (πολλῶν λόγων, *ibid.*) about Cyrus' death,
this one appeared to him most convincing, says Herodotus,
indicating a degree of personal judgment: ὅδε μοι ὁ πιθανώτατος
εἴρηται. Why this one? Although we cannot be sure about the
other versions Herodotus has in mind, we can probably see why
this one attracted him. First it is 'most convincing' in exemplifying
the 'wheel of human affairs': from highest success (204. 2), Cyrus

has now fallen to deepest humiliation and thus once more confirmed Solon's wisdom. But it also is an adequate conclusion and expression of Cyrus' career in Herodotus' work, from his first to his last conversation with Croesus: the first led him to spare a prisoner's life and to awake himself to a new sense of humanity. The last entails his responsibility for another prisoner's, a noble youth's, self-destruction, and results in his own speechless death, followed by a symbolical drowning in blood. The fact that one and the same Croesus is his guide in both directions, to humanity first as well as on the road to barbarism later (it was Croesus who invented the guile of which Tomyris complains at 214. 5), makes it highly doubtful to me that Herodotus should ascribe to the harmonious scene which depicts the two humble kings' first conversation (1. 86ff.) any other reality than that of a beautiful, but transient and vain vision of peaceful humanity among human beings. If that idealizing conversion of the two kings did not come first, one might perhaps take Cyrus' career as a rarer example of unenlightened despotism, a tale transmitted from mankind's uneducated quarters. But with Croesus insisting on having been educated by bitter experience and therefore being a qualified counselor in human affairs, and with the brutalized Cyrus being converted once more by this advisor, any more optimistic interpretation is foreclosed. On the contrary, the pessimism implied in Herodotus' narrative may be seen as confirmed from another corner, viz. by Croesus' last appearance in the History (in Book 3), when he, sensibly this time, tries in vain to give advice to Cyrus' insane son. Apparently, it is mostly blindness and insanity that, by winning victories over sound judgment, triggers and forms a course of action: Candaules introducing his own end, Croesus attacking Persia, Cyrus crossing the Araxes upon Croesus' advice, Cambyses proving his alleged 'sanity' by his savage behavior. This, of course, is complementary to the well-known fact that the prudent warner (Gyges; Solon; Croesus before Cambyses) rarely finds open ears in Herodotus.

Negative as such a statistic may appear to a surveying eye, it does not represent the essence of Herodotus' findings: the essential characteristic of this (in)human insanity is that it can neither be accounted for nor be controlled. For even where blindness has been healed and enlightenment has taken its place, no guarantee can be given that a permanent result is achieved. The intellectual problem of closing the knowledge gap is as unsolved in the end as it was in the beginning when Solon vainly tried to make Croesus aware of his true situation. For in the end, when Croesus vainly tries to make Cambyses aware of the dangerous consequences of his behavior, there is – quite apart from the fact that insane Cambyses would not listen anyway – no criterion to explain why the advice springing from Croesus' mind happens to be sound this time. The reader can indeed sympathize with Cambyses' caution towards the unreliable advisor. And the events that form the middle links of the chain, between Solon and Cambyses, do not in any way solve the problem either, but rather – and this is seen to be their function – expound it, i.e. they state it and thus make it known more fully.

A long and painful process of learning, described step by step in detail by our author, does not provide the learner himself (nor one who joins his course upon watching his experience) with a clue to apply his recent learning appropriately to a similar situation which contains recurrent features. What is more, his new learning leads him to the same blind self-reliance and certainty which had characterized his irrational drive when he set out to ruin himself for the first time. But if the acquisition of μαθήματα can be transformed into the same conceited human self-righteousness as do success and greed, then Herodotus has found a noteworthy explanation for the savage balance he records of human history.

An Athenian generation gap

W. G. FORREST

THE MAIN THESIS of this paper and much of the argument has
already been glanced at in my *Emergence of Greek Democracy*, but at
the cost of some repetition I think it may be useful to state it again
rather more bluntly and baldly. It is, I think, important – it may
even be true. The paper was first given at Yale in the autumn of
1968 to an audience which included both Adam Parry and
Christopher Dawson. It seems proper, therefore, to print it in a
volume which is a memorial to both; proper too to offer it in the
casual form in which it was delivered without much more than a
passing bow to that demand for scholarly paraphernalia which
both of them knew so well how to keep in its place. The only
alterations I have made to the text are due to the shrewd and
friendly criticism that they gave at the time or afterwards; they
and others, colleagues and students in New Haven and elsewhere.

Of colleagues I shall not speak, but it is well known that students
are revolting. In some places they have been more revolting than
in others, but overall the pattern has been roughly the same; for
some reason or other they no longer want to sit back and be
coddled in the cosy comfort of capitalist prosperity, or for that
matter communist prosperity. They want instead to stop wars,
help their less fortunate fellow beings and do other strange things
like that. For some reason...but the reason is not easy to see.
Probably we are too close to see it, and I therefore turn now for
relief to another striking case of student revolt, rather perhaps
alumni revolt, where our vision may be clearer because there is less
evidence to cloud it. I do this not because I believe that the past
is likely to illuminate the present – *pace* Thucydides it rarely does
– but for fun, for relief.

The starting point is the oligarchic revolution of 411 B.C., the
only politically interesting interruption of the, for Greece, remarkable domestic peace which Athens enjoyed from 508 till 322 B.C.;

[37]

a moment when for a short four months a handful of men did away
with the democracy which had been created by Kleisthenes in 508
and had then quietly taken its full form after the reforms of
Ephialtes in 462. I say 'a handful' rather than the traditional
'Four Hundred' partly because I do not wish to become involved
in any of the technical problems which this nasty episode raises,
partly because no one knows how many men took a positive part
in promoting it (my guess would be nearer fifty than four
hundred),[1] mainly because I do not wish to limit responsibility to
those who had official recognition under the new régime. Who
would like to give a number to the group which took over in
Greece in April 1967?

No, our problem is with the character of the few men we know
who can be associated with the event – Antiphon, Kritias,
Phrynichos, Peisander, Aristokrates, Theramenes, Alkibiades –
and with the nameless and numberless others who may have been
like them.

With the exception of Antiphon who was born about 480 B.C.,
all these men were near contemporaries, born within a few years
of each other about the middle of the century. The only nearly
fixed date is the birth of Alkibiades, 450 B.C., but none of the others
needs to be or even can be moved by much outside the decade 455
to 445 B.C.[2] They also belong to the same circle, not the same
political circle in any technical sense, but to the same social circle.
They were all, with the possible exception of Phrynichos, members
of the upper class. Phrynichos, [Lysias] said, was of humble,
shepherd origin. But no one much believes what Lysias said when
he was arguing a case, still less [Lysias]. And there is the harder
evidence in Aristophanes that Phrynichos had at least made the
Algonquin circle by 422.[3] All these boys were *Kaloi Kagathoi*; they
were gentlemen either by birth or by adoption.

They were gentlemen and most of them were growing up or had
just finished growing up in the 420s; their first experiences of
politics, the first political issues they will have known about from

1. Fifty might well decide to quadruple themselves to imitate a known
Solonian model; four hundred, less likely in themselves, are still less likely to
have dreamed up a Solonian precedent.

2. For such evidence as there is see J. K. Davies, *Athenian Propertied Families*
(Oxford 1971), s. nn.

3. [Lysias] xx. 11; Ar. *Wasps* 1302.

direct adult experience, will have been those of the years just before and just after the death of Perikles. It is on these men in these early years that I should like to concentrate, or rather, since we know nothing about any of them except Alkibiades and very little about him, on other men of the same age-group and of the same background of whom we do know something.

Two such upper-class youths have left direct testimony to their outlook, Aristophanes in the *Knights* of 424 and another of unknown name whose work comes to us among the writings of Xenophon and is known as the Ps. Xen. *Ath. Pol.*, more usually and much less accurately as the Old Oligarch. Others have said revealing things about the class in general, Aristophanes again, Thucydides, Plato and perhaps Euripides. With these sources, and some imagination, we can divine what this generation thought at the time, how they behaved at the time, and why many of them, the less reputable among them, behaved as they did later, in 411.

But first a few words about the political background of the 420s. Here I merely offer three propositions.

(1) That in one sense everyone in Athens during the Archidamian War was a democrat. An oligarch is a man who wishes to set up an oligarchic constitution and, if he is a practising politician, a man who tries to set up an oligarchic constitution or at least makes propaganda for one. There is no suggestion, no credible suggestion, in the sources that any such existed in Athens; some old grumblers no doubt there were in odd corners of the *agora,* but they have left little mark. Everyone who mattered was prepared to accept the given constitution and, in that sense, was a democrat.

(2) That in another sense very few members of the upper-class under the age of about fifty would be a democrat. Here I mean not someone who merely accepted the *status quo* but someone who believed positively in democracy. To the upper-class Athenian who grew up in the 460s, before Ephialtes' reforms, or even in the 450s when the democracy was still being tightened up, fundamental constitutional questions mattered. Some, like Perikles, became democrats; others, probably the majority, would believe in the existing Kleisthenic system; others again, a few, might even want to go back to earlier and purer aristocratic forms. But almost all would be concerned, deeply concerned, one way or the other. But to the young man of the 430s the questions were different. For one

thing democracy was there and was obviously there to stay: for another the horror that many of their elders had felt in 462 must have been tempered when it was discovered that democracy meant Perikles, a man who had, after all, been to the right kind of school, wore the right kind of tie, had the right kind of accent – who was a gentleman; when it was discovered, moreover, that democracy not only worked but worked to their own economic advantage (no one in Athens was growing poorer between 460 and 430). Then, in 429, the gentleman died but democracy went on; by now, however, so firmly established that I cannot conceive that anyone seriously contemplated its overthrow – it was no longer an issue and only a freak could have felt passionately about it. Older men still would, they would still get excited about the status of the Areopagos or the competence of the law-courts as old men do – Aristophanes makes fun of such old-fashioned characters in the *Acharnians* and the *Wasps*, the old anti-Spartan hoplites, the old democratic dikasts. To the young these old men were laughable; for them democracy was taken for granted, was not something you worried about, for or against.

(3) That there was no major issue for these young men of the twenties to get excited about. How to administer the democracy; how to run Athens' empire (the existence of the empire, like that of democracy, was taken for granted); how to win the war which Sparta had started in 431; who, if anyone, was to take Perikles' place as προστάτης τοῦ δήμου after his death, someone like Perikles himself or someone like the upstart Kleon. These were the questions of the time and none of them, except minimally the last, has that nice touch of principle about it which young men thirst for. Like most young men they would have been quite prepared to set the world to rights, but there was nothing that seemed particularly wrong; they were ready to rebel, but there was nothing to rebel about, and certainly no chance of winning.

The result was twofold. For one thing the young turned their attention to the only question with a smack of principle about it – the appearance of the so-called demagogues. This was a new phenomenon, men who were not of the traditional ruling class but yet had the audacity to try to rule. We do not make the mistake of taking Aristophanes' or others' word for it that these men were far below the proper level, men from the street; far from it. The fantastic economic growth of Athens since the time of Solon, together with the new political machinery introduced by Kleisthenes had made it possible for new families to nose their way forwards. By the middle of the fifth century several had arrived, not at the very top, but near enough to matter. Kleon, for example, the arch-demagogue, represented as the essence of low-born vulgarity when he acquired real authority in the 420s, was the son of a man who had been a Choregos in 460–59, an office limited to the higher property-classes, and who had entered into a nexus of marriage-alliances with others of his kind and with some decayed aristocrats, alliances which remind one of nothing so much as the panic searches for birth or wealth that were so characteristic of early nineteenth-century England – and which may even be found in contemporary America.

In the 450s such men were important but obscure. By the 420s at least one of them was seeking and reaching a leading position. That was intolerable. But it was a change from a Rolls-Royce administration to a Jaguar administration. No more than that. But, of course, for owners of Triumphs who were soon to inherit Rolls-Royces that was enough. There is nothing more despicable than a Jaguar.

Here then was something wrong, and the young men turned their desire for trouble in general against Kleon and others like him in a way that the poor man certainly did not deserve. We see their attitude in that of Bdelykleon in Aristophanes' *Wasps*, of the young aristocratic knights who make up the chorus of the *Knights* – and in case anyone thinks that this only reflects the hostility to Kleon of young Aristophanes let us remember that the Athenian knights had in fact had a quarrel with Kleon two years before;[4] that the so-called Old Oligarch shows a similar hatred – but of that later. We see the whole attitude perfectly summed up by Eupolis, another of the same generation, in his play the *Demes*, a few years later, in 416:[5]

> Once upon a time our city's Generals came from the best families, first by wealth and first by birth. We used to pray

4. Details of the quarrel are obscure but do not concern us. For a recent discussion see W. R. Connor, *Theopompos and fifth century Athens* (Harvard 1968), pp. 50ff.
5. Frg. 117 (12).

to them as if they were gods – and so they were, and we
prospered. But now we go on campaign at random, electing
as our generals – garbage.

But simply to hate Kleon and abuse him was not enough, and
this brings us to the second result and at the same time from the
political to the intellectual background of these same pupils. They
were all pupils of the sophists. A quick reading of Plato's *Gorgias*,
dramatic date probably 427, will make it far clearer than I can
what the effects of this training were.

We have the harmless, in one way harmless, gentle, clever old
Gorgias; we have his bright, but not over-bright graduate student
Polus. Clearly to Plato neither mattered very much. Gorgias is
Gorgias and nothing can be done about it; Polus is something of a
menace but only in a very limited way – he wants to be a professor
like his tutor and might even be quite a good one at Oxford or
Cambridge (Mass.). But Kallikles, the third character with whom
Sokrates discusses the powers of rhetoric is a very different matter.
He is to become a man of action; brilliant and unscrupulous, he
has learnt from Gorgias all the tricks of persuasion that he has to
offer and is now bent on using them to turn himself into a new
Perikles; he has learnt that conventional morality is bunk and is
out to take Perikles' place with no thoughts of anything except the
pure joy of power that the position will give. He accepts democracy, but in this acceptance there is no sign of preference for
democracy as such. It is simply the society in which men like
Kallikles, in the circumstances of the time, are most likely to
succeed. Neither for the *demos* whom he is supposed to serve, nor
for democracy itself does Kallikles care a fig. And whether or not
that is a fair summary of the character of Kallikles as he appears in
the dialogue, it is at any rate an accurate description of what I
imagine to have been the outlook of the more dangerous among his
aristocratic contemporaries.

Young men were drawn to the sophists for many reasons. Two
of these deserve mention. First they were drawn because the
sophists offered to teach them a skill, the art of persuasion, with
which they thought they might overcome, outdo in the eyes of the
demos such unpolished monsters as Kleon or Hyperbolos, believing
that tutored mediocrity would somehow be more effective than

untutored genius. Secondly they were drawn because in a way the sophists might seem to be giving them a substitute of sorts for what they lacked in real political life; those issues of principle I spoke of before. Political theory had been invented as a subject and with this subject mastered in twelve easy lessons it must have been a great consolation to forget about the hard facts of real-life Athens where change was out of the question and to create a fantasy Athens which could be reformed and revolutionized, chopped and changed and bashed about to fit the requirements of the ideal state which each and every one of them was busy constructing according to his personal tastes.

These were the attractions; note also two of the effects. (1) that their education would serve to increase the sense of class superiority that they already felt towards Kleon and his like, (2) that constitutional theorizing would lead to the production of theoretical constitutions. By the time they took their degrees they all would have somewhere among their lecture notes a little piece of paper which said 'The Areopagus should do so-and-so; the Boule should do so-and-so; and the rest'. The importance of the first is immediate; that of the second doesn't appear until 411 – then it is vital. But of that later; we must now turn to the two documents I mentioned earlier, the Old Oligarch and the *Knights*. The second is non-controversial – it was produced in spring 424 and was written by Aristophanes at the age of roughly twenty. The second is more difficult. We do not know what the Ps. Xen. *Ath. Pol.* is, nor who wrote it, nor when it was written – come to think of it that's not true – I do.

To take the most important point first – what is it? It is not, as many scholars have assumed, a political pamphlet, that is to say a manifesto or a piece of propaganda; it is, on the contrary, a purely theoretical work, a political analysis. On the whole my feeling is that it was intended to be spoken rather than read but it is not a speech for delivery with a specific political purpose in an active political assembly; it is a lecture for the class-room or the study-group. This for the simple and conclusive reason that a practical political document will not give the opposition full marks on every subject as the Oligarch does and will make some practical recommendations, will leave the reader with some idea of what he is supposed to do or think which the Oligarch does not. But the

word 'lecture' is misleading; the author is demolishing one by one
a series of arguments that have been put before him, every section
begins with some variation of the formula 'It is held that so-and-
so is the case...but' and may I add paradoxically at the moment
that he is demolishing arguments *against* the Athenian *demos*. In
other words we should perhaps substitute for 'lecture' 'debate'
and if we do the nature of his opponent in this debate is clear.
'It is held that there is no Eunomia in Athens but...'; 'We are
told that the Athenians do not know how to handle slaves but...';
'It is taken for granted that the Athenian hoplite army is inferior
to that of her enemies...'; 'there is no physical training, no
gumnastike in Athens but...' Only one state in Greece was famous
for Eunomia, hoplites, physical training and the beating-up of
slaves, only a Spartan or someone with very Spartan tastes would
rake up such a collection of charges. So we have one of two set
speeches in a debate between an Athenian (that the speaker is
Athenian cannot be doubted) and a Spartan or violently laconizing Athenian on the subject of Athenian democracy, the Spartan
speaking against, the Athenian for, but speaking for in a very
peculiar way. His whole defence rests on the assumption that
anyone, including the *demos*, has a right to look after his own
selfish interests and on the argument that Athenian democracy is
organized in the best interests of the *demos*. He does not regard
himself as a member of that *demos* – he despises it, hates it but he
justifies it none the less.

When was the debate held? Learned men have put it as early as
440, intelligent men have put it as late as 416, some less intelligent
have even gone below that. There is in fact no doubt that it
belongs to the Archidamian War, to be precise to August 424,
but to avoid unnecessary argument I shall now make only a more
limited claim for somewhere between 429 and 424.[6]

And who took part in the debate on the Athenian side? His
name we shall probably never know but three things are clear.
(1) He was of the upper class – his whole approach shows that.
(2) He was a pupil of the sophists – this has been said often enough
and needs no argument. From his primary assumption – αὐτὸν
μὲν γὰρ εὖ ποιεῖν παντὶ συγγνώμη ἐστίν – down to the last trick
of style his approach is sophistic. (3) He was a young man, a very

6. For my views on the date, see *Klio* 52 (1970), pp. 107–16.

young man. There is nothing crusty or settled or even disciplined about him; he is experimenting with language as he is with thought and is none too competent with either. What we have is undergraduate journalism, not sober or, I would say, original political thought. I have nothing against undergraduate journalism but it is fairly easy to distinguish.

By now the answer should be fairly obvious; this is a second-level sophistic *epideixis* (he finishes with the words τούτῳ τῷ τρόπῳ ᾧ ἐγὼ ἐπέδειξα), a performance delivered by some quite competent pupil in the class-room, an artificial defence of Athenian democracy against a perhaps slightly less artificial attack. 'Next week, gentlemen, Mr Smith will prepare a paper in which he will set out the criticisms that one of the Spartan prisoners on the Akropolis might express against Athenian democracy; Mr Jones will be prepared to reply. Mr Smith might find it useful to consult my advanced student Kritias who is working on the Spartan Constitution at the moment; Mr Jones may find it helpful to remember the principle recently enunciated by my colleague and former pupil Thrasymachos that justice is the interest of the stronger – it has interesting implications for this subject.'

What can we infer from Mr Jones' performance about his politics? Strictly speaking, nothing, for both the questions and the situation are unreal but we can infer much about his approach to politics and one of the most interesting things about it is that it is precisely the same as that of Aristophanes in the *Knights*. It is also much the same as that which I have inferred for their contemporaries from the political background – not surprisingly, since I have carefully doctored the latter to make it fit.

The most important point, once again, is that the stability of democracy is undisputed. But now this stability is analysed. Sea-power depends on the *demos* and the *demos* depends on sea-power for its profits. The *demos* knows that these profits reach it safely only under a democracy, *ergo*, so long as Athenian sea-power lasts and the profits come in, there will be democracy. There is inefficiency and corruption in this democracy (a point that Aristophanes makes all the time) but the *demos* finds it worthwhile to put up with this in order to get its benefits. The demagogues are much less competent than clever young men would be in running the country but again they add to the *demos*' pleasure because they strengthen the democracy and increase the benefits. Therefore they are not to be got rid of. In fact it is no use hoping to change any details, however much in need of change they may be. All minor points are necessary side-effects of democracy and since democracy cannot be shifted, with all its weaknesses, it must be accepted.

Aristophanes in 424 is equally young but is neater, funnier, cleverer and writes better Greek; but the thought is the same. You will remember that Nikias and Demosthenes, the honest slaves, are in despair because their master Demos listens only to the wicked slave, Paphlagon, the tanner Kleon.[7] There is, it seems, no answer until at last an oracle is found. Kleon will be overcome by one even more despicable than he – a sausage-seller. The serious-minded undergraduate sees no hope; the comedian equally sees no hope but being a comedian invents the fantasy of someone worse than Kleon who will be miraculously transformed into his country's saviour. Notice especially the lines which the comedian inserts into the working-out of his fantastic idea. The chorus attack Demos for his stupidity in being the dupe of the dema-gogues: 'How easy you are to lead astray; how you love flattery; you believe anything an orator says. Your wits are all astray.' The Demos replies 'Your wits are none too strong if you think I'm really such a fool. Don't you realize that I put on this act deliber-ately? Here I sit being served by all and of course I keep one thief in my retinue; he makes his profits but in the end I get mine and when I'm done with him out he goes on his ear' and so on. What better parallel could there be to the Oligarch's belief that the *demos* looks after its own interests?

To sum up: democracy is there, unshakeable, so long as Athens' navy survives; the *demos* lacks restraint, lacks sense (or appears to), lacks *sophrosyne* and *eunomia* but it can afford to lack them, it prospers on its *misthoi*, the festivals, the pay for service and all the rest and prospers all the more, the more corrupt, venal and horrible its ministers are.

7. The standard identification of Slaves A and B with Nikias and Demos-thenes was challenged by K. J. Dover in *Maia* 21 (1969), pp. 123–5; but while he is clearly right to deny any respectable manuscript authority for the identi-fication and to point out some inconsistencies, I cannot believe that an Athenian audience of 424 could have failed to see the characters as we see them -- Nikias and Demosthenes.

Given this view of the world of politics what does the young man do, what does the so-called Old Oligarch do? He may want to be a politician or he may not. If he does, the only course open to him is the course adopted by Plato's Kallikles, the course adopted in real life by Alkibiades. He must learn the tricks and join in the demagogic rat-race. He must beat the demagogues at their own game. He must be more extreme, more flattering, more irresponsible than they. Some more honourable men, no doubt, stood aloof; some took to drink and democracy, like Phrynichos;[8] many just took to democracy. Alkibiades did, and so did many others.

Now I do not want to suggest that there were no decent men born in upper-class families about 450, nor that this particular age-group was or could be quite so sharply distinguished from its neighbours as I have implied. Such generalizations, such clear-cut distinctions don't work in real life. But I would claim that this age-group was more distinguishable than most, that contemporaries in fact distinguished it and that its most marked characteristics were its cleverness, its unscrupulousness, its ambition, and its lack of any ideals which might have made the ambition worth while. Let me list the slender evidence.

I have already mentioned the parts played by clever young men in Aristophanes, Bdelykleon, the Knights, even Pheidipiddes in the *Clouds*. Let me add the long and very significant attack on these same young men in the parabasis of the *Acharnians* of 425 for their lack of sympathy, their sense of superiority, their over-cleverness, their selfishness. Aristophanes himself was one of them and shared many of their prejudices but he was broad-minded enough, intelligent enough, sympathetic enough, to avoid their worst failings. He too was a pupil of the sophists and proud of it but he had what many of them lacked – humanity – and this, plus a touch of genius, made him the comedian that he was. Plato too was aware that they had existed for we cannot suppose that his Kallikles was meant to represent a single individual, nor can we doubt that it was his awareness of the failings of men among whom he had grown up, these men, that impelled him to the search for principle in politics that produced the *Republic*. So possibly was Euripides. In that puzzling play the *Supplices*, perhaps another document of the 420s, we hear more than once directly or by implication of the

8. For details see n. 2 above.

Neoi and their pernicious effects on state affairs.[9] Those who see
Alkibiades everywhere see him here. I do not, but I do feel a
recognition by Euripides that in some way or other, harmful
rather than the reverse, the young as a group were likely to cause
trouble. The nature of the trouble is made clearer by Thucydides
in a speech made by a democrat in another great democratic city
where democracy really was threatened, by Athenagoras in
Syracuse in 415. This is a speech on Syracusan preparations
against the Athenian invasion. With no apparent relevance
Athenagoras bursts out in the middle of it with the words: τί καὶ
βούλεσθε, ὦ νεώτεροι;

Nothing could be clearer than Athenagoras' identification of
the young with the oligarchs, at least with the vocal oligarchs, nor
more impressive than his insistence on their claims to superior
intelligence. Notice the superb contempt of his conclusion, Ἀλλ'
ἔτι καὶ νῦν, ὦ πάντων ἀξυνετώτατοι, εἰ μὴ μανθάνετε κακὰ
σπεύδοντες, ἢ ἀμαθέστατοί ἐστε... (Thucydides, vi. 39–40).

Fortunately it doesn't much matter whether Athenagoras said
these words or not, nor that the speech is said to have been given
in Syracuse rather than in Athens and in 415 not 424; intellectual
movements are international and the only modification I would
introduce in transferring the whole thing to Athens is the deletion
of positive proposals for oligarchy. Athens had not reached that
stage in the 420s; she did in 412.

In 413 the Athenian navy was destroyed in Sicily. It is difficult
for us to appreciate just how profound the effect on Athens was.
We have never experienced anything like it. The immediate
political result was a desperate desire to abandon power, to shift
responsibility on to someone else, on to anyone willing to take it –
to the *probouloi* in 413, the Four Hundred in 411.

At the same time there seemed a chance of survival in an
alliance with Persia, and, so they were told by men who were still
prepared to think about politics, only oligarchs can talk to
Persians. Sicily provided the necessary psychological conditions,
the prospect of Persian aid the practical inducement for Athens to
accept oligarchy. But we need more than these two points to
explain the revolution, above all to explain the attitude of the men

9. *Supplices* 160, 190–1, 250; for the date see Zuntz, *Political Plays of
Euripides* (Manchester 1963), ch. 3.

who organized it, and what we need is precisely the intellectual background that I have been talking about so far.

Democracy, they had been taught, depends on sea-power – the sea-power was gone. The *demos* wants democracy because of the profits – the profits were gone too. At one stroke the fantasy issue of principle on which they had lived for the last ten or fifteen years became a real issue, the ideal world of theoretical constitutions became the real world. They looked at their lecture-notes again and saw that, by all the rules, oligarchy was a practical possibility. For ten years or more, like Kallikles, they had played at being democrats. Phrynichos, Peisander as well as Alkibiades had all been 'demagogues' and so had many others; they had had no choice and it was only play – as Alkibiades says at Sparta in 415 'We have acted as leaders of the people, but since democracy was the form of government at Athens we had to conform to the prevailing conditions' or again 'As for democracy anyone with any sense knew what that meant...nothing new can be said about a system which is generally recognized as absurd' – περὶ ὁμολογουμένης ἀνοίας – agreed, that is, by the smart young men.[10] Now the play was over and they had a choice. Phrynichos, Peisander, Alkibiades and many others chose oligarchy. Not all. Aristophanes did not, nor did another near contemporary, Lysias. Some went so far, others went to extremes. The whole respectable upper-class crowd broke up and reformed but when it had reformed a large part of it had turned its thoughts to revolution. The lecture notes were still there, the theoretical constitutions were brushed up and they set about carving up Athens to fit their theories.

And here let us note again the importance of their theoretical approach. There is a world of difference between the peaceful revolution of 462 and the bloody lunacy of 411 and it is in very large measure to be explained by the theorizing that lay behind the latter. Ephialtes had, in some sense, a theory of democracy. But Ephialtes' beliefs were born in the real world of politics and were designed to be applied to real life. He thought as he did because he had evidence in real life to support him and he acted when and how he did because, as an able politician, he saw how much he could do and chose the moment to do it not by looking up his books but by looking at Athens and Athenians. Glance at

10. For their earlier careers see n. 2 above.

the model constitutions which appear as chapters 30 and 31 of the
Ath. Pol. and you will see at once that this is in a different world.
These models were never put into effect but that is irrelevant. The
mere fact that they could play any part at all in practical politics
in 411 is enough to show how absurd the whole thing was. At no
point do they make contact with reality: they do not belong in the
council-house but in the professor's study – and heaven help the
state which chooses such a professor as its one-man commission on
the constitution.

The revolution, then, had its roots in the past, and in conclusion
I offer two further illustrations of this continuity in what had been
simply respectable but now became oligarchic thinking. One battle
cry was *sophrosyne*, now being used as a euphemism for oligarchy
(they dealt a great deal in euphemisms – *eunomia*, *ta panta
eutaktein*, the best of all, μὴ τὸν αὐτὸν τρόπον δημοκρατεῖσθαι).
Primarily this pointed the contrast with the democratic lack of
sophrosyne which had, they thought, led to Sicily. They, the clever,
would never have made such a mistake. But Sicily was only the
confirmation of a much older idea. It is there in Aristophanes; it
is there even more clearly in the Old Oligarch where he argues
that rule by the χρηστοί would bring good government but cut the
people's pleasure; it is there in the whole business of intellectual
superiority I spoke of earlier. It is a false and frightening doctrine,
but none the less popular for that.

Again the most immediate practical demand they made was for
an end to *misthophoria* – a reasonable enough demand in the
circumstances of 411 when Athens could not afford to continue
public pay. But again it goes back and the fact that it has this
earlier history is suggestive. The attachment of the *demos* to its
misthoi appears again and again in Aristophanes. Let me quote one
passage from the *Knights*, 'If two orators proposed, one to build
triremes, the other to increase state-pay, the salary-man would
beat the trireme-man in a canter.' And, of course, it is almost the
central point of the Old Oligarch's thesis. Both disapprove,
Aristophanes good-humouredly, the Oligarch peevishly, but more
important, both give the impression that the chief motive the
demos has for democracy is the personal profit involved. In the
Wasps Aristophanes recognizes another, the simple desire for
power. But neither, indeed no one, suggested that there might be

something else, the principle of the thing. Aristophanes of course would hardly mention a principle even if he recognized it – he was a comedian. But the Oligarch would not have recognized it even if it had been thrust under his nose. He and others like him didn't believe in principles. They had none of their own and were not likely to believe that others had.

Their argument I suspect was a simple one. The *demos* loves democracy because of the profits. Profits are no longer possible. Remove them and you remove the desire for democracy. Here then is our chance. The belief that profit is the only motive among ordinary men is a common one, popular among modern supporters of private enterprise as it was among fifth-century oligarchs and it was as false then as it is today. In 482 the Athenian *demos* had voted, of its own free will, for triremes rather than cash, that same *demos* in 411 recovered from the shock of Sicily, threw out the Four Hundred and survived, though divided and suspicious, survived incredibly and superbly for six years more with new triremes and no cash against a combination of Spartan arms and Persian money. Men like Peisander, Phrynichos and the rest couldn't understand such behaviour; it didn't belong in their educated world – that was one reason, perhaps the chief reason why they failed.

Athens failed too in the end but it must be clear by now where I would put the blame. Not with so many history books on the Athenian people, history books which, by an unhappy marriage of Thucydides and Plato, produce a story of democracy and corruption advancing hand in hand from the restrained dignity of the days of Perikles, through the first debauches introduced by Kleon to the hideous degeneracy of wild-eyed monster Kleophon. The Athenian people was not free from corruption, selfishness, stupidity and cruelty; no people is. But for something like a hundred years it chose leaders, Themistokles, Aristeides, even Kimon in his limited way, Ephialtes, Perikles, Kleon; later a reformed Alkibiades, Thrasyboulos and a half-reformed Theramenes (for some of the oligarchs learned their lesson in 411); it chose leaders, some ἐκ τῶν μεγίστων οἰκιῶν, some not, with whose help it directed its government, conducted its wars and administered its empire fairly, tolerantly, sensibly, justly and on the whole unselfishly. It did fail but it failed because it produced and on some occasions listened to a group of men who did not share its beliefs, whose own personal ambition, whose lack of *sophrosyne* if you like, destroyed what they were too clever to understand.

Today things are different. The young are on the left, not on the right. They are arguing not against principles but for them, even if they have only a very hazy grasp of what those principles are, and so I love them as I do not love Kritias. But one thing is the same. That neither side seems to understand the other – that is intelligible enough – but also that quite often they don't try to understand the other. It was because the *demos*, right though they were, didn't try to understand the opposition that it executed Socrates. Which was a pity. If it had spared him we might never have been faced with the awful Plato.

Thucydides' judgment of Periclean strategy*

GEORGE CAWKWELL

IN THE SPEECH which Thucydides put into the mouth of Pericles[1] at the end of Book 1, successfully urging the Athenians not to submit to the Spartan demands, Pericles asserted his confidence that Athens could survive in war (1. 144. 1), and when Thucydides summed up Pericles' life he declared that this military estimate was sound. 'When the war began, he appears in this matter too to have realized in advance the power of the city ...and after his death his foresight with regard to the war was recognized still further' (2. 65. 5f.). But was Thucydides right? Was Pericles' strategic estimate so justified by the war?

There is no real question of what Pericles' strategy was.[2] Pericles himself set it out clearly enough (1. 143. 3–144. 1), and Thucydides reiterated it in the summing up (2. 65. 7). Nor has it ever been shown that it was plainly inept.[3] Yet doubts remain. It was tried for so short a time that it cannot be thought to have been properly tested, and to commend it one is forced in some degree, like Thucydides, to argue the ineptitude of what replaced it. But perhaps all possible Athenian strategies might in the long run have failed. In any case it is hard to believe that so great a war could have been satisfactorily fought to a conclusion on a purely defensive strategy. Frustration is more likely to prompt invention and resource than to compel submission. Pericles might, also, have

* I wish to take this opportunity to thank the Master and Fellows of Jonathan Edwards College, Yale, for inviting me to visit Yale in 1969 as Robert Bates Visiting Fellow, and the members of the Classics Department for their great kindness on that occasion.

All references in this paper are to Thucydides, unless otherwise stated.

1. See Note A at end.

2. See Note B at end.

3. For E. Meyer, *Geschichte des Altertums*, IV, pp. 296ff., G. Busolt, *Griechische Geschichte*, IV. 2, pp. 901f. ('grundsätzlich richtig'). H. Delbrück, *Geschichte der Kriegskunst*, pp. 121ff. J. Beloch was critical (*Griechische Geschichte²*, III. 1, p. 300).

been proved over-optimistic financially speaking: the large naval expeditions of 431 and 430 were perhaps too costly to be continued for a decade without the 'forced contributions' (βίαιοι εἰσφοραί) Pericles himself declared unsatisfactory for financing a war (1. 141. 4), and the increased dependence on costly imports at a time when a large capital reserve was being put into circulation as sailors' pay would tend to cause inflation (and probably did, even though the plague, which Pericles could not have foreseen, reduced the populace so much that the full financial effect of his strategy was not felt).[4] All in all, it is not immediately obvious that the strategy so briefly followed would have enabled Athens to 'win through'. Why then was Thucydides so firm in recommending its author?

The answer lies in consideration of Spartan strategy. The war fully exposed the weakness of the Spartan position in 431, and this paper aims to make this clear and to show that Pericles, and therefore Thucydides, judged well.[5]

There is a plainly discernible difference in Sparta about the

---

4. The raising of jury-pay (Schol. Ar. *Wasps* 88, 300) was perhaps to compensate for the rise in the cost of living. Sea-transport was expensive, especially in time of war (7. 28. 1), and the loss of cereals from Attica enforced costly replacement. But perhaps Pericles dealt with the problem. The δεκάτη of the first Callias Decree (line 7) is, *pace* Meiggs–Lewis, p. 161, probably the δεκάτη τῶν ἐκ τοῦ Πόντου πλεόντων exacted at the Bosporus (Xen. *Hell.* 1. 1. 22; 4. 8. 27 – Polybius 4. 44. 4 could only be taken to prove that it did not exist before 410 if we could be sure that such a tax earlier must have been mentioned in a literary source; given Thucydides' lack of interest in finance, the probability is all the other way, that Polybius' statement derives, perhaps indirectly, from Xenophon). But it would be very strange if the δῆμος were to levy a 10% tax on its food: so I suggest that 10% was paid at the Bosporus on the value of the cargo by ships not bound for Athens but that ships bound for Athens were by some method exempt; the tax thus served before the war to draw the necessary imports to Athens. During the war as the second Methone decree shows (Meiggs–Lewis, no. 65, lines 34–41) the system was different. Save for privileged states like Methone, or Mytilene (as an autonomous ally) (3. 2. 2), all exports from Byzantium other than to Athens were banned, and the Hellespontophylakes, known only from this inscription but necessary whenever Athens was taxing the Pontic trade, were now required to seize any ship that broke the ban (ἀζέμιος in line 40, relating to the ship, not the captain, suggests this, 3ημία being of course a 'penalty' not a 'tax'). In this way, perhaps, Pericles adapted the system, to compensate for the loss of Attic cereal.

5. The subject has been fully treated only by Brunt, *Phoenix* 19 (1965), 255–80. I have not included in the notes references to parts of that article, but it will be clear that we overlap and that my debt is large.

strategy of the Archidamian War. On the one hand, there was what may be labelled the 'conventional' strategy of ravaging and seeking so to bring on a decisive battle or to enforce submission. Hence the major invasions of 431 and 430,[6] which, despite Archidamus' warnings (1. 81. 6), were expected to bring a quick decision (5. 14. 3, and cf. 1. 141. 5). On the other hand from the outset there were plainly notions of what may be labelled the 'adventurous' strategy. The Corinthians were represented as declaring before the war, 'You have other ways of fighting the war, viz. causing revolt amongst their allies, which is the most effective means of depriving them of the revenues their strength depends on, and fortifying strong-points to menace their land, as well as other measures, at present unforeseeable' (1. 122. 1). Once war had been decided on, Sparta had it in mind to seek help from Persia and elsewhere, and to assemble a naval force of 500 ships[7] (2. 7. 2, and cf. 1. 82. 1), which would have well outnumbered the Athenian navy (2. 13. 8). Until 425, the Spartans appear mainly to have stuck to the 'conventional',[8] but the 'adventurous' clearly had some part. Persian aid was sought repeatedly (4. 50. 2), and, although in the Archidamian War nothing came of the appeals to Sicily and Italy for naval forces, Sparta made trial of the sea. In 429 Cnemus gathered a substantial enough fleet[9] for the attack on Acarnania, and before the second sea-fight Phormio roundly

6. Plut. *Per.* 33. 5 and *Mor.* 784E number the Peloponnesian army of 431 at 60,000, not an incredible figure if it included light-armed. Androtion (*Die Fragmente der griechischen Historiker*, 324) F 39, though corrupt, proves that there were at least 20,000. (See Jacoby, *ad loc.* on these figures.) Certainly the invasions were large. They involved two-thirds of the available forces (2. 10. 2; 47. 2); presumably Thucydides gave this information here, as for the force that sought to distract Athens in 428 (3. 15. 1), because they were notably large armies.

7. 'An impossible number' according to Gomme *ad loc.* But hopes were high in 431. Sybota had seen a fleet of 150 ships; Syracuse had voted a fleet of 100 (Diod. 12. 30. 1; under 439/8 but perhaps shortly before the war – hence the Leontine and Rhegian appeals of 433/2) and it was not yet clear that it would not be built (no large Syracusan naval force is encountered during the Archidamian War); financial help was to be sought from Persia (2. 7. 2 and 1. 82. 1), possibly naval help too.

8. Presumably the point of Archidamus' attack on Plataea in 429 was to lure the Athenians out in defence of an ally, whom they could not be expected to desert (cf. 2. 73. 3). For the rest, Attica was invaded annually down to 425, save for 426, when earthquake warned off (3. 89. 1).

9. 2. 86. 4 (seventy-seven ships).

declared to the Athenian sailors 'The issue is of great importance to you: either you will destroy the hopes the Peloponnesians have of their fleet or you will make more real to the Athenians their fears about control of the sea' (2. 89. 10). There followed shortly the (abortive) attack on the Piraeus (2. 93f.), and the next year at Olympia the Spartans put before the allies a proposal to send help to Mytilene in revolt (3. 8. 1), the mysterious Meleas having been sent out even before the revolt began (3. 5. 2).[10] Forty-two ships were sent (3. 26. 1), a sizeable force, specially prepared (3. 16. 3), clear proof of intent to exploit those 'other ways' of war. There followed the intervention in Corcyra with a still larger fleet (3. 69. 1 and 2), and in the following year came the foundation of Heraclea in Trachis (3. 92), partly a bastion for Sparta's allies in central Greece but partly a base for attacks on Euboea, all important to Athens in the Decelean War (8. 95. 2), earlier not unimportant (2. 14. 1, and cf. Ar. *Wasps* 715f.).[11]

Thus 'adventure' played a part. Yet very little came of it before 425. Basically, Sparta lacked the naval power and the Spartiates to send abroad, and, until the capture of the men on Sphacteria, she had no will fully to exploit her other resources of manpower. No doubt prudent voices counselled caution, but above all the 'conventional' must have seemed sufficient. The Spartans had entered the war, as already remarked, confident of a quick decision (5. 14. 3), and in summer 430 Athens appealed for peace (2. 59. 2). Thucydides makes much of Pericles' apologia, little of

10. Had Meleas been sent by the state? If so, the apologia the Mytilenaeans deemed necessary (3. 9–12) reads oddly. Also, how is one to explain his companion, Hermaeondas of Thebes? Perhaps this was a private mission, contrived by those who wished to get Sparta involved with 'other ways' of war. Meleas is designated by Thucydides Λάκων: only one other such designation occurs (8. 55. 2) and by it Thucydides means some special status, not Spartiate, nor perhaps περίοικος (cf. 8. 6. 4; 22. 1), Λακεδαιμόνιος being a general term used perhaps when Thucydides is not sure of a man's class. So perhaps Meleas was, like the Argilian man (1. 132. 5), a sort of person who could be sent abroad on private business.

11. It is perhaps more likely that Thucydides inferred the reasons he gives (3. 92. 4) for the foundation from the way in which the city was used than that he had information from Sparta which would have betrayed the intention to go by land to the Thracian district of the Athenian Empire. But did anything happen in the way of naval attack on Euboea? Thucydides does not let on, but the celebrated fragment of Philochorus concerning an expedition to Euboea in 424/3 (F 130) may have been concerned with such Spartan activity.

the Athenian appeal; he gives no hint of the terms Athens proposed or was prepared to accept. His brevity over such contemptible weakening should not blind us to the effect it must have had on Spartan conduct of the war.[12] To Spartan eyes it must have seemed that the strategy of ravaging was beginning to bite, and that it continued to do so right down to 425. In that year the Spartans sought peace, 'thinking that the Athenians previously were desiring a truce and were prevented by Spartan opposition'.[13] In this opinion the Spartans may have been somewhat mistaken: Athens might have been prepared to return to the Thirty Years Peace and no more. But for Spartan strategy the main point was clear. The strategy which had compelled some readiness to treat, would in due course compel more. There was no need seriously to think of fortification in Attica, a not entirely simple matter in any case. Annual invasion and devastation were doing their expected work.

Pylos changed all that. From then on the 'conventional' strategy was denied them (4. 41. 1), and, to man the 'adventurous', Sparta at long last accepted the reform proposed perhaps first by the regent Pausanias[14] and shortly afterwards begun and treacherously stopped, viz. the use of helots to fight Sparta's wars (4. 80. 2f.). This was a radical change. Sparta could not risk sending far abroad more than a handful of Spartiates, but once she had decided to use her helots the 'other ways' of war were open. The northern campaign of Brasidas could begin.

Thus the 'adventurous' strategy, unalloyed, took over from the largely 'conventional' early years, and its successes measured in revolts of Athens' allies seemed to promise more. There was, however, clearly a difference about how to proceed. Brasidas intended to continue setting cities in revolt; after the capture of Amphipolis he called for reinforcements and began to build ships

12. He does not dwell on another important influence on Spartan opinion, viz. the incidence of the plague. Plagues were of divine origin (cf. 2. 54. 4; 2. 64. 2). Spartan feelings of guilt about the war (7. 18. 2) must have been much assuaged, and confidence in the rightness of their cause greatly increased, by the partial incidence of the plague (2. 54. 5).

13. The present tenses (ἐπιθυμεῖν and κωλύεσθαι) are to be noted.

14. For this suggestion, see my article 'The Fall of Themistocles' in B. F. Harris (ed.), *Auckland Classical Essays presented to E. M. Blaiklock* (Oxford 1970), p. 52.

on the Strymon (4. 108. 6). In Sparta there were those who
thought otherwise, who wished to recover the prisoners of
Sphacteria and end the war. The reinforcements were not
promptly sent out (4. 108. 7 and cf. 132. 2); instead, the year's
truce was made in hopes of a full peace being concluded (4. 117.
1f.). This division of opinion showed after the Peace of Nicias.
Clearidas, who had been picked to be harmost of Amphipolis (4.
132. 3), refused to hand over the city (5. 21. 2), loyal to Brasidas'
plan to use it as a base for further 'adventures', not as a diplomatic bargaining counter.

In this difference of opinion, Brasidas' opponents were surely in
the right. The energy and dash of Brasidas were no lasting substitute for naval power. Until Athens had lost the best part of her
fleet in Sicily and until Persia had begun to contribute money to
pay for a large Peloponnesian fleet, there was little real hope for
the 'other ways' of war. The cities which had revolted when
Brasidas appeared, had in due course to suffer the consequences of
Sparta not being able to sustain them. Even the small force sent
under Nicias (4. 129. 2) was sufficient to check Brasidas and set
about the recovery of the lost cities. Sparta was right to use what
she still had to secure peace. In 421 the 'adventurous' strategy had
its limits.

But was the debate purely strategic? Brasidas had been associated
with much of the 'adventurous' before 425. In 429 he had been
one of the three counsellors sent out to Cnemus to help him make
a more effective bid for naval control of the Corinthian Gulf (2.
85. 1). The attack on the Piraeus was partly his (2. 93. 1). Coun-
sellor again in 427, he took part in the intervention on Corcyra
(3. 69. 2, 76), and in 425 he played a lively part in the attempt to
land by ship on Pylos, a paradoxical situation as Thucydides
remarked (4. 11. 4, 12. 3). He was indeed uncharacteristically
'energetic' (4. 81. 2 δραστήριος). The 'adventurous' strategy
accorded well with his character. But was there more to it? Did
differing strategies serve differing policies?

The best starting-point for this inquiry is the peace negotiations
of 425, which were an appalling betrayal of the lofty promise with
which Sparta had begun the war. Sparta had promised to free
Hellas. A proclamation had been issued to this effect (2. 8. 4, 4.

85. 1, and cf. 3. 32. 2). For Sparta to appeal for peace was a complete *volte face*. Earlier they had thought that to free Hellas they would quickly 'destroy the Athenians' (4. 85. 2). In 425 they ended their appeal with these very remarkable words: 'And consider what advantages are likely to be found in this course. If you and we concert policy, the rest of the Greek world, being weaker, will, you may be sure, pay us the greatest honour' (4. 20. 4). The spirit of these words is none other than that of the appeal of Trygaeus in the *Peace* (1082), 'to make peace and share rule over Hellas', as the course of the assembly in 425 made plain. When Cleon bade the Spartan ambassadors openly declare what they had in mind to propose, 'they thought that, if they decided to make some concession under stress of the disaster, it was not possible to speak out in an assembly in case, after saying and failing to obtain it, they should be denounced before their allies' (4. 22. 3). That is, what they had in mind was a betrayal of their allies' cause and could not bear publication.

Thus in 425 there were Spartans willing to go back on the proclamation of 431 and to do a deal with Athens, of the sort of which the Peace of Nicias was, leaving Athens in control of her empire and Greece no freer than before, a ghastly confession that Greece could not be freed. Against all this Brasidas acted, and spoke. He began his speech to the Acanthians as follows: 'I and my army have been sent out by the Lacedaemonians to give reality to the claim which we made in our proclamation at the beginning of the war, namely that we would fight the Athenians for the freedom of Hellas.' He was the liberator, but not all supported him. Not only was he denied the prompt reinforcement he needed (4. 108. 7) but also he saw fit to give the Acanthians a very remarkable assurance: 'I have come to free the Hellenes and I have obliged those in power at Sparta with the most solemn oaths to guarantee that any state I bring over to alliance will be left independent' (4. 86. 1). Clearly he had not been able to trust people in Sparta to take his view of his mission, and the Acanthians too needed such reassurance, for Brasidas' report of these oaths helped them to decide on revolt (4. 88. 1). Thus after 425 the 'adventurous' strategy was the instrument of a radical policy of liberating Hellas, against which those who would do a deal with Athens chose to contend.

The difference of policies is similarly linked, perhaps, to the difference of strategies in the early years. If Hellas was to be liberated, the 'adventurous' strategy, as Archidamus had foreseen, would in all likelihood be forced upon Sparta (1. 80–2), but it is curious that the first real moves in this direction belong to 430. In that year Spartan ambassadors were caught on their way to the King (2. 67):[15] Thucydides speaks of their purpose as if this was the first attempt to persuade Persia to help Sparta. Likewise with the fleet. Despite the grandiose plans of 432/1 (2. 7. 2) the first Peloponnesian fleet appears in 430, in the attack on Athens' ally, Zacynthus. These matters may be by chance, but it is to be noted that Brasidas was eponymous ephor from autumn 431 to autumn 430 (Xen. *Hell.* 2. 3. 10). In view of the importance of the ephors in the making of policy at Sparta, it is reasonable enough to guess that his influence lies behind the 'adventures' of summer 430. It was also within his year of office that Athens appealed for peace (2. 59). The rejection is therefore not surprising. Brasidas perhaps demanded no less than what Sparta had begun the war for, the end of the empire.[16] When Athens would not talk sense, he resolved to stick at nothing to make her see it: the help of Persia would have to be sought, the fleet built up and used. His year as ephor ended too late for action in 430. In summer 429 he was out to help Cnemus (2. 85. 1). The 'adventurous' strategy, which alone could secure the radical end, was in play.

The internal history of Sparta is dark indeed, and it may be argued that to see the strategic issue in political terms is to go far beyond the evidence. The case of Archidamus might prompt caution. In his speech before the war, he attacked the complacency of those who thought that the war would be quickly ended by the

15. The date is late summer (2. 67), i.e. after the Athenian peace negotiations (2. 59), but during the ephorate of 431/430.

16. The formulae of diplomacy were not many – normally there was agreement either ἔχειν τὰ ἑαυτῶν ([Dem.] 7. 18) or ἔχειν ἃ ἔχουσι, as in 410 (Diod. 13. 52. 3). There could be variants such as ὅσα πολέμῳ χωρία ἔχουσιν ἑκάτεροι ἀποδίδοσθαι – hence the curious instructions given to the commander at Plataea in 427 (3. 52. 2): in 425 it would seem that the Spartans wanted this formula but Cleon demanded the places lost in the Thirty Years Peace ἃ οὐ πολέμῳ ἔλαβον. One can only guess what the Athenians offered in 430; perhaps they were ready to accept the demands of the embassy of 1. 139. 1. Perhaps Brasidas' board of ephors replied with the demand of the final embassy of 1. 139. 3 – τοὺς Ἕλληνας αὐτονόμους ἀφιέναι.

'conventional' strategy. So, strategically speaking, he advocated the 'adventurous' and advised delay until it was possible (1. 80–5), but, politically speaking, he may have had in mind much less than the liberation of Hellas. At least he saw fit to issue one final appeal to Athens before he invaded Attica (2. 12. 1f.), and he could hardly have expected Athens to submit to the extreme demand of the liberators: presumably he would have been content with much less, the moderation rather than the end of Athenian Empire. So do strategies and policies necessarily accord? But all this was early in the war. It was the failure of 431 and 430 to produce more than an offer to negotiate that brought into the open a division endemic in Sparta ever since the Persian Wars.[17]

In the Persian Wars Sparta had held the hegemony of Greece, but the liberation of the islands and the Greek cities of the Persian Empire and the continuing war with Persia raised a serious dilemma for Sparta. On the one hand, the war had to be fought[18] and, if Sparta did not choose to lead, Athens would, an unpalatable alternative; so Sparta had to continue. On the other hand, Sparta was a land power and the war would be naval; she did not dare send large numbers of Spartiates far from the Peloponnese and hegemony might require them; so Sparta had to retire. The conduct of Pausanias enforced retirement, and after a debate in which those who wanted Sparta to contend for the hegemony were outvoted by those who, led by Hetoemaridas, were content that Athens should lead (1. 95. 7, Diod. 11. 50), Sparta settled back within the Peloponnese. But the dilemma remained and Sparta continued to divide on whether to oppose Athens or to treat her as partner.

As long as Athens vigorously prosecuted the war with the willing support of the Delian league, Sparta was, or had to be, content. Certainly Pausanias' second voyage to the Hellespont indicated some divisions in the state, for he went out to the Ἑλληνικὸς πόλεμος (1. 128. 3), by Thucydidean usage 'war against Greeks',

17. For the following three paragraphs cf. G. E. M. de Ste Croix, *The Origins of the Peloponnesian War* (London and Ithaca, N.Y. 1972), chapter 5. (Whom he calls 'hawks', I call 'liberators'!)

18. The Spartan attempt to withdraw the Greeks from Asia and settle them in Greece itself miscarried (Hdt. 9. 106).

and in some way on official business, for he bore the *skytale* (1. 131. 1), but he was recalled and suppressed, and comparatively easily.[19] If he did indeed first propose to use the helot manpower as the instrument of large overseas policies (cf. 1. 132. 4), the plan and awakened helot ambitions came to nothing (4. 80. 3f.). He no doubt had supporters among the Spartiates; he had his 'enemies' (1. 132. 1) and presumably his friends; one of the board of ephors in whose year he was killed sought with a nod to secure him sanctuary (1. 134. 1); but if he was hostile to Athens, there is no evidence that his hostility led him in his last years to propose action. With Thasos in 465 it was different. For the first time one of the Hellenes appealed to Sparta for protection against Athens and the issue could not be shirked. Sparta promised to invade Attica if Thasos were attacked (1. 101. 2). But the promise was secretly given, which suggests that it may have been given not by the assembly but by the ephors, as to the Potidaeans in 432 (1. 58. 1); in the assembly the policy might have been opposed: for after the earthquake which set off the helot revolt and prevented the promised invasion Sparta saw fit to appeal to Athens for help (1. 102. 1) and the name of the son of the man who brought the appeal is suggestive of his sympathies. He was Periclidas (Plut. *Cim.* 16. 8, Ar. *Lysis.* 1138), father of the Athenaeus, who helped negotiate the truce of 423 (4. 119. 2). Presumably his son's name reflects Atticizing, as Cimon's son, Lacedaemonius, reflects Laconizing (Plut. *Cim.* 16. 1). The appeal was made, one may guess, not because Sparta was *in extremis*, for the first shock was over and Ithome under siege (1. 102. 1), but because there was an influential body of opinion that favoured concord with Athens, and Cimon's celebrated call to the Athenians to save Athens' partner (Plut. *Cim.* 16. 10) succeeded because there were known to be Spartans who wanted partnership. Thus the division of the Archidamian War asserted itself in the 460s.

It next appears at the time of the making of the Thirty Years Peace. In the invasion of Attica in 446 King Plistoanax, who in 421 was most eager for peace with Athens (5. 16. 1), withdrew and

19. Only 'some' of the ephors (1. 133. 1) overheard the conversation between Pausanias and the Argilian man. The whole story is improbable (cf. Cawkwell, 'The Fall of Themistocles'), perhaps a fabrication to silence Pausanias' sympathizers.

the Peace followed shortly after. What Sparta expected in 431, she doubtless had expected in 446, viz. the prompt submission of Athens: not only was Attica open for the first time since the outbreak of the First Peloponnesian War, but also Euboea was in revolt (1. 114. 1). So why did Plistoanax withdraw? Later he was charged with doing so for a bribe (2. 21. 1), and likewise one of the ephors who had accompanied him, Cleandridas (Plut. *Per.* 22. 3, Diod. 13. 106. 10, Suda *s.vv.* Ἔφοροι and εἰς τὸ δέον). The charge only reflects the lack of good strategic reasons for withdrawal. They must have wanted not to crush Athens. And not only they: the Peace was made, even though Sparta could perfectly well have returned to the attack,[20] less favourably than in spring 446, but no less than in 431; the assembly was not compelled to accept the decision of Plistoanax; there must have been ample support for his view of how to deal with Athens. The attacks on him and Cleandridas must have followed later, perhaps under the next ephors[21] who may have sought, as happened in 421/420, to undo the peace they had inherited. At any rate the attacks argue plainly enough the division in the state, between those who wished to crush, and those who wished to come to terms with, Athens. It need, therefore, cause no surprise if the same division is there in the Archidamian War, affecting policy and so strategy.

It is found also in the period of the Decelean and Ionian War.

20. If discussions began on the plain of Eleusis, there would be a long time needed for exchange of embassies, etc. Spartan kings had no power to make treaties.

21. Plistoanax was recalled in the nineteenth year of his exile (5. 16. 3), and it is commonly supposed that he returned shortly after Cleomenes in 427 led the invasion on behalf of the young Pausanias, son of Plistoanax (3. 26. 2), which puts the exile in 445. This may be right, but, since Plistoanax is not again mentioned by Thucydides until 421, his return and exile could well be later. (In 427 Cleomenes, as regent, led the invasion presumably because Archidamus, who had commanded the expeditions from 431 to 428, was ill (and dying): Agis took over in 426 in place of his father.) So the hypothesis may be proposed, that Plistoanax was recalled in 425, when the Spartans were seeking peace, and was exiled in the ephorate of 444/443 when the consequences of the Thirty Years Peace were exposed in the ostracism of Thucydides son of Melesias who perhaps came to Sparta (Plut. *Mor.* 802C). Such accusations of bribery need have been made no more promptly at Sparta than at Athens. (Plut. *Per.* 22. 3 suggests that the prosecution followed hot upon his return from Attica, but that would have brought back him from exile before the invasion of 427.) Cleandridas went off in time to join in the founding of the colony to Thurii, if his name lies behind the corruption of Photius *s.v.* θουριομάντεις.

One figure dominated the later years, Lysander. The final victory
was his, and he received the most extravagant honours throughout
the Greek world (Plut. *Lys.* 18). To secure the liberation of Hellas
he had worked closely with Cyrus (Xen. *Hell.* 1. 5. 1ff., Diod. 13.
70, and cf. Xen. *Oec.* 4. 20ff.), for he had seen that without Persian
money Sparta could not gain complete victory. He was the true
heir of Brasidas, resolved to stop at nothing. Against him stood
those who were responsible for the appointment of Callicratidas,
his successor as nauarch. He was not an especially prominent
figure, as far as we know, but he interested Xenophon who
recorded with Panhellenist zest the succession in command. When
kept waiting at the court of Cyrus, Callicratidas departed in
disgust saying 'the Greeks are most wretched because they pay
court to barbarians for money' and adding 'if I get home safely,
I will do all in my power to reconcile the Athenians and the
Spartans' (*Hell.* 1. 6. 7).[22] The price of reconciliation would be
abandonment of the cause of liberating Hellas. Clearly there were
others prepared to pay it, most notably Endius, son of Alcibiades,
and heir to his father's friendship with the family of Alcibiades of
Athens (8. 6. 3), prominent in negotiations with Athens, first as
one of the three envoys who 'were thought to be well-disposed to
the Athenians' (5. 44. 3) sent to try to prevent the Athenian–
Argive alliance of 421, later again one of three envoys sent to
secure the ransom of captives (*F. gr. Hist.* 324 F 44), above all as
chief of the embassy sent to secure peace after the battle of Cyzicus
in 410 (Diod. 13. 52. 2). His speech on that occasion (if faithfully
given by Ephorus,[23] from whom Diodorus chose to quote so
notable an instance of Laconian brevity) was concerned to plead
for a peace on the basis of each side keeping what it held at the
moment. Since Athens still held much of the empire, this was to
abandon a multitude of Greeks to their masters. One looks in vain
in the speech for a hint of the proclamation of 431. He wants to do
a deal.

As already remarked, the politics of Sparta are dark. Few names
can be added. Philocharidas who assisted in the making of the

22. Echoed by Teleutias (Xen. *Hell.* 5. 1. 17), in protest against the medizing
of Antalcidas.

23. Ephorus may well have taken the text almost *verbatim* from the *Hellenica
Oxyrhynchia.*

truce of 423 (4. 119) and of the Peace of Nicias (5. 19) seems to be a supporter of Endius (5. 44. 3, *F. gr. Hist.* 324 F 44). No more is heard of Athenaeus (4. 119. 2, 122. 1) after 423. No doubt like Plistoanax (5. 16. 1) he was content with the Peace of 421. One can only suspect the sympathies of King Pausanias, who later thwarted Lysander and let the Athenians off the hook in 403 (Xen. *Hell.* 2. 4. 29f., etc.), his allies being Endius, eponymous ephor in that year (*ibid.* 2. 3. 10), and Nauclidas, also ephor and opponent of Lysander (*ibid.* 2. 4. 36). But in a sense names are not necessary. For Endius to offer the terms of 410, there must have been ample support for a negotiated settlement, let Hellas like it or not.

When Endius sought peace in 410, the Persians were still taking a very ambiguous attitude to the war. Until Cyrus came down with clear orders, armed with, as it were, *maius imperium* (Xen. *Hell.* 1. 4. 3, etc.), prudence must have suggested that total defeat of Athens was not likely. Very much more so was this the case before the Sicilian disaster and it is no surprise that Thucydides gives the Sicilian expedition a prominent place on the road to ruin (2. 65). Before it, Sparta could do no better than make a deal and a deal was essentially a disaster: for it would mean that the Greeks would have to face the fact that Sparta could not do what she had proclaimed, viz. liberate them. Not only that. If Sparta could not change the situation, she would have inevitably to suffer whatever it was she had feared from the growth of Athenian power (1. 23. 6). It may be debated what exactly Sparta feared, but since hopes of Sparta presumably nourished in the allies of Athens the will to resist,[24] once those hopes were dead the power that Sparta feared would be so much more fearful and so much more irresistible.

All this was seen by Pericles. Master of politics and of strategy, he saw that if Athens acted rightly, Sparta could do no more than make a deal – with catastrophic consequences. That was why Thucydides commended his strategy, and Thucydides was right.

Note A

Discussion of the strategy of the Peloponnesian War depends on the view one takes of the 'strategic' parts of the speeches in Book 1

24. As with Mytilene before the war (3. 2. 1).

(esp. 80–3 Archidamus', 121–2. 1 the second Corinthian, 141–3 Pericles'). Were they written 'late', in the knowledge of the events of the Decelean–Ionian war, or do they in some sense represent the sort of discussion that actually went on in 432/1? Certainly the speeches are artificially contrived: Pericles answers the Corinthians almost point by point; Archidamus (82. 4) and Pericles (143. 5) use the word ἀληπτότεροι, not met in classical prose outside this book (being used at 1. 37. 5 by the Corinthians). But artificial contrivance does not prove that the speeches were written 'late'. In view of Thucydides own profession (1. 22), the presumption must be all the other way; artifice could transmute the raw material 'early' as well as 'late'. The *onus probandi* must lie with those who would discount the speeches as reflecting the ideas current in 432/1.

The proof would have to consist in showing that the speeches allude to events of the later part of the war. First, the references to ἐπιτειχισμός and αὐτομολίαι (122. 1 and 142. 4) might be supposed to derive from the fortification of Decelea and the large numbers of slaves that deserted thereafter (7. 27. 5). But there were desertions before the Archidamian War began (1. 139. 2) and ἐπιτειχισμός was not only planned in 422/1 (5. 17. 2) and familiar in principle perhaps to the Old Oligarch ([Xen.] *A.P.* 2. 13) but also perhaps intended in the attack on Epidaurus in 430 (2. 56. 4) – an ἐπιτείχισμα against the Peloponnese, as Heraclea was declared to be against Euboea (3. 92. 4), i.e. a base rather than the refuge Pylos turned out to be. The idea could well have been mooted in 432/1, long before the Decelean War. Again, the idea of ἀπόστασις συμμάχων (122. 1 and 81. 4) might seem more appropriate later. But Mytilene had actually proposed revolt before the war (3. 2. 1), and Archidamus and the Corinthians could well have thought of revolt spreading. Again, the optimism about equipping and training a fleet (82. 1, 121. 4, 142. 2f.) might be thought to reflect later Spartan naval activity. But there were the highest hopes in 432/1 (2. 7. 2), far higher than the hard experience of the Ionian War could allow. The only serious point concerns the idea of luring away Athens' mercenary sailors with higher pay (121. 3, 143. 1). This indeed happened in the Ionian War (Xen. *Hell.* 1. 5. 4f.) and, as far as we know, not earlier. If, however, nothing can be allowed to have been thought before it actually happened, the proposal to borrow from Delphi and Olympia (*ibid.*) should, strictly taken, make very curious reading – for no such borrowing took place before the 360s and 350s! (Of course, Athens may have provided the idea by borrowing from Athena, which began as early as 440.) But the procedure is unsound. None of these ideas was unthinkable in 432/1. Indeed, it is to be noted that the Corinthians do not develop Archidamus' suggestion of an appeal to Persia: their failure to do so is perhaps more of a pointer than the supposed anachronisms. All in all, proof of 'lateness' is lacking.

It is a nicer question whether these speeches were written under the influence of events of the Archidamian War. De Ste Croix, *The Origins of the Peloponnesian War*, p. 209 argues that the Athenian failure before 425 to occupy Methana, a position of great usefulness for attacks on Epidaurus and Troezen (4. 45. 2), suggests that ἐπιτειχισμός was not seriously considered until Demosthenes occupied Pylos despite the scepticism of colleagues (4. 3. 3). The truth, however, may be that Pericles was not prepared to establish and maintain a fort other than one directly menacing Laconia; a city seized, like Epidaurus, was a different matter. Of course if, as I believe but cannot argue here, the Old Oligarch wrote early in the Archidamian War, the point may be settled; quite apart from that, it seems quite probable that the idea would be current. Naxian refugees had been settled in forts on Naxos in 499 (Hdt. 5. 34. 3), presumably not just for the view. By 427 the Samian exiles in Anaia were asserting themselves (3. 32. 2), and there is no reason to suppose that they would not as soon as possible raid Samos (cf. 4. 75) as well as organize hostilities against the Athenians (3. 19. 2). Surely exiles living in the Peloponnese before the war (cf. 8. 64. 4) were capable of thinking out means of hostile action against their own countrymen. Ἐπιτειχισμός was no great leap of the imagination. What Thucydides wrote for 432/1 could well have been thought in that year. (There is a slight query about the remark of Archidamus at 81. 6 expressing scepticism about quick decision in the war, whereas, when he spoke on the borders of Attica in 431, he seemed to expect that Athens would come out and fight (2. 11. 6), and he would have thought that a general engagement would be decisive. But he may have meant no more than that the Athenians would try to attack those engaged in ravaging who were off their guard.)

All in all, there is no reason to regard the speeches as unsafe evidence for what was thought about strategy in 432/1.

Note B

> 'Pericles (having planned an offensive war) lost his striking power, first because Potidaea revolted, next because of the Plague. Forced to the defensive, he left that as his testament. Thucydides was reluctant to face the fact of this failure, and accepted the testament, siding with the defeatist officer class against the revived offensive of Cleon (4. 27. 5, 28. 5, 65. 4, 73. 4; cf. 5. 7. 2). This is why Pericles' huge effort against Epidaurus (6. 31. 2; motive, cf. 5. 53) is recorded as a minor futility (2. 56. 4); why Phormion's first campaign in Acarnania (2. 68. 7–9 of 432?) is left timeless; why we hear nothing of the purpose of the Megara decree; why, when that nearly bore fruit at last, Thucydides suggests that the capture of Megara was of no great moment (4. 73. 4; but cf. 72. 1).'

Thus Wade-Gery in *Oxford Classical Dictionary*², p. 1069. (He continues, 'Such criticisms hardly detract much from his singular truthfulness'!) As far as I am aware, he never fully developed this view of Periclean strategy save in lectures, and it may seem mere shadow-boxing to set about an answer here, but, if he were right, our whole view of Pericles and of Thucydides would have to be radically altered and some sort of statement seems due. Much of the quoted passage seems extraneous. We cannot here go into the purpose of the Megara decree, or Cleon's alleged strategy, nor defend Thucydides' not dating Phormio's campaign in a merely explanatory paragraph. But the 'minor futility' of the attack on Epidaurus is very relevant.

First, it is worth remarking that one argument that might be used to support the thesis of an 'offensive' strategy is of no force. At the start of the war the Athenians reviewed the alliances with the islands covering the western side of Greece, πέριξ τὴν Πελοπόννησον καταπολεμήσοντες (2. 7. 3). The word καταπολεμεῖν might be taken in the sense of the Latin *debellare*; it is used in Alcibiades' speech at Sparta in a passage culminating in τοῦ ξύμπαντος Ἑλληνικοῦ ἄρξειν (6. 90. 3). So does it argue 'offence'? But clearly it is not the equivalent of *debellare*; cf. 4. 86. 5 where it

evidently means 'carry on the war', and 6. 16. 2 where it is used
to describe the condition of Athens at the end of the Archidamian
War. Again, 6. 90. 3 may echo 2. 7. 2, but the grandiose concep-
tions of Alcibiades prove nothing about Pericles'.

As to the expedition to Epidaurus, there is nothing very mysterious about its large size. If the purpose was merely to ravage, the
more hands the better. In 431 the force sent out consisted of 1000
hoplites, 400 archers and 100 ships (2. 32. 2). Experience may well
have suggested that larger forces were needed. When the force
landed, patrols were needed to give advance warning of attacks,
and cavalry was obviously better than men on foot, presumably in
431 the archers; roads had to be blocked by hoplites, for otherwise
ravaging parties were very vulnerable; for ravaging, the crews of
as many ships as possible would have to be used. Further, a ravaging force may have divided so as to land on adjacent beaches and
ravage as widely as possible in a short time, and the protecting
troops with each division would be correspondingly reduced. So
there was safety and effectiveness in numbers. When one adds that
in 430 Pericles had either to take as many hoplites as possible or
to leave them in the city to succumb to the plague (2. 57. 1) or the
temptation of going out to fight, morale being not high in the
weeks before the appeal for peace (2. 59), it is clear that the large
numbers of 430 do not necessarily indicate some 'offensive' design.

But what was the purpose of the operations round Epidaurus?
Thucydides says nothing. Has he something to conceal? Wade-
Gery cites as an explanation 5. 53, where Alcibiades and the
Argives aim to take Epidaurus to shorten the route from Athens
to Argos. But that was in 419, when the Argive–Spartan treaty
had expired. So 5. 53 is not relevant to 430.

Thucydides must have known the purpose of the expedition, if
not from Pericles, from subordinate officers; Pericles was too good
a general not to make his intention clear. It is unthinkable that
Thucydides sought to mislead. His 'singular truthfulness' also
makes it hard to believe that he deceived himself. That however
has been believed in various matters. What is uncomfortable is
that the theory makes Thucydides too stupid to see that there is a
discrepancy between his narrative and the 'testament'. If one can
provide an explanation of his brevity here, which does not belittle
his intelligence, it would be preferable.

The explanation is, of course, that Thucydides would not for a second have dreamed that there was anything to explain. Pericles' strategy was radical in its abandonment of Attica. Archidamus could not believe that the Athenians would not fight (2. 11. 6). For the rest it was conventional. Ravaging was a normal way of fighting. If Epidaurus could be taken at a rush, so much the better. But there was nothing for a Greek to explain about Epidaurus just as at 2. 56. 6 there was nothing to explain about Prasiae. The Epidaurus expedition is not a problem.

Finally, one must note that Pericles in 431 set out his strategy in his speech at 2. 13. 2. How do these words relate to the 'testament'? One presumes that Thucydides made notes at the time of the speech. Are we to suppose that Pericles was seeking to exonerate himself in advance? Or have we another 'late' speech tainted with Thucydidean 'double-think'? The truth is disappointing. There is no problem.

The speeches in Thucydides and the Mytilene debate*

DONALD KAGAN

I

THERE ARE few arguments of longer standing in the scholarship on Thucydides than the one concerning the speeches in his *History*, and none is more important for understanding it and its author. The main question is: did Thucydides try to reproduce the arguments put forward by the speakers on each occasion as accurately as he could, or did he feel free to invent arguments and even whole speeches? In spite of the long debate there is little agreement, yet we cannot understand Thucydides' ideas and purposes or the events he describes without answering that question. It is remarkable, therefore, that students of Thucydides and his *History* have found it possible to take up a position on the question without considering closely the arguments surrounding the interpretation of 1. 22 or even to take no clear position on the matter at all. Examples are legion, but two will suffice to make the point. A recent study of the funeral oration of Pericles coolly asserts that Thucydides' role in the speeches can go so far as 'the invention of whole speeches or the concentration of several speeches into one'.[1] The author makes no defense of that assertion, resting content with a reference to the work of Eduard Schwartz, among others. He takes no note of an article by A. W. Gomme, quite famous and over thirty years old, which confronts the arguments of Schwartz and those holding similar views and annihilates them.[2] Neither Flashar nor his authorities refute or reject the arguments put forward by Gomme; they ignore them. Yet Flashar's

* Part of this essay is based on a chapter in my forthcoming book, *The Archidamian War*.

1. Hellmut Flashar, 'Der Epitaphios des Perikles', *Sitzungsberichte der Heidelberger Akademie der Wissenschaften* (1969).
2. 'The Speeches in Thucydides', *Essays in Greek History and Literature* (Oxford 1937), pp. 156–89.

entire case rests on the premise that Thucydides invented speeches
and attributed them to historical characters, a premise that has
been powerfully attacked but which is not defended.

So excellent a Thucydidean as Jacqueline de Romilly seems to
avoid the critical question almost completely. She treats Pericles'
speeches as expressions of his own views,[3] yet she says that the
debate between Cleon and Diodotus over the fate of Mytilene was
'composed by Thucydides in such a way that the systematic contrast between them, although rather improbable in an actual
debate, brought out the wisdom of one solution compared with the
folly of the other. We cannot discover what resemblance there was
between the ideas expressed in Thucydides and those put forward
in real life by Cleon and his opponent.'[4] The clear implication here
is that Thucydides was free to invent any argument he liked
regardless of what may actually have been said. In still another
place, discussing the speech of the Athenians at Sparta in Book 1,
Mme de Romilly finds it 'difficult to believe that the Athenians
actually spoke',[5] which implies that Thucydides may have invented a whole speech. Thus even so careful a scholar finds it
possible to treat the speeches in any way that seems convenient,
without consistency and without any confrontation of Thucydides'
own account of his method. It is plain that Gomme's essay has not
had the influence it deserves, and that is excuse enough for taking
up the argument once again.

Thucydides begins his statement on his treatment of the speeches
by mentioning the difficulty he and his informants had in remem-
bering accurately what was said: χαλεπὸν τὴν ἀκρίβειαν αὐτὴν
τῶν λεχθέντων διαμνημονεῦσαι. As Andrewes has put it: 'However
much we water down the meaning of these words, and some
scholars have wished to dilute it very much, it is of basic importance that Thucydides should bring the speeches actually delivered
into the question at all and suggest that they might be of concern
to his readers.'[6] It is the next clause, however, that has caused the
most trouble: ὡς δ' ἂν ἐδόκουν ἐμοὶ ἕκαστοι περὶ τῶν αἰεὶ παρόντων

3. *Thucydides and Athenian Imperialism*, tr. by Philip Thody (Oxford 1965),
p. 111.

4. *Ibid.*, p. 160.   5. *Ibid.*, p. 243.

6. A. Andrewes, 'The Mytilene Debate: Thucydides 3. 36–49', *Phoenix* 16
(1962), 65–6.

τὰ δέοντα μάλιστ' εἰπεῖν, ἐχομένῳ ὅτι ἐγγύτατα τῆς ξυμπάσης γνώμης τῶν ἀληθῶς λεχθέντων, οὕτως εἴρηται. Andrewes' paraphrase seems neutral and accurate: 'they are written as I thought each speaker would most fittingly speak about the particular occasion, keeping as close as I could to the general sense of what was actually said'.[7]

This complete statement has been thought ambiguous, for the first clause plainly calls for some imagination and special perception on the part of Thucydides (ἐδόκουν ἐμοὶ...τὰ δέοντα μάλιστ' εἰπεῖν) and may seem to run counter to the second which calls chiefly for accurate reporting. The supporters of what we may call loose construction of this passage naturally wish to emphasize the force of the first clause and to diminish the importance of the second. One way to do that is simply to say that the emphasis in the sentence belongs on the first clause and, as John Finley does, that the participial clause has only 'a purely secondary, limiting force'.[8] Once again Andrewes' reponse is correct and to the point: 'This is clearly no answer. If the clause has a limiting force, then it limits, and the force is not nullified by calling it secondary. It is not, as many critics take it, a matter of weight or balance: the question is whether the author means what he says, and we have no general license to disregard participles.'[9]

The second way is to say that the participial clause does not mean what it appears to mean and what almost all readers without a *parti pris* have taken it to mean. This is the way Eduard Schwartz dealt with the problem. He argued that ἡ ξύμπασα γνώμη does not mean 'the general sense (*der Gesamtsinn*)' but rather 'the general intention (*die Willensrichtung im ganzen*)', or 'the practical purpose of the speech (*der praktische Zweck der Rede*)'. τὰ ἀληθῶς λεχθέντα does not mean 'the authentic wording' but only that the various speakers did rise to speak on the occasion designated.[10] Even this concession to the obvious is retracted a few lines later when Schwartz tells us that 'the Athenian embassy which, without being instructed to do so, defends the Athenian

7. *Ibid.*
8. J. H. Finley, *Thucydides* (Cambridge, Mass. 1942), p. 95.
9. Andrewes, 'The Mytilene Debate', p. 66.
10. Schwartz' views are stated most clearly in his review of Taeger's *Thukydides* in *Gnomon* 2 (1926), 79–80. The relevant passages are cited and analyzed by Gomme, 'The Speeches in Thucydides', pp. 156ff.

policy in Sparta, is a fiction', which is obvious to anyone who knows how to read Thucydides.[11] I am unable to resist quoting Gomme's sarcastic but accurate summary of this view:

> We may believe, in most cases, that the debates referred to actually took place, and that the general tendency of the speeches, their practical aims, were as Thucydides records: ...Even within these limits we must not be simpletons: we must understand of course that when Thucydides says that Athenian delegates were at Sparta on other business and requested permission to address the assembly on the question of war and peace, he is saying quite plainly that there were no Athenians there and that no Athenian speech was made.[12]

It is important to emphasize Schwartz' departure even from his own tendentious and unlikely interpretation of ἡ ξύμπασα γνώμη almost immediately after its enunciation, for if it does not mean 'the general sense' or even 'the general intention' of a speech really given it means nothing. Schwartz, therefore, has not re-interpreted the passage but deprived it of all meaning in his attempt to get around the awkward but undeniable fact that Thucydides claims to present the most accurate account possible of what was actually said in speeches that were really spoken.

The clause ὡς δ' ἂν ἐδόκουν ἐμοὶ ἕκαστοι περὶ τῶν αἰεὶ παρόντων τὰ δέοντα μάλιστ' εἰπεῖν presents little difficulty for the view that Thucydides tries to report actual speeches accurately. The subjective and imaginative faculties come into play in two ways. Without recording devices or shorthand stenographers memory alone could not hope to achieve an accurate record, and Thucydides acknowledges the need to reconstruct rather than record. Thus the statement may be taken to refer to the form rather than the content of the speeches.[13] It is also likely that Thucydides received reports of some speeches that were less complete than others. He may have been told of the general line of argument and given a few quotations and details and supplied the rest of the speech from what seemed to him τὰ δέοντα. That, however, is as

11. *Idem.*
12. 'Speeches in Thucydides', p. 158.
13. Andrewes, 'The Mytilene Debate', p. 66.

far as his words permit us to go. Seen in this light there is no contradiction between the two clauses.

Some scholars who have seen that Thucydides' words are to be understood in their obvious sense and taken seriously have nevertheless found it impossible to grant that he carried out his promise throughout his work. Unable to believe, for whatever reason, that some of the speeches Thucydides gives us are historical, they seek escape from a difficult problem of interpretation by resorting to the time-honored device of explaining it away as the result of early and late levels of composition. Even so excellent and sensible a scholar as Andrewes, who fully understands the force of Gomme's arguments and the impossibility of treating the speeches as free inventions, has been led some distance astray. He is attracted by the theory put forward by Max Pohlenz, which has rightly attracted few others, that Thucydides began by trying to adhere to the principles of 1. 22, to stay, that is, as close as possible to what was really said, 'but diverged from it later'. Andrewes argues that just as Thucydides changed his style of narrative between the flat style of Books 2–4 and the more polished and dramatic mode of 6–7, 'his practice with regard to the speeches changed likewise'.[14]

This attempt to deal with the problem, however, is no more satisfactory than tampering with the meaning of Thucydides' words. The method of dealing with Thucydidean problems by creating hypotheses about the composition of passages in the *History* at different times, though it has been practiced for well over a century,[15] has produced less agreement among scholars with the passage of time. The decision as to whether a particular passage was composed earlier than another is in almost all cases completely subjective. It is surely bad method, therefore, to try to solve a puzzle by means of an enigma, to explain *ignotum per ignotius*. But even if we allowed the legitimacy of the method it is hard to deny that 1. 22 is one of the least likely of all passages to be relegated to an early and unrevised layer. Book 1 is widely regarded as very polished and finished, therefore 'late'. It is more important, however, to point out that the analogy of a variation in narrative style between 'early' and 'late' passages to a change in the

14. *Ibid.*, p. 67.
15. The question of composition seems first to have been raised in modern times by F. W. Ullrich, *Beiträge zur Erklärung des Thukydides* (Hamburg 1846).

method of presenting speeches is quite inappropriate. Thucydides, after all, never promised his readers to write one kind of narrative rather than another, since that would have had little or no effect on the accuracy and credibility of his history, but he did promise to give an accurate account of speeches that were actually spoken. Thus, if he departed from the method described in 1. 22 without saying so, he deceived his readers and his general reliability is seriously impugned.

Andrewes sees the problem, but his response to it is unsatisfactory: 'The only real surprise is that he should have left 1, 22 as it stands. One could not, with this very reflective artist, put that down to inadvertence, but it is perfectly possible that he let this sentence stand provisionally because he had not yet thought out the formula which would replace it and define what had become his practice. That would not be the only revision which Thucydides failed to complete.'[16] According to Andrewes, it appears, we are to understand that Thucydides began his work by trying to report speeches accurately, altered his practice along the way so as to present fictional speeches alongside, or instead of, real ones, had time to contemplate the inaccuracy of his original statement on the subject, but decided to let it stand provisionally until he could think of another way of describing his practice. If all this is true it is no wonder that he died before making the change. What, after all, could a man say who introduced fictional speeches after making many assertions of the importance of accuracy and his efforts to achieve it, who criticized his predecessors for giving inaccurate accounts and introducing poetry and myths instead of telling the truth, and who boasts of excluding the fabulous element from his own work?[17] Great skill would be required to make those statements compatible with the admission that while some of the speeches were accurate accounts of what was said, others were fictional creations of the author.

None of the attacks on the obvious meaning of 1. 22 withstands even moderately close scrutiny, and there is no reason to doubt that what Thucydides said there was meant to hold true for his entire history. The real reason for questioning the passage does not arise from the words themselves but from the apparent discrepancy

16. 'The Mytilene Debate', p. 67.
17. I. 21–2.

between the statement of method and Thucydides' practice. As Andrewes put it: 'It is really not possible to believe that the Melian Dialogue adheres closely to what was actually said, and other speeches arouse in less degree the same mistrust.'[18]

But if we grant that Thucydides said he was trying to record real speeches accurately and meant what he said we cannot allow the possibility that a speech is invented in any important way without destroying the credibility of Thucydides. The fact is that no one has shown that there is a single speech in the *History* that could not have been given in something like its Thucydidean form. Critics have been ready to pit their own judgments of what was appropriate for a speaker to say against the Thucydidean report, but their arguments have no more weight than that.[19] I myself have examined all the speeches reported from before the war and during the Archidamian War without finding any that seemed implausible in the context, much less impossible.[20] The authenticity of even the Melian Dialogue, the most incredible of all the speeches to the critics, has found an able defender.[21]

There is yet another reason, I believe, why many have been unwilling to accept the obvious meaning of i. 22. Many of the speeches stand out in the great *History*. They often carry broad, far-ranging, speculative statements about politics and the nature of man and society. They seem to give the work structure and to be arranged in patterns that are not accidental. They seem, in short, to be the work of a single architectonic mind, not merely the scattered statements of different men. To say that Thucydides merely reported these speeches is to make the obvious artistry of his work unacceptably accidental.

There can be no doubt that the *History* of Thucydides is a unified work of art created by a single man and that the speeches are fundamental to its construction. I would go further and say that they are often used to express points of view with which Thucydides agrees, to expose the weaknesses in positions with which he disagrees, to set forth the character and ideas of major actors in

18. 'The Mytilene Debate', p. 66.
19. For an exposure of many such arguments see Gomme, 'Speeches in Thucydides', pp. 168ff.
20. See D. Kagan, *The Outbreak of the Peloponnesian War* (Ithaca 1969) and *The Archidamian War* (Ithaca 1974).
21. A. Amit, 'The Melian Dialogue and History', *Athenaeum* (1968), 216–35.

the historical drama. None of this, however, requires that the speeches be invented. The speeches of real statesmen, soldiers and politicians often reveal important things about them, their values and ideas, and the character of the people to whom they speak. In difficult times they are likely to discuss important questions of permanent interest from one point of view to another. But Thucydides did not record all the speeches that were given during the war, far from it. His speeches represent a rigorous selection from many possible choices. There are many instances where we can be sure that speeches were given that were not recorded and many more when such speeches are likely. A few obvious examples come quickly to mind. Thucydides gives us the speeches made at Athens by the Corinthians and Corcyraeans, but none of the many speeches by Athenians that must have been spoken in the two assemblies that debated the Corcyraean alliance.[22] He presents the speech given by Pericles in response to the final Spartan embassy before the war, but he omits the speeches of the ἄλλοι τε πολλοί who came forward to speak on either side of the question of war or peace.[23] We are given Pericles' final speech denouncing the sending of peace missions to Sparta but not the debates that produced the peace offer that was actually made. And these are but a few of the many speeches we can be sure were presented but not reported.

Thucydides, therefore, selected what speeches he wished to report, and we may be sure that he did so with the purpose of portraying that truth about human affairs which was the main goal of his work. His artistry lies in that process of selection, a process not fundamentally different from the one which led him to present certain facts in his narrative and to omit others that he certainly knew. Scholars who wish to understand the mind and art of Thucydides must seek to discover not why Thucydides invented a particular speech, any more than they should ask why he invented a certain battle or meeting of an assembly. Instead they must ask why he chose to report a speech *in extenso* instead of paraphrasing it or omitting it, just as they must ask why he chose to report the introduction of the *eisphora* in 428 but not the trebling of the tribute in 425.

Since we are obliged to accept the essential authenticity of the speeches reported, it is never enough to ask why Thucydides

22. I. 44.   23. I. 139. 3–4.

wished to give us a particular speech; it is necessary also to ask why the speaker spoke it. The two questions are linked, and both must be asked on each occasion if we are to understand it as fully as possible. I believe this is the best method for interpreting the speeches in Thucydides, and the debate on the fate of Mytilene puts its effectiveness to a fair test.

II

The Athenian assembly that met to consider the fate of Mytilene must be seen in the light of the particular historical moment when it took place. Athens was in the fourth year of a war that the Athenians had been told they would win easily, chiefly by adhering to a defensive strategy. Their strength, as they knew, lay in their reserves of money, the unquestioned superiority of their fleet, the security of their empire and the invulnerability of their walls. A mere demonstration of their determination and the futility of attacking them, it was thought, would bring the Spartans to their senses and the war to an end within a year or two, certainly not much longer. All their confidence, all these optimistic expectations had now been shattered. Their money was swiftly being exhausted, and their fleet had been reduced by the shortage of men and money to the point where it could not prevent an enemy fleet from penetrating to the heart of the empire. A more daring enemy commander could have assisted a general rebellion and brought the Persian power into the arena against Athens. The plague, assisted by the crowding that resulted from the defensive strategy, had leaped over the walls and caused more deaths than an enemy army would have. That plague had raged, on and off, since 430, and there was no reason to believe it would not come again. Meanwhile, the enemy had suffered no serious harm nor shown any signs of losing interest in the war. The only strategy employed by Athens was plainly a failure, and for the moment no other strategy seemed possible. Athens had been forced completely onto the defensive and had only escaped disaster by a hair's breadth thanks to the sluggishness of the enemy commander. Next time the Athenians might not be so lucky. The display of Athenian weakness on the sea that permitted the Spartans to sail unhampered to Ionia and return unharmed would soon be well known and was

likely to encourage further rebellion. The situation of Athens was
perilous in the extreme, and the assembly meeting to decide the
fate of Mytilene, whose rebellion had just been crushed, must have
known it.

We get some sense of the fear and anger felt by the Athenians
from their decision to put to death Salaethus, the captured Spartan
envoy to the rebels, apparently without a trial. The decision of the
assembly appears to have been unanimous. The fate of Mytilene
was more controversial and produced a debate. Thucydides has
chosen not to report this meeting in detail nor to reproduce any
of the speeches made in it, yet he gives us enough information
direct and indirect to reconstruct its course in a general way. We
may believe that the embassy from Mytilene was permitted
to speak first, just as the Corinthians and Corcyraeans were
permitted to present their views to the assembly in 433
that decided on the Corcyraean alliance. The Mytilenaean
embassy, which had been composed when both factions were
negotiating with Paches, must have been made up of both
oligarchs and democrats.[24]

Thucydides gives no direct evidence of what the Mytilenaeans
said, but some of their arguments may possibly be deduced from
what the Athenians said later about the matter of responsibility for
the rebellion. A major subject of debate among the Athenians at a
second meeting of the assembly was whether all the Mytilenaeans
were guilty or whether only the oligarchical government was
responsible. Ronald Legon has plausibly suggested that the subject
was first introduced by the embassy from Mytilene at the first
meeting.[25] With him we may believe that the embassy split when
facing the angry Athenians; the oligarchs tried to spread the blame
as widely as possible in the hope that the Athenians would not
destroy a whole people, while the democrats, probably represented

24. Ronald Legon, *Phoenix* 22 (1968), 208; T. J. Quinn, *Historia* 20 (1971),
408, n. 19, denies the phrase ποιοῦνται κοινῇ ὁμολογίαν (3. 28. 11) need mean
that the Mytilenaean demos was engaged in dealings with the Athenians. That,
however, is certainly its obvious sense, and Quinn's own suggestion, 'that there
was one agreement for government and demos, not two separate ones', is
strained. Legon's suggestion is convincing and I accept it.

25. Legon, *Phoenix* 22 (1968), 208–9; Quinn, *Historia* 20 (1971), 408, n. 19,
of course, does not accept this and presumes that the question of who was guilty
was raised by the Athenians.

by their more politically conscious and active leaders, must have argued that the rebellion was inspired by the oligarchic ruling faction which coerced the demos into obedience. 'They would have asked that punishment be confined to the real culprits, the members of the oligarchic regime.'[26]

After the ambassadors from Mytilene had spoken it was time for the Athenians to decide. The debate centered on the motion proposed by Cleon son of Cleaenetus, to kill all the adult males of Mytilene and put the women and children to death. We know that there were several speakers (ἄλλαι γνῶμαι ἀφ' ἑκάστων ἐλέγοντο), and there may even have been other proposals, but Thucydides tells us only of the motion of Cleon and that the chief opposing speaker was Diodotus son of Eucrates. It is possible to see in this debate a split between the two factions that had significant support in 427, the moderates following the cautious policy of Pericles, represented by Diodotus, and the more aggressive faction led by Cleon. Since Sparta's rejection of peace proposals in 430 had discredited the advocates of peace, and lack of men and money had prevented any offensive actions by Athens, there were no important grounds for disagreement, and the moderates had remained in control. The aggressive faction, however, which had been critical of what seemed to them the half-measures taken by Pericles and his successors since the first reinforcements had been sent to Corcyra in 433, must have been frustrated by the unhappy results of moderation. That frustration was turned into anger by the rebellion of Mytilene, and Thucydides tells us the Athenians in general shared that anger. They were angry because the Mytilenaeans rebelled in spite of the privileged status they enjoyed, because the rebellion was not a sudden aberration but had plainly been long and carefully prepared: most of all they were angry because the Mytilenaean revolt had brought a Peloponnesian fleet into the Aegean and to the shores of Ionia.[27]

Presumably Cleon used these and other arguments; we are not told what Diodotus said in rebuttal. Cleon carried the day, and a trireme was sent to Paches telling him the decision and ordering him to carry out the sentence immediately. Meanwhile the Athenians were having second thoughts. Once their fury was spent

26. Legon, *Phoenix* 22 (1968), 209.
27. 3. 36. 2. I consider οὐκ ἐλάχιστον here to be an example of litotes.

KSG

they began to consider the unreasonableness and frightfulness of their action which seemed to treat the innocent and guilty alike. The ambassadors from Mytilene, among whom were probably some of the Athenian *proxenoi*, and their supporters in Athens, Diodotus, no doubt, and other moderates, perceived the change in sentiment and took advantage of it. They easily persuaded the generals to get the prytanies to call a special meeting of the assembly to reconsider the matter.[28]

On the very day after the assembly had decided the fate of Mytilene a second assembly met to discuss the question again. Thucydides, introducing Cleon into his history for the first time, although he had played a prominent role in Athenian politics for some years, calls him 'the most violent of the citizens and at that time by far the most influential with the people'.[29] It is a rare instance of direct characterization of an individual by Thucydides, and its harshness is uniquely applied to Cleon. The speech that follows seems amply to justify the epithet.[30] Bullying and rhetoric aside, Cleon's main points were these: the Mytilenaeans must be punished severely because their rebellion was without cause and unjust, the result of unforeseen good fortune which turned, as usual, into wanton violence (ὕβρις); justice, therefore, required swift and severe punishment. No distinction should be made between common people and oligarchs, for both took part in the rebellion. Not only justice but expediency requires that the punishment be severe. Cleon believes that lenient treatment merely encourages rebellion while uniformly harsh punishment will deter it. This last point is not merely an exercise in criminal theory or a rationalization for Cleon's passions. It is the central point of his argument and represents an important departure from the Periclean policy of imperial management.

The criticism of Periclean administration of the empire is clearly implied. 'We should never have treated the Mytilenaeans differently from the others and then they would not have reached this point of insolence. In general, it is the nature of man to despise

---

28. 3. 36. 5. For the constitutional questions, see Gomme, *A Historical Commentary on Thucydides*, vol. II (Oxford 1956), p. 298.

29. 3. 36. 6.

30. For an interesting discussion of this speech see A. Andrewes, *Phoenix* 16 (1962), 64–85.

flattery and admire firmness.'[31] The implication is that the
Athenians in the past ought not to have permitted Mytilene to
retain its autonomy but should have reduced it, and, presumably
Chios as well, to subject status. Even more plain is the following
reference to what Cleon considers to be past errors:

> Consider your allies: if you impose the same penalties upon
> those who rebel under constraint by the enemy and on those
> who rebel of their own free will, tell me who will not rebel on
> the smallest pretext when the reward for success is freedom
> and the price of failure is nothing irreparable?[32]

The reference, no doubt, was a general one, for even in the dark
days of the First Peloponnesian War, when rebellions in the empire
and especially on Euboea threatened the safety of Athens, when
the decrees of Cleinias and Clearchus tightened Athenian control
of the allies, when the rebellious Colophonians had Athenian
colonists planted among them and a democratic government
imposed in place of their former constitution, when Athenian
cleruchies were scattered throughout the empire, the Athenians
under the leadership of Pericles never imposed so harsh a punishment.[33] The harshest treatment imposed by Pericles, the one the
Athenians inflicted on Hestiaea after the First Peloponnesian War
and which Xenophon lists among the atrocities committed by
Athens alongside Melos, Scione, Torone, and Aegina,[34] deprived
the victims of their lands, but not their lives as Cleon now proposed.[35] But closer in time, and probably more vivid in the minds
of Cleon's audience, was the treatment of Samos and Byzantium
in 440. The Samians, in spite of the serious threat their rebellion
posed and the difficulty Athens had in putting it down, escaped
not only with their lives but with their property as well. They lost
their walls and ships and were compelled to accept a democratic
government, but they received no garrisons or cleruchies. They
even were free of tribute, paying only a war indemnity that was
not crushing. Byzantium suffered hardly at all. She was permitted

---

31. 3. 39. 5.   32. 3. 39. 7.
33. See Kagan, *Outbreak*, pp. 116–19.
34. Xen. *Hell.* 2. 2. 3.
35. For an account of the Athenian settlement of Euboea in 446 see **Kagan,**
Outbreak, pp. 126–7.

to return to her condition before the revolt, paying a tribute only
slightly higher than before.[36] We can easily imagine that Cleon
and his friends were the accusers in the trial of the generals who
had taken the surrender of Potidaea but allowed its citizens to
escape without personal harm.[37]

It was such lenient treatment, Cleon implied, that had led to the
Mytilenaean rebellion. If the Athenians continue that failed policy
of softness, misplaced pity and clemency, 'we shall risk our lives
and money against each rebellious state. If we happen to succeed
we will recover a state that has been destroyed, only then to be
deprived for the future of its revenue, which is the source of our
strength. If we fail we will add new enemies to those we have
already, and the time we should devote to fighting our present
enemies we will spend combatting our own allies.'[38]

Cleon's argument is not directed merely toward the fate of
Mytilene; it is a full-scale attack on the imperial policy of Pericles
and his followers. In its place he recommended a calculated policy
of terror toward imperial rebels, at least in war-time. He proposed
and carried a proposal to put the people of Scione to death after
their rebellion in 423,[39] and he sold the women and children of
Torone into slavery after he recaptured that rebellious town in
422.[40] Cleon's speech was a breach in the common front that had
informally existed between the moderate supporters of Pericles and
the more aggressive Athenians who followed Cleon since the peace
proposals of 430 had been made by the Athenians and rejected by
the Spartans. It was a signal that Cleon and his friends were
no longer willing to put up with the policy of the moderates or
with their leadership and that henceforth they would challenge
both, advocating more aggressive policies and more daring
leadership.

The debate between Cleon and Diodotus that Thucydides
reports in direct discourse is often used as evidence for the coarsen-
ing of the Athenian spirit and the decline in the morality of the

36. *Ibid.*, pp. 176–7.

37. Thucydides, 2. 70. 4; Aristoph., *Knights*, 438. See G. Busolt, *Griechische
Geschichte*, III. 2, p. 962, n. 1.

38. 3. 39. 8.   39. 4. 122. 6.

40. 5. 3. 4. The captured men were sent back to Athens and were later sent
home after the conclusion of peace. It is likely that if Cleon had lived he would
have argued for harsher treatment.

Athenians caused by the war,[41] but there is little reason to do so. The dramatic way in which Thucydides presents the debate has obscured some of his own remarks.[42] We must remember that Cleon and Diodotus were only two among several speakers and that they represented the extreme positions.[43] It is not only intrinsically likely that the other speakers addressed themselves to the questions of justice and humanity, but Cleon's speech is obviously a rebuttal to such speeches. Finally, we must not forget that the second assembly was called precisely because the Athenians were worried by the possible cruelty and injustice of their actions. We must understand Diodotus' emphasis on expediency and his avoidance of emotional appeals to mercy and other humane sentiments in the light of the entire debate, much of which we don't have, and particularly as a response to the speech of Cleon.

Cleon had implied that to speak in favor of leniency was softness at the least and corruption and even treason at most. It would be bad tactics indeed to argue for humanity in the face of such an assault. It seems, in fact, to be natural for men in such circumstances to try to cloak any humane reasons they may have in a pose of toughness even greater than that of the enemy. One is reminded of the arguments used by Dean Acheson and Harry Truman in behalf of the Marshall Plan in response to the charges of isolationists and Republicans that it was the product of do-gooders, sacrificing American interests to humanitarian softness. The plan was, in fact, motivated in part by the humane desire to feed and reconstruct a starving and shattered continent, but its supporters defended it almost exclusively in terms of tough self-interest.[44] In the same way Diodotus tells the Athenians to vote for his proposal, without undue regard for pity and clemency, but merely out of calculations of expediency.[45]

41. E.g., Finley, *Thucydides*, p. 177.
42. Andrewes, *Phoenix* 16 (1962), 64–85, has pointed this out. My understanding of the circumstances surrounding the debate owes much to his article.
43. 3. 36. 6 and 3. 49. 1.
44. A. W. Gomme, *More Essays in Greek History and Literature* (Oxford 1962), p. 158, has noticed a similar phenomenon. 'In 1945 English newspaper correspondents in Berlin were stressing the need for food to be sent to the starving inhabitants, and assuring us that this was not from pity or kindness towards a wicked and defeated enemy, but because under-nourishment can so easily caused typhus and typhus might spread to allied troops.'
45. 3. 48. 1.

His main task, after the necessary defense against the rhetoric of Cleon was cleared away, was to defend the imperial policy laid down by Pericles and supported by Diodotus and the other moderates. He did so vigorously and skillfully, relying on two main arguments. First, he claimed that relying on the certainty of the death penalty for unsuccessful rebels was not an effective deterrent for rebellion. Men rebel because they think they will be successful; no threat of punishment, therefore, can prevent them. A better policy would be, 'not to punish excessively free men who revolt but to guard them zealously before they rebel and anticipate them before they even think of it'.[46] Gomme is right to say of such a statement that it is 'sound, but easy advice to give, and difficult to follow' and to notice its similarity to the advice Pericles offered at the start of the war, 'keep a firm hand on the allies'.[47] It is precisely the advice of a man who believes that the principles of the present imperial system are sound and simply require better administration. Diodotus, in fact, directly reaffirms his confidence in the present system. 'Consider what your policy is now: if a city, having rebelled, realizes that it will not succeed, it may wish to reach an agreement while it is still able to pay the indemnity and the tribute in the future.'[48] The Athenians must have been reminded of the surrender of the Samians and Byzantines, who had yielded before it was necessary to destroy them. The Samians were still paying installments of the war indemnity and the Byzantines their considerable assessment of tribute, both of which were contributing to the power of Athens; neither state had tried to renew its rebellion. Diodotus' audience might well believe that the surrender of Mytilene had been influenced by these examples of Athenian moderation.

With these happy results Diodotus contrasts the possible consequences of accepting the innovation proposed by Cleon.

> 'What city will not make better preparations than now, and hold on to the very last when besieged, if coming to terms swiftly or at leisure has the same effect? And how will it not be harmful to us to spend money besieging an enemy who will

46. 3. 46. 6.
47. 2. 13. 2; Gomme's remarks are addressed to sections 4 and 6 of 3. 46 on p. 322 of the second volume of his *Commentary*.
48. 3. 46. 2.

not surrender and to be deprived of its revenue for the future, for that is the source of our strength against our enemies?'[49]

Diodotus' second argument rests on a flat contradiction of Cleon's assertion that the common people of Mytilene were no less guilty for the rebellion than the oligarchs. The character of the disagreement makes it likely, as we have argued above,[50] that the subject has been debated before, whether by Cleon and Diodotus at the first meeting or by other speakers, and probably introduced by the Mytilenaeans themselves. On Cleon's side is the fact that there is no evidence that the people ever resisted the rebellion until hunger impelled them. On the side of Diodotus there is the fact that it was a rebellion by the demos that brought about the capitulation, and the suggestion, not denied by Cleon, that the people may have been forced to join in the rebellion.[51] It is not possible to judge the question simply. Thucydides' narrative does not suggest opposition to the rebellion before the Athenian blockade had taken its toll, but Cleon's remark that the common people joined the revolt, 'thinking there was less risk in going with the oligarchs',[52] implies that refusal to join would have been punished.

The larger question of whether the Athenian Empire was generally popular among the lower classes is also important for Diodotus. He asserts that 'Now the *demos* in all the cities is well disposed to you and either does not rebel along with the oligarchs or, if it is compelled, is immediately hostile to those who made the revolution, so that you go to war having the majority of the opposing city as an ally'.[53] Once again we cannot be sure whether Diodotus is right; there is evidence in both directions, and the debate among modern scholars waxes.[54] The case immediately at

49. 3. 46. 2–3.
50. See above, p. 80.
51. Diodotus 3. 47. 2; Cleon: 3. 39. 6 with the analysis of Legon, *Phoenix* 22 (1968), 209–10.
52. 3. 39. 6, τὸν μετὰ τῶν ὀλίγων κίνδυνον ἡγησάμενοι βεβαιότερον.
53. 3. 47. 2.
54. The first important monograph on the rebellion on Lesbos was written by W. Herbst, *Der Abfall Mytilenes* (Köln 1861). Since then the matter has received a great deal of attention, but until recently most of it centered on the debate at Athens in 427 on the disposition of the defeated island. (For bibliography see D. Gillis, *AJP* 92 (1971), 40, n. 5.) The debate over the nature of the Athenian Empire inspired by the provocative article of G. E. M. de Ste

hand, the rebellion of Mytilene, does not, as we have seen, give unequivocal support to Diodotus. In fact, he seems to realize that the evidence in his favor is far from conclusive, but this does not trouble him unduly, for he is less interested in describing the facts than in prescribing a policy. In general, after putting down a revolt, the Athenians should blame as few men as possible. To kill the people along with the noble instigators of rebellion would play directly into the hands of the oligarchs. Future rebellions would find the common people hostile to Athens, once it was known that the same fate awaited nobles and commoners, instigators and unwitting followers, guilty and innocent. 'Even if the *demos* were guilty you should pretend otherwise so that the only group that is still friendly to you should not become hostile.'[55]

It is a policy of firm but moderate and judicious treatment of the allies that Diodotus puts forth clothed in the language of *Realpolitik*. But though this language may have been forced on him by the circumstances of the debate, and though we may credit him with considerations of humanity as well, we should not doubt that his chief concern was political or that he believed in the effectiveness of the policy he proposed. It was the program of Pericles, and, up to the rebellion of Mytilene, it had worked well. There was no reason to believe that Mytilene was anything but an isolated case. The policy of calculated terror proposed by Cleon was not only offensive but was probably unnecessary and would likely be self-defeating. Diodotus proposed instead that the Athenians pass judgment only on those whom Paches had sent to Athens as the guilty parties, but not to harm the other Mytilenaeans.[56]

We may more readily believe that the question was less one of humanity than of policy when we realize that the number of people arrested by Paches as 'most guilty' was a little over 1000.[57] That number was probably not less than one-tenth of the entire adult male population of the rebellious towns on Lesbos.[58]

Croix, *Historia* 3 (1954), 1–41, has led to a more careful study of the causes of the revolt and its course. (For a good bibliography of the literature to this point see again Gillis, *AJP* 92 (1971), 40, n. 4.) The keenest insight into these questions is provided by Legon, *Phoenix* 22 (1968), 200–5.

55. 3. 47. 4.   56. 3. 48.

57. 3. 50. 1. The number has been questioned by many scholars who have thought it impossibly large. See Busolt (*G.G.* III. 2, p. 1030, n. 2.)

58. Beloch, *Die Bevölkerung der Griechisch-römischen Welt* (Leipzig 1886), p. 235.

Diodotus did not propose that these men should be put to death, but he must have known that would be the result. In the event, the vote was extremely close; the show of hands was almost equal, but the proposal of Diodotus won. Cleon took immediate advantage of the situation to propose that the assembly should vote the death penalty for the 'guilty' 1000, and his motion passed. Thucydides does not suggest that the vote on this question was close.[59] Busolt rightly compares these proceedings with the trial of the Athenian generals after the battle of Arginusae.[60] Lesbians received no proper trial, either singly or even *en masse*. The assembly simply assumed them guilty on the basis merely of Paches' opinion, and voted the death penalty. The case of Salaethus was multiplied a thousandfold. We do not know how Diodotus voted; there is no record that he objected.

This analysis shows, I believe, that the arguments attributed by Thucydides to Cleon and Diodotus were among the ones they used, for they make perfect sense in the context, properly understood. Yet some modern scholars have found them impossible to accept. The speech of Diodotus, says one, does not bear the stamp of a real individual: 'No one could have talked to an Athenian assembly in this rather impersonal and abstract manner and carried his point.'[61] 'This analysis of ἀνθρωπεία φύσις as the foundation of political psychology could hardly be imagined as part of a speech in the *ekklesia*; even an Athenian assembly would have preferred the popular slogans to the undiluted abstract concentrate.'[62] Such arguments are not unusual in modern scholarship, but they have no value. First we must remember that the speeches reported by Thucydides are much compressed. The arguments put forward by the speakers are necessarily reproduced in the words chiefly of Thucydides. Speeches that might have taken an hour are presented in much shorter compass. Besides, we have no warrant to decide what manner of argument might have persuaded an Athenian audience. The evidence of the contemporary tragedians, and especially Euripides, in fact, suggests that an audience of average

---

59. 3. 50. 1.

60. *G.G.* III. 2, p. 1030, n. 1.

61. F. M. Wassermann, 'Post-Periclean Democracy in Action: the Mytilenean Debate (Thuc. III, 37–48)', *TAPA* 87 (1956), 34.

62. *Ibid.*, p. 39.

Athenians was ready to award the prize to plays filled with abstract
and difficult arguments as well as complicated and unusual
language. These points are well made by John Finley,[63] and I
quote some of his relevant conclusions:

> 'numerous passages in Euripides show that ideas and forms of
> argument attributed by Thucydides to his speakers were
> known in Athens at or near the time when their speeches were
> allegedly delivered. The parallels were taken to prove, not
> that the speakers used those arguments, but that they could
> have... These parallels tend to show that the speeches of
> Thucydides are not anachronistic but that, on the contrary,
> they expound ideas which the historian knew to have been
> familiar at the time when the speeches were delivered. They
> therefore create a strong presumption that he thought of his
> speeches, not primarily as setting forth his own ideas, but as
> conveying the actual policies of the speakers.'

The speeches 'reflect a rhetoric generally used' and

> 'one can at least say that a broad common ground between
> the speeches of Thucydides and the debates of the dramatist
> is that in both alike the concrete issues at hand are looked on
> as not, so to speak, interpretable in and through themselves,
> but only through the more universal laws which they
> exemplify' (50–3).

The style of Diodotus' speech, then, and its mode of argument
point, if anything, to an accurate report by Thucydides of the
speech he really gave.

Andrewes has seen the weakness of the argument against
authenticity based on 'the involved and elevated style of Diodotus' discourse on retribution and deterrence'.[64] Although he
sees this style as one of 'the most surprising features' in the debate,
he concedes that it may not be a real problem. 'It is not indeed
easy to estimate how far the assembly, as Kleon is made to allege,
actually enjoyed this style of argument, but if Kleon spoke up for
deterrence Diodotus was entitled to argue in reply that terrorism

---

63. 'Euripides and Thucydides', *Three Essays on Thucydides* (Cambridge,
Mass. 1967), pp. 1–54.
64. P. 73.

would be ineffective.' To that we might add, with Finley, that the speech's abstract rhetoric was typical of the time. No more is Andrewes troubled by Diodotus' unemotional concentration on arguments from expediency and exclusion of considerations of justice and humanity. He points out that such arguments must already have been used on the previous day and by other speakers on the same day. He recognizes, moreover, that Diodotus' speech is shaped to a large degree by Cleon's.

> 'In face of Kleon's charge that anyone who speaks for Mytilene must have been bribed (38. 2, 40. 1, cf. 42. 3), of his rejection of the use of reason (37. 3, etc., cf. 42. 2), of his attempt to whip up cooling emotions (40. 7, cf. 42. 1, 44. 4), Diodotus is compelled to spend a good third of his time laboriously establishing his right merely to speak at all, and when it comes to his substantive case he must at all costs show that he is as careful of Athens' interest as Kleon, or more so.'[65]

In spite of these compelling arguments he has adduced, Andrewes, nonetheless, finds that the whole debate 'does not read much like an authentic report, *though it is not easy to pin down the elements which contribute to this impression*'.[66]

The main source of his discomfort seems to be Cleon's speech. It is harsh, angry and cruel, not only in the policy it advocates but in its manner and general sentiment. Cleon warns the Athenians not to be tender-hearted and to avoid being led astray by the three things most damaging to an empire, pity, clemency, and a delight in eloquence.[67] A love of fine speeches hardly seems in place in such a catalogue, but its mention is part of the angry indictment Cleon levels at what he thinks is the levity and instability of the Athenian people. They refuse to recognize the hard fact that their empire is a despotism held together by fear of the power of Athens, not gratitude for her benevolence.[68] They are easily deceived by excessively clever men and elaborate arguments. Ignorant but modest and self-restrained men are better for a state than clever ones who think themselves wiser than the laws, but the Athenians are easy prey for clever speakers who lead them lightly to change

65. P. 72. 66. P. 73, my italics.
67. 3. 40. 2. 68. 3. 37. 2.

their minds and even their laws. It is such behavior that exaspe-
rates Cleon and convinces him that democracies are unable to
govern empires. For Cleon the matter is simple: the Mytilenaeans
have done wrong by rebelling from Athens and conspiring with her
enemy in war-time. The crime is all the more terrible because it
was unprovoked (indeed the rebels had a privileged position),
because it was premeditated. Justice requires that they be
punished. Nor should any distinction in guilt be made between
oligarchs and democrats, for all took part in the rebellion. The
safety of Athens also required swift, fierce and undistinguishing
punishment for the rebels, for anything clsc would cncourage
future rebellions. The conclusion of Cleon's speech is fittingly
harsh and unappealing.

> 'Don't become traitors to yourselves, but remembering as
> well as you can what you suffered at their hands and how you
> would have given anything at that time to crush them, now
> pay them back without softening in the face of their present
> helplessness and without forgetting the danger that just
> threatened us. Punish them as they deserve and present an
> example to your other allies that whoever revolts will be
> punished by death. For if they know that you will have less
> need to neglect your enemies to fight your allies'.[69]

Most of this speech Andrewes understands and explains
persuasively. It is the attack on the habits and gullibility of the
assembly that troubles him. 'Kleon's assault on reason is dragged
in with a certain appearance of effort... And his striking description in 38 of the Athenians revelling in an oratorical ἀγών is
developed to unexpected lengths... Kleon's comment on Athenian
delight in sophistry is prolonged well beyond its immediate tactical
usefulness.' Andrewes 'cannot help suspecting that Thucydides
through these speeches was trying to say something that he himself
thought important about the assembly and its leaders'.[70]

Here Andrewes has fallen into the trap of allowing Thucydides
to invent and to present his ideas in the guise of words spoken by
another. It is not merely the language whose authenticity he
questions, which would be acceptable; he suggests the development by Thucydides of a whole topic hardly treated by Cleon at

69. 3. 40. 7–8.   70. 73–5.

all. This is a clear violation of the principle Andrewes has earlier described with intelligence and accuracy, but it is not necessary. The speeches were public ones spoken in Athens at a time when Thucydides was probably present. If he were not, then there would be no shortage of witnesses and little likelihood that so important and spectacular a debate would be forgotten. If ever it were possible to receive and give an accurate report this was such a time. Even if we given credence to Pohlenz' theory, and we should not, this was only the fourth year of the war, not very long for Thucydides to have abandoned his original principle so soon. But let us think of the peculiarities that have driven Andrewes to such desperate expedients. Are they so great? Cleon pursues an irrelevant argument at too great a length. Is he the only politician to have done so? It is not hard to believe that the inelegant argument of Cleon is included because he used it and, perhaps, because Thucydides was not unwilling to present it as evidence of Cleon's vulgarity. It is also possible, of course, that the discourse on the dangers of sophistry and rhetoric refers pointedly to the earlier speech of Diodotus or to others not reported by Thucydides. It does not, in any case, warrant any suspicion about the authenticity of the debate. Let me emphasize the point. No evidence or argument has ever been adduced that compels or even supports the belief that the speeches of Cleon and Diodotus are Thucydidean creations rather than essentially accurate reports of what was said. That belief can only arise from a general theory of the Thucydidean invention of speeches, a theory which does not withstand criticism.

It is not my purpose here to consider the important question that remains: why did Thucydides choose to give us the two speeches he has selected and not any others? That question, of course, can not be answered with any certainty, though several attractive ideas may be and have been suggested. The debate serves splendidly as a characterization of two imperial policies that competed in Athens at the time, continued to do so throughout the war, and are always possible choices for any imperial power. It also provides a sharply defined picture of Cleon at his most unattractive – ruthless, coarse, and hostile to reason at the same time as he employs sophistic techniques. Verbal resemblances between both speeches and speeches of Pericles may subtly indicate the way in which the policies and government of Pericles were undermined by lesser politicians. All these reasons, and possibly others, may have contributed to make Thucydides report the speeches of Cleon and Diodotus in the way that he did. There is no reason, however, to believe that they compelled him to invent their arguments and certainly not their speeches.

Xenophon, Diodorus and the year 379/378 B.C.
Reconstruction and reappraisal[1]

DAVID G. RICE

I. Introduction

THREE RECENT ARTICLES, published in *Historia*,[2] have raised again the difficult problems of historiography and history surrounding the events in the year 379/8. The two major continuous accounts of Xenophon and Diodorus are in many instances contradictory. Plutarch also supplies information concerning this period, but he has been regarded with suspicion as a later writer who is not an exacting historian. The tendency of most modern scholars has been to prefer the evidence of the contemporary witness, Xenophon, to the clumsy and suspicious accounts in Diodorus or Plutarch. This attitude should now be altered.

The recent work by I. A. F. Bruce on the *Hellenica Oxyrhynchia* has, in my judgment, provided real reason to believe that Diodorus may very well have had access, through his main source Ephorus, to accounts of the history of Greece after Thucydides which are no less reliable, if not superior to, the information contained in Xenophon's *Hellenica*.[3] It is clear enough that Xenophon is a contemporary witness to much of what he reports, but he is

1. A first draft of this paper appeared as chapter 3 of my doctoral dissertation, 'Why Sparta Failed: a Study of Politics and Policy from the Peace of Antalcidas to the Battle of Leuctra, 387/71 B.C.' (Yale University 1971). My thanks to my director, Donald Kagan, and to my readers, Charles Hamilton, Ramsey MacMullen, and J. J. Pollitt for many helpful criticisms. I owe a special debt to my first teacher, the late C. Bradford Welles, with whom I first discussed the importance of Diodorus.

2. A. P. Burnett, 'Thebes and the Expansion of the Second Athenian Confederacy: *IG* 11² 40 and *IG* 11² 43', *Historia* 11 (1962), 1–17; J. Buckler, 'Theban Treaty Obligations in *IG* 11² 40: a Postscript', *Historia* 20 (1971), 506–8; A. MacDonald, 'A Note on the Raid of Sphodrias', *Historia* 21 (1972), 38–44.

3. I. A. F. Bruce, *An Historical Commentary on the Hellenica Oxyrhynchia* (Cambridge University Press 1967). See especially pp. 20ff.

subject to bias in favor of the Spartans, and, more specifically, to bias in favor of his friend, benefactor and hero – Agesilaus. Attempts to establish the relative superiority of one or another of the accounts through methods of *Quellenforschung* have not yielded very suitable results, nor do they focus on the events themselves. The *Hellenica Oxyrhynchia* emphasizes the importance of factional politics as a key to understanding the shifts in foreign policy in Greece during the fourth century.[4] It seems reasonable for modern historians to do no less.

In the following paper I hope to test the validity of *P*'s approach by examining all the sources dealing with the events of 379/8 with an unprejudiced eye, to seek an understanding of the factional politics in each state, and then see if politics helps to explain changes in policy. The following pages will offer a narrative, chronological analysis of the events from the retaking of the Cadmeia by the Theban exiles to the establishment of the Second Athenian Sea League. In every case I have tried to examine and weigh evidence, to accept or reject testimony solely on the basis of what most probably happened. It may well seem that there is too much *Realpolitik* in what follows. It seems to me that while statesmen are subject to the usual human foibles of anger, fear, prejudice and the like, they usually make their decisions on the basis of principle, interest, or their reading of a particular situation. The results of the following analysis will no doubt appear conjectural to some; it is to be hoped that the conjecture will also appear reasonable, perhaps even convincing.

II. The recovery of Thebes

By 379 Sparta had successfully completed her plans for the organization of mainland Greece. Under the leadership of Agesilaus, she had dealt with matters close to home, and done so with a firm hand. In the seven-year period since the Peace of Antalcidas Sparta had disciplined her allies in the Peloponnesian League,[5]

4. See V. Bartoletti (ed.), *Hellenica Oxyrhynchia* (Leipzig, 1959), sections 6. 2–7. 2, pp. 6–7.
5. As can be seen in the campaigns against Mantineia in 386, cf. Xenophon, *Hellenica* 5. 2, 1–7 and Diodorus 15. 12. 1; and against Phlius in 384/79, cf. Xenophon, *Hellenica* 5. 2. 8–11; 5. 3. 10–25.

and had so cowed Athens that the latter did not dare risk military action against Sparta. She had also checked the pretensions of Thebes to hegemony over the Boeotian Federation and, by means of carefully placed garrisons at Orchomenus, Thespiae, and Thebes, which were in turn supported by oligarchic factions loyal to her interests, had made sure that central Greece would remain loyal to Sparta under any conceivable circumstances. In addition, the successful campaign against Olynthus had checked the possible growth of a new power in north-east Greece which, combined with Athens and Thebes, might be dangerous to Sparta.[6] The years since the Peace of Antalcidas had been ones of steady victory for Sparta and for the architect of Spartan policy, Agesilaus. The future seemed to demand only Spartan diligence in overseeing what she had gained.

Sparta's military success had the political result of putting into power in the Greek states factions which were loyal to her and obedient to her foreign policy. In Thebes, for example, the faction of Leontiades was in charge, though supported by a Spartan garrison and harmost stationed on the Cadmeia.[7] The leading members of the anti-Spartan faction in Thebes, since the death of their leader Ismenias, had taken refuge in Athens, where they found sympathy and some support in their plight, no doubt, from those Athenians opposed to Spartan policy and methods.[8]

During the period 387/79 a conservative faction had been in control at Athens, whose leader was very likely the distinguished politician Callistratus of Aphidna.[9] It was his policy to maintain

6. For the status of Orchomenus, see Diodorus 15. 37. 1; for Plataea, Xenophon, *Hellenica* 5. 2. 10 and 14; for Thespiae, Xenophon, *Hellenica* 5. 4. 10–55 and Diodorus 15. 27. 4; for Thebes, Diodorus 15. 20. 1–3; 16. 23. 2–3; 16. 29. 2, and Xenophon, *Hellenica* 5. 2. 25–36. For Sparta's position see Diodorus 15. 23. 3–4; Xenophon, *Hellenica* 5. 3. 27; Isocrates, *Panegyricus* 121; *Peace* 99; *Archidamus* 63. For Olynthus see Xenophon, *Hellenica* 5. 3. 26; Diodorus 15. 23. 2–3.

7. Xenophon, *Hellenica* 5. 2. 35–6; Diodorus 15. 20. 2; 15. 25. 1.

8. Xenophon, *Hellenica* 5. 3. 31.

9. The position of Callistratus of Aphidna in Athens is a complicated one, and requires a fuller discussion than I can offer here. I react strongly against the view of Raphael Sealey in 'Callistratus of Aphidna and his contemporaries', *Historia* 5 (1956), 178–203. Sealey is very cautious in accepting the worth of *P*, and believes that the Athenian factions in 395, headed respectively by Thrasybulus, Cephalus, and Agyrrhius did not disagree in principle, but only in tactics. For Sealey, it would appear, politics and principles are never

friendly relations with Sparta, and at the same time to encourage Athens to maintain a limited and cautious presence in the Aegean, confined mostly to those cities and islands which were on the vital grain route from Athens to the Crimea. It was in keeping with this policy that Athens had allied herself with Chios in a simple defensive alliance.[10] The terms of this treaty are notable in that they lay special emphasis upon the fact that the treaty in no way violates the Peace of Antalcidas.[11] Although Sparta might not like

the real issue between factions. For him the only struggles are for personal power and advantage. It is important to note that *P*, who is an excellent and perhaps even contemporary source, closely connects policies with social, economic, and political groups. It seems to me we can do no less.

If the above is reasonable, what then of Callistratus? A few details of his career are known: his uncle was Agyrrhius, a leading democrat; he prosecuted Andocides and the other ambassadors who accepted peace with Sparta in 391; he served on the board of *strategoi* in 378 as a financial expert and proposed that the contributions to the Second Athenian Sea League be called 'contributions' rather than 'tribute'; he prosecuted Timotheus, a leading pro-Theban imperialist in 373, and as *strategos* in 372 broke Spartan naval power, and shortly after negotiated a treaty with Sparta at Theban expense. The rest of his career was relatively insignificant, but indicates that he maintained a fairly hostile attitude towards Thebes and towards her friends in Athens. Clearly then, if put to the test, he would prefer to deal with Sparta, and, in the period of his influence at Athens, the leading Spartan statesman was Agesilaus, and he shared Callistratus' views about Thebes. If *P* is correct in linking the fortunes of factions in one state with their corresponding numbers in other states, then Callistratus' fortunes would most likely rise or fall in relation to what happened to Agesilaus in Sparta, and vice versa. Plutarch remarks that the Theban exiles claimed to have a letter from Callistratus to the pro-Spartan oligarchs in Thebes, and, whether such a letter existed or not, the mention of it was enough to get them admitted. The fact that Callistratus prosecuted Andocides and his friends is not necessarily proof of hostility to Sparta. With what faction was Andocides dealing in Sparta? It was likely not that of Agesilaus, but the Lysandrians, for the terms accepted would have threatened Athens on the sea, and this was not what Callistratus wanted. The fact that Callistratus served as financial officer of the league and suggested a sweeter name for the taxes does not strike me as the action of one who must have been an enthusiastic supporter, but rather one who tried to save what he could and hope for better things later. If anything, Callistratus' policy was one of cautious Athenian presence in the Aegean, and expansion where safe, of hostility to Thebes, and of friendship to Sparta, particularly to Agesilaus.

10. See *IG* II², pp. 34 and 35 = Tod, p. 118.

11. See *IG* II², pp. 34 and 35 = Tod, p. 118, lines 6–12, 17–24. Compare Xenophon, *Hellenica* 5. 1. 31. *IG* II², p. 36 = Tod, p. 119 which is apparently an alliance between the Chalcidians and Athenians, is dated by Kirchner to 384/3. Kirchner believes that this decree should be interpreted as part of the Athenian diplomatic offensive at Olynthus, as summarized by Cleigenes of

it, Athens was within her rights in seeking an alliance with Olynthus, and this was quite understandable as an attempt to assure that Athens' vital trade and grain interests were not threatened by a hostile state in north-east Greece. It is also significant that Athens broke off the treaty discussions when Sparta chose to attack Olynthus.[12] Athens did not become involved in any sort of offensive alliances or treaty discussions until 378, when she made several alliances of a more aggressive nature with such states as Byzantium and Methymna.[13] It seems reasonable to conclude that until the events of 378, Athens was pursuing a very moderate policy in foreign affairs: she sought to protect and even expand her influence in the Aegean, but would take no risk which might provoke Sparta. Such, we may well believe, was the policy of Callistratus and his friends.

Sparta was not, however, unopposed in her policy. Since the Corinthian War, it is true, those factions in Greece opposed to Sparta and her policy had not been in control of the government in their respective states. The succession of violations of the Peace of Antalcidas committed by Sparta, however, provided fuel for their opposition. The Athenian imperialists in particular, who had watched Sparta increase her prestige while Athens was eclipsed, must have welcomed the Theban exiles as living proof of one further example of Sparta's policy as *hegemon* of Greece. It is likely that these Athenians would be most sympathetic to their plight and most willing, if an occasion permitted, to aid them to return to Thebes and win back what Sparta had taken. A favorable occasion was the only requirement, and this was provided when Phillidas, the secretary to the Theban polemarchs, visited Athens and spoke with the exiles, among whom was Melon, one of his old friends.[14] From him the Theban exiles learned that there were at least some

Acanthus in Xenophon, *Hellenica* 5. 2. 15ff. The decree is badly mutilated, and it is almost impossible to determine what its terms and purpose are. It is of course usual Athenian policy to be concerned with the vital grain route to the Black Sea, and anything affecting north-east Greece and/or the islands would be of interest to the Athenians. They certainly do not seem to have had an aggressive foreign policy during the years 386/79, however, probably due to nervousness about Sparta and Persia.

12. Xenophon, *Hellenica* 5. 2. 11ff.

13. *IG* ii², pp. 41 and 42; see also Diodorus 15. 28. 3.

14. Xenophon, *Hellenica* 5. 4. 2ff.

Thebans who opposed the polemarch Leontiades, and thus the Spartans, and who would be willing to employ violent means, if necessary, to overthrow their tyranny. It was still a risky business, however, to attempt such a *coup* without support from a state such as Athens. Diodorus tells us that the Athenians did in fact support the Thebans:

> 'When the Lacedaemonians maintained a garrison unjustly in the Cadmeia and had exiled many important citizens, the exiles gathered, secured the support of the Athenians, and returned by night to their native city. Having first slain in their own houses those who favored the Lacedaemonian cause, whom they surprised while still asleep, they next rallied the citizens to the cause of freedom and obtained the co-operation of all the Thebans.'[15]

Xenophon tells a different story.[16] Although Diodorus is surely right in thinking that the Thebans got Athenian help, Xenophon must be closer to the truth when he places that help after the victory of the Theban exiles and not before it. Athens would certainly not have risked angering Sparta by aiding the rebellious Thebans before they were successful. Indeed, it is hard to believe that all the Athenians would have been willing to risk angering Sparta at any time. It is likely that it was the imperialists of Athens who provided support at this early point. It was probably such men, among whom were two of the generals, who waited at the border to see the outcome of the attempted *coup*.

Plutarch adds the detail that the exiles went to the house of Leontiades and gained access by announcing that they had come from Athens with a letter for Leontiades from Callistratus.[17] It is very likely that the exiles used Callistratus' name. It is plain that Leontiades had secret dealings with Callistratus, and was prepared to receive messages from him with alacrity. Even if the story is not true, though we have no good reason to doubt it, it is plain that the general position of Callistratus was understood to be such as to make the story plausible. Xenophon reports that the Theban exiles

---

15. Diodorus 15. 25. 1–2. Unless otherwise noted, translations are derived from the appropriate volume of the Loeb Classical Library.
16. Xenophon, *Hellenica* 5. 4. 2ff.
17. Plutarch *De Genio Soc.* 597d.

were successful, and only then summoned the Athenian volunteers, led by two of the generals, who were encamped across the border in Attica:

> 'After this they (the exiles) immediately made proclamation to all the Thebans, both horsemen and hoplites, to come forth from their houses, saying that the tyrants were dead. The citizens, however, so long as night lasted, remained quiet out of distrust; but when day came, and what had taken place was evident, then both the hoplites and the horsemen speedily rushed forth with their arms to lend aid. The returned exiles also sent horsemen to fetch the troops of the Athenians who were on the borders under two of the generals. And the latter, knowing the purpose for which they had sent out the horsemen, came to their aid.'[18]

If the Thebans failed, then the Athenians could return home quietly with no harm done; if the exiles were successful, the Athenians could help them complete the *coup*, and thereby secure Theban friendship and support. This would in turn increase their stature at home and help them reduce the influence of Callistratus and his faction, and gain control themselves. It was a good gamble for the imperialists, and was successful. The exiles entered Thebes, found the polemarchs either drunk or asleep, killed them, rallied their fellow citizens, and prepared to attack the Spartan garrison which was billeted on the Cadmeia.[19]

At this point our two sources again diverge. Diodorus states that the Spartan harmost sent to Sparta for aid and that the Thebans, believing that an army would soon come to his relief, asked Athens to come with full forces. The Athenians voted to support the Thebans, and dispatched 5000 hoplites and 500 cavalry under the leadership of Demophon.[20] The Spartans defended themselves for a

---

18. Xenophon, *Hellenica* 5. 4. 9. Clearly only after their victory was complete did the Thebans summon the Athenians.

19. Xenophon, *Hellenica* 5. 4. 2–9; Diodorus 15. 25. 2.

20. Diodorus 15. 25. 3–15. 26. 2. Accame in *La lega ateniese del sec. IV A.C.* (Rome 1941), p. 18 believes the account of Diodorus wholeheartedly. P. Cloché in chapter 2 of *La politique étrangère d'Athènes de 404 à 338 av. J.C.* (Paris 1934) argues that the Athenians followed a very cautious policy until the time of Sphodrias. I can find little evidence in support of Accame's position. It

while, but when their food ran out they surrendered on terms and returned to the Peloponnese. The relief column from Sparta arrived too late, and the Spartans contented themselves with punishing the commanders who had abandoned Thebes.

Xenophon, on the other hand, tells us that the Spartan harmost sent to Plataea and Thespiae for help. The Thebans and Athenian troops from the border came up and laid siege to the Cadmeia; the Spartans became frightened and asked for terms. The Thebans agreed to let them withdraw on terms, but, as the Spartans marched out, the Thebans attacked anyone in the group whom they recognized as members of the faction of Leontiades, although the Athenians did their best to save as many as possible.[21] The Spartans later executed the harmost, because he had not waited for relief, and called out the ban against Thebes.[22]

The account of Xenophon again appears to be the more likely story. It is hard to believe that the Athenians were ready to fight the Spartans so quickly as Diodorus indicates, especially since it was not yet clear that they would need to. So far as they knew at that moment, the Spartans might be willing to ignore the Athenian assistance and leave Athens in peace, while fighting only against Thebes. This seems all the more likely since there is no evidence that Callistratus had lost power in Athens. Surely he would be reluctant to embark on a war with Sparta. It is clear that the

certainly appears that the faction of Callistratus played a significant role in Athens at the time when the exiles returned, since the exiles entered Leontiades' house on the basis that they carried a letter from Callistratus. If Callistratus is an important figure at this time, then it is likely that Athenian policy would be cautious.

21. Xenophon, *Hellenica* 5. 4. 10–12. See also Plutarch, *Pelopidas* 7–12; *De Genio Soc.* 596. Also Nepos, *Pelopidas* 3.

22. Xenophon, *Hellenica* 5. 4. 13. In general it seems to me that the account of Xenophon is more accurate in detail than that of Diodorus until the time of Sphodrias. From that point on Diodorus supplies more reliable evidence, especially in light of the solution to a chronological problem offered in section VIII of this paper. Diodorus, no doubt following Ephorus, believed that the Athenians were involved in the return of the exiles in an earlier and more official fashion than in fact they were. As a consequence of this mistake, he places the expedition of Demophon too early. It seems best to believe that the Athenians changed factions and policy only after Sphodrias' acquittal.

The return of the exiles probably took place in December 379 or early in January 378. See the arguments of Burnett in 'Thebes and the Second Athenian Confederacy', pp. 16–17; K. J. Beloch, *Griechische Geschichte*, III: 2, p. 234.

generals, who had led an Athenian force to assist the Theban rebels, were acting on their own, without official authorization. Even they were unwilling to provoke Sparta unduly, for when the victorious Thebans tried to attack the pro-Spartan faction as it filed out of the city, the Athenian troops intervened to save them. The Athenian imperialists might well have been satisfied to have achieved the restoration of a free Thebes hostile to Sparta. At home they could gain political advantage by pointing to the success of their judicious conspiracy with the Theban exiles; secure the downfall of Callistratus and his conservative faction; and permit the Thebans and Spartans to contend for the dominance of central Greece, while they could safely turn Athens' attention to her traditional sphere of influence – the sea. All of this might well be accomplished without violence on Athen's part. At the moment there was no need to borrow trouble.

The Theban exiles no doubt hoped that Sparta would take some time to organize an expedition, for they knew that Sparta was split into factions, and that Agesilaus might not win support for a major expedition against Thebes. Such an interval would give them time to consolidate their gains and, if necessary and possible, make an alliance. It is this interval that Diodorus has missed by telescoping his account too much.

The Athenian expeditionary force returned to Athens, and for a short time the *status quo* remained in being. The Theban anti-Spartan faction was in control at Thebes. The next move was up to Sparta.

III. The Spartan reaction

The news of the restoration of the anti-Spartan exiles to Thebes caused the Spartans no small concern. Sparta was now threatened by possible attack from a now vigorous and hostile Thebes, perhaps even with support from Athens. In addition, those factions opposed to Sparta in Greece could point to Thebes as an example of what could be accomplished in throwing off the Spartan yoke if only the Greeks would rise. The possibilities of rebellion both within and without the Peloponnese were now much more feasible and likely. Sparta knew that some response was necessary.

It was at this point that ambassadors from Thebes arrived at

Sparta and sought peace terms. One source for this information is Isocrates, who tells us that the Thebans

> 'were punished by the gods, and, after the Cadmeia was captured, they were forced to take refuge here in Athens. By this they furnished the crowning proof of their perfidy; for when they had again been saved by your power and restored to their city, they did not remain faithful for a single instant, but immediately sent ambassadors to Lacedaemon, showing themselves ready to be slaves and to alter in no respect their former agreements with Sparta. Why need I speak at greater length? For if the Lacedaemonians had not ordered them to take back their exiles and exclude the murderers, nothing would have hindered them from taking the field as allies of those who had injured them, against you their benefactors.'[23]

Isocrates is certainly distorting the events. His account appears in the *Plataicus*, delivered some time between 373 and 371 B.C., when Athens and Thebes were not friendly. His charge that the Thebans were perfidious might suit Athenian sentiment, but had no basis in fact. There is no reason whatever to believe that the new government of Thebes offered to return to the old alliance with Sparta. Most likely their embassy came to assure the Spartans that Thebes had no aggressive intentions, and was willing to live in peace with Sparta, if the Spartans agreed. Such a proposal could not be construed as a betrayal of Athens, which was also at peace with Sparta. In any case, we must remember that the Athenian state had not yet committed itself to support of Thebes against the Spartans. Such assistance as had been given was offered by the two Athenian generals unofficially and, as we shall see, they were repudiated by the state. We may however believe the fact presented by Isocrates, that the Thebans did send an embassy immediately after their victory. No doubt they hoped that their success had undermined the power of Agesilaus, and looked to the factions opposing him for the establishment of a more moderate policy.

In these hopes the Thebans were disappointed. Agesilaus was able to persuade the ephors to deal harshly with the Thebans. As Isocrates noted, the Spartans demanded that the Thebans expel the newly-restored anti-Spartan faction, and receive back those

23. Isocrates, *Plataicus* 29.

members of the faction of Leontiades who were still alive. These terms were unacceptable to the Thebans. They chose to fight, and Sparta obliged them by first punishing the harmost who had been stationed in the Cadmeia, and then calling out the ban against the Thebans.[24]

The choice of a commander for the expedition was a critical one. In the campaign against Mantineia years earlier, the choice had been between Agesilaus and Agesipolis. The former advocated a strong hand against all Greeks, whether inside or outside the Peloponnese; the latter urged a milder, conciliatory policy towards Sparta's allies, as his father Pausanias had before him. The choice of commanders in a very real sense reflected the internal political struggles in Sparta.[25] Here again, regarding the question of who should lead the army against Thebes, politics played an important role. It was Agesilaus who had urged a strong anti-Theban policy, and it was this policy which had failed. No doubt conservative Spartans, such as the peace-maker Antalcidas, could point an accusing finger at Agesilaus and the fruit of his aggressive extra-Peloponnesian policy. The friends of Agesipolis, who now looked to his brother Cleombrotus, could object to Agesilaus' misdirected imperialism and the high-handed interference in the government of Thebes, a non-belligerent. Agesilaus was in deep political trouble. If he led out an army against Thebes, his opponents at home would have an opportunity to overthrow his policy, especially if he were unsuccessful in overthrowing the new Theban leadership. Perhaps Agesilaus reasoned that it would be much safer to let Cleombrotus lead out the army. His appointment would ease the pressure on Agesilaus. The opposition forces at home would be deprived of a strong leader, and Agesilaus would be in Sparta to keep a watchful eye on the home front. Meanwhile, if Cleombrotus were successful, he would merely vindicate the

24. Xenophon, *Hellenica* 5. 4. 13.

25. See note 5 above. It seems that Agesilaus wished to ensure the subservience of Agesipolis to his policies. In having him made commander, Agesilaus hoped either that he would succeed, and thereby only advance the policy of Agesilaus, or, if he failed, then Agesilaus could come to the rescue and emerge with glory both as the architect and agent of a successful policy, while Agesipolis only won disgrace. The intervention of Pausanias helped to extract his son from this difficult situation, and enabled Agesipolis to use the victory over Mantineia as a tool for his own political advancement.

wisdom of Agesilaus' policy, and would gain no credit for himself.
If Cleombrotus failed, however, he would be proven incompetent.
Agesilaus would of course be compelled to come to his rescue. He
would win a victory at Thebes, recoup his popularity at home, and
vindicate his policy. In any case, Agesilaus had to keep opposition
at home divided, if only for a short time. Xenophon himself
confirms the political overtones in the choice of a general:

> 'Now Agesilaus said that it was more than forty years since
> he had come of military age, and pointed out that just as other
> men of his age were no longer bound to serve outside their
> own country, so the same law applied to kings also. He, then,
> on this plea would not undertake the campaign. It was not,
> however, for this reason that he stayed at home, but because
> he well knew that if he was in command the citizens would
> say that Agesilaus was making trouble for the state in order
> that he might give assistance to tyrants. Therefore he let them
> decide as they would about this matter. But the ephors, hear-
> ing the stories of those who had been banished after the
> slaughter in Thebes, sent out Cleombrotus – this being the
> first time he had had a command – in the dead of winter.[26]

The Spartan ephors chose to accept the story told by their Theban
friends, and did not accept the offer made by the Theban embassy.
The ephors selected Cleombrotus as leader of Sparta's army.[27] The
young king could hardly refuse. No doubt he was eager for a
command and eager to make a name for himself. He may well have
weighed the possibilities and concluded that it might be possible to
deal with Thebes in a way whereby he could further his own
career and also promote his own policy. The faction that he might
be expected to support, if he followed his family policy, was in
charge at Thebes. If he could settle the matter by compromise and

26. Xenophon, *Hellenica* 5. 4. 13–14.
27. The language of the last sentence in the quotation, if taken literally,
seems to suggest that it was the continual urging of the Theban exiles which
led the ephors to select Cleombrotus as the general. If Xenophon is to be taken
literally, we may suggest two explanations. The simpler is that the Thebans
wanted Cleombrotus because he was the king, and therefore the token of a
serious Spartan commitment. A variant of this, however, is that the Theban
exiles were advised to make this request by Agesilaus in pursuit of his own ends.
The evidence permits only speculation.

diplomacy, in the way that his brother Agesipolis had dealt with Mantineia, and his father had dealt with Athens long ago, he could hope to undercut Agesilaus' influence at home and abroad. His success would cause Spartan policy to shift in the direction of a milder attitude towards friends and allies of Sparta, and perhaps even to seek other directions for Spartan extension. Therefore he led out the expedition against Thebes.[28]

The Spartans advanced into Boeotia along the road through Plataea, avoiding the Athenian peltasts under Chabrias, who were on guard duty on the road to Eleutherae.[29] The Athenians were no doubt alarmed at the Spartan expedition, and wished to make sure that the attack would not be directed against them. The Spartans advanced through Plataea and Thespiae, which were loyal to them, and halted at Cynoscephalae.[30] Cleombrotus lingered there for some sixteen days, and advanced no further against the Thebans. He left Sphodrias at Thespiae with a detachment of soldiers, and returned to Sparta, much to the puzzlement of his troops:

> 'Meanwhile Cleombrotus proceeded to conduct the soldiers under his command back homeward by the road which leads through Creusis, the troops being vastly puzzled to know whether there was really war between them and the Thebans, or peace; for he had led his army into the country of the Thebans and then departed after doing just as little damage as he could.[31]

He might explain his inactivity by pointing out that the Thebans had not come out to fight, but that would be a very lame excuse, for it was Sparta which was the aggressor and it was the job of Cleombrotus to take the initiative. The fact is that the faction now

28. Xenophon, *Hellenica* 5. 4. 14.
29. See A. W. Gomme, *Historical Commentary on Thucydides* (Oxford 1956), vol. I, pp. 10–15. Gomme discounts the use of peltasts in Greek warfare, even after Iphicrates' use of them in the Corinthian War. Xenophon talks as if the use of peltasts by both Sparta and Athens was a common practice. If Eleutherae was in fact located in the mountain passes on the borders of Attica, it would be imperative to use peltasts, which would be the only effective force for that kind of terrain. One wonders what type of infantry the harmost Sphodrias was leading on his unlucky raid.
30. Xenophon, *Hellenica* 5. 4. 14–15. See also *Hellenica* 6. 4. 5.
31. Xenophon, *Hellenica* 5. 4. 15–16.

in control at Thebes was hostile to Agesilaus and might possibly be
made friendly to Cleombrotus. If Cleombrotus meant to pursue
the policies of his father Pausanias and his brother Agesipolis, that
is, to win the support of dominant factions in Greek states, his best
plan would be to win the Thebans over, not to alienate them. We
may well believe that Cleombrotus dallied at Cynoscephalae for
sixteen days in the hope that the new rulers of Thebes would come
out and offer to talk. We need not believe that Cleombrotus was
seeking only his own advantage. He may well have believed that
the aggressive and brutal policy of Agesilaus brought trouble to
Sparta, and that the more genial policy pursued by his father
Pausanias was better for his country.

   In any case his hopes were disappointed; the Thebans did not
come out to parley. If he moved against Thebes now, he would
only be furthering the policy of Agesilaus, and not accomplishing
anything towards increasing his political influence in Sparta.
Cleombrotus must have concluded that his chances for developing
factions loyal to him in Thebes and elsewhere, as his brother had
done in Phlius and attempted to do at Olynthus, were hopeless.[32]
In order to make political headway at home, he would have to
force a change in foreign policy that would ensure that Sparta was
headed in a direction he could control. Cleombrotus therefore left
one-third of his forces, a sizeable amount of money, and explicit
directions to the harmost Sphodrias at Thespiae. This was certainly
much more men and money than would be needed by an ordinary
garrison commander, even in time of war. Perhaps Cleombrotus
thought of the sizeable group of Spartans who might be a source of
support for him – the old faction of the Spartan admiral Lysander,
which had long been leaderless. Perhaps Cleombrotus decided that,

---

32. See the references mentioned in note 5 regarding Phlius. Xenophon in
Hellenica 5. 3. 10 remarks that the Phliasians were praised by Agesipolis for
sending him a large sum of money for his campaign against Olynthus. Clearly
he had been successful in winning them over to his side. He may very well have
judged that the campaign against Olynthus would offer him another chance to
win over Olynthus to Sparta by a show of force and good treatment, rather than
by a harsh and heavy-handed violence. One wonders whether Agesilaus'
campaign against Phlius at this time was prompted not only by a desire to
ensure the city's loyalty, but also to remove an effective supporter of his
political rival Agesipolis. Unfortunately, the young king died while on the
Olynthus campaign, and there is no way of knowing what he might have done
had he been successful at Olynthus.

in keeping with Lysander's policy, he must turn Sparta's attention away from land adventures on the Greek mainland and towards conquest abroad, in the Greek cities of Asia Minor and perhaps even against the Great King himself. To accomplish this he must first remove Athens as a potential source of opposition.[33] In that case Sphodrias' instructions might include not merely procedures for the acquisition of mercenaries, but also orders to attack the Peiraeus, to strike at the source of Athens' strength, her harbor and her ships.[34]

33. The policy of Lysander is best discussed by Charles Hamilton. See 'Spartan Politics and Policy, 405–401 B.C.', *AJP* 91 (1970), 294–314. See also his dissertation, 'Politics and Diplomacy in the Corinthian War' (Cornell University January 1968).

34. Diodorus and Xenophon disagree on the order of events. Xenophon is certainly to be preferred. Diodorus places the arrival of Cleombrotus just after the Spartan garrison evacuated the Cadmeia: see 15. 25. 2–3. Diodorus' order of events is:

1. Exiles, supported officially by Athens, go out and take the Cadmeia.
2. Spartan garrison, *circa* 500 in number, sends for help to Sparta.
3. The Thebans seek help from Athens, and she sends an expeditionary force under Demophon.
4. Allied army besieges Thebes, Spartan garrison surrenders, army from Sparta arrives, attacks, is unsuccessful, returns home.

Plutarch's *Pelopidas* supplies the information that Cleombrotus led the Spartan relief force.

Xenophon's account, *Hellenica* v. 4. 2–18, is as follows:

1. Attack by exiles.
2. Athenian volunteers come to their aid.
3. Spartan harmost in Thebes seeks aid from Thespiae and Plataea.
4. Thebans defeat relief force from Plataea.
5. Spartan garrison surrenders.
6. Sparta calls out the ban against Thebes and sends Cleombrotus with an army to Thebes.
7. Cleombrotus advances and retreats.

It would be more logical to seek help from Plataea and Thespiae, rather than wait the time necessary to assemble reinforcements from Sparta, even if that were only a short time (as Grote thinks; see *A History of Greece*, vol. vii (London 1862), p. 79). It is most unlikely that the pro-Theban faction in Athens was strong enough to persuade the Athenians to vote for a treaty with Thebes. There was no reason to believe that Thebes, even with Athenian aid, could resist a full Spartan army. Nor was it likely that the pro-Spartan faction would have tolerated such a violation of the Peace of Antalcidas. Diodorus continues his account by saying that Athens and Sparta maintained a truce until the time of Sphodrias. An Athenian expedition of the size of Demophon's would surely have been considered by Sparta as a *de facto* declaration of war. Diodorus has

IV. The Athenian reaction to the Theban restoration

We have no detailed information regarding the immediate Athenian reaction to the return of the anti-Spartan exiles to Thebes. It is most likely that after the restoration of these exiles the conservative group in Athens was not willing either to move to support the Thebans or the Spartans. The Athenian imperialists, strongly anti-Spartan, would have desired, no doubt, to help the Thebans in an official and active way, but in the absence of supporting evidence we must doubt that the Athenians received a Theban embassy and voted to send a large military expedition to Thebes under Demophon, as Diodorus believes.[35] On the other hand, since there was support for Thebes from a significant portion of the citizenry, the conservatives were not likely to find overwhelming support for Sparta among the Athenians. For the moment, then, Callistratus and his conservative associates allowed the *status quo* to remain unshaken. They could argue that since Thebes had been *de facto* a member of the Peloponnesian League,[36] a quarrel between Thebes and Sparta should be settled by Sparta and her allies, and that the Athenians should not interfere. So the Athenians vacillated, while Sparta sent out Cleombrotus and his army. The Athenians, no doubt, were alarmed, since they could be blamed for indirect support of the Theban democrats, for they had not only sheltered them in their exile, but also some Athenians had participated in their return. The Athenians therefore sent out Chabrias and a force of peltasts to protect their frontier. The Spartans at this point did not wish to quarrel with Athens, so Cleombrotus avoided them in his march to Boeotia.[37]

While military operations were taking place, the Spartans were not inactive on the diplomatic front. Three Spartan ambassadors

misplaced these events; they take place only *after* the acquittal of Sphodrias had alienated Sparta and Athens. The alliance with Thebes and the Second Sea League should be placed after, and not before, the Sphodrias affair. The raid of Sphodrias is the catalyst, though Diodorus is right regarding the motives of the Athenian imperialist; see 15. 26. 1.

35. Diodorus 15. 25. 4–15. 26. 3. As argued in note 33 above, these events should be dated after Sphodrias, not to the time of the recapture of the Cadmeia.

36. See Donald Kagan, *The Outbreak of the Peloponnesian War* (Ithaca 1969), chapter 1.

37. Xenophon, *Hellenica* 5. 4. 14.

arrived at Athens. Their names were Etymocles, Aristolochus and Ocyllus, and the first of these was numbered among the friends of Agesilaus.[38] Why would these ambassadors have come to Athens? It was in keeping with the policy of Agesilaus to ensure that Athens remained docile and friendly to Spartan interests. The actions of the two generals and the Athenian volunteers, who had acted without authorization of the state, represented a threat to the peaceful relations between the Athenians led by the faction of Callistratus and the Spartan government influenced by Agesilaus.[39] Agesilaus wished to make sure that the Athenian faction friendly to him was not overcome by the imperialist group, which was friendly to Thebes. The ambassadors from Sparta may well have pointed out that the price for continued good relations between the two states was the repudiation of the two generals. Athens was not willing at this time to go to war with Sparta over Thebes, especially since a Spartan army was in the field. This army might very well reinstate the Theban oligarchs and then turn against Athens. The Athenians might be charged with violating the principle of autonomy contained in the Peace of Antalcidas, since Athenians had participated in the Theban *coup*. The Athenians were frightened, and dealt harshly with the generals, as Xenophon tells us. The Athenians

'were so fearful that they brought to trial the two generals who had been privy to the uprising of Melon against Leontiades and his party, put one of them to death, and, since the other did not remain to stand trial, exiled him.'[40]

38. Xenophon, *Hellenica* 5. 4. 22. Xenophon himself remarks that Etymocles was a friend of Agesilaus. See *Hellenica* 5. 4. 32.

39. The best analogy is that of the relations of Cimon, the Athenian politician and statesman, with Sparta after the Persian Wars.

40. Xenophon, *Hellenica* 5. 4. 19.
The trial of the generals took place most likely during Munychion 378. The chronology of events to this point as I see them is as follows:

December 379	Return of the exiles to Thebes.
Beginning of	Athenian unofficial assistance.
January 378	Retreat of Spartan garrison.
January 378	Thebans send embassy to Sparta and it returns.
	Sparta calls out the ban and attacks Thebes.
February 378	Cleombrotus on the march, spends time at Plataea, Thespiae, and then sixteen days at Cynoscephalae.

Up to this point, then, the Athenians had not broken with their past policy: to favor Sparta, i.e. the faction of Agesilaus, and not to embroil themselves in quarrels on the mainland, except when such quarrels might affect their interests in the Aegean. For the present the *status quo* continued: Athens waited, Thebes expected a Spartan attack, and Sparta anticipated Cleombrotus' victory.

V. Sphodrias

The Spartan army had accomplished nothing during its campaign against Thebes.[41] Cleombrotus decided, therefore, to return home, fearing, no doubt, that there was little he could do to strengthen his political position at home by lingering in Boeotia. To attack Thebes now that his plan for negotiation had failed would only serve the interests of Agesilaus. On the other hand, the faction which he might be expected to support in the light of his family's traditions[42] was already in power in Thebes, and he had

21 February– 7 March 378	Election of new Athenian generals. (For dating see N. G. L. Hammond and H. D. Scullard (eds.), *The Oxford Classical Dictionary*, 2nd ed. (Oxford 1970), p. 1017, where it is stated that the election of the generals takes place in early spring. C. Hignett, *A History of the Athenian Constitution to the End of the Fifth Century* (Oxford 1952), p. 245, notes that the election takes place in the seventh prytany, February/March. See also Aristotle, *Constitution of the Athenians* 44. 4 and the discussion in J. E. Sandys, *Aristotle's Constitution of Athens* (London 1912), pp. 177ff. Benjamin D. Meritt is not so sure; see 'The Election of Athenian Generals', *Klio* 52 (1970), 277–82, but has nothing to say on this particular problem, for he is concerned only with later evidence.) Generals for this year included Timotheus, Chabrias, and Callistratus; see Diodorus 15. 29. 7. At this point there seems to be no change in policy at Athens.
March 378	Arrival of Spartan ambassadors. Trial and condemnation of two Athenian generals. Raid of Sphodrias.

41. Xenophon, *Hellenica* 5. 4. 14ff.

42. Curtius remarks in *The History of Greece*, trans. by A. W. Ward (New York 1874), vol. IV, p. 381, about Sphodrias that 'He was known as an adherent of Cleombrotus, whom it was accordingly sought to hold accountable as the real originator of the attempt; but it is too strikingly contradictory to the policy of the young king and his family.' Curtius is right in remarking that this would be a contradictory situation, but it seems likely that Cleombrotus was forced by political circumstances to adopt a more aggressive policy. It was the policy of

not been successful in developing support for Sparta among the other cities in Boeotia.[43] The position of Cleombrotus was precarious. Not only had he accomplished nothing against Thebes, but in the eyes of his troops he had not even tried. His own soldiers 'wondered whether there was a war against the Thebans or peace, for he had led the army against Thebes and then led it away having done no harm at all'.[44] Cleombrotus had good reason to fear returning to Sparta with no more accomplished. Not only would he expect attacks from his enemies, but even his supporters might turn against him after a disgraceful failure in his first command. A bold stroke was necessary to redeem his reputation and sustain his position. When he left Boeotia, therefore, he left Sphodrias in command of the garrison at Thespiae, supported by a force of men and money far beyond what was allotted to a typical harmost.[45] This action was not casual, and was soon to plunge Greece into war.

The exact circumstances of Sphodrias' mission have been the subject of considerable controversy.[46] The dispute focuses on the

---

his family to secure Sparta's interests by a moderate treatment of allies. If that family policy failed, it would be possible and likely that Cleombrotus would be forced to seek other means. Is it too much to imagine that Cleombrotus, who had witnessed his own brother's attempts to make political headway against Agesilaus, may well have decided that the traditional policy could no longer retain viability under the given political realities, and that as an ambitious young man he had to look elsewhere in order to circumvent Agesilaus?

43. See Grote, *History of Greece*, vol. 10, p. 83.

44. Xenophon, *Hellenica* 5. 4. 16.

45. Xenophon, *Hellenica* 5. 4. 15.

46. Accounts of the raid of Sphodrias and subsequent events may be found in the following secondary sources: Grote, *History of Greece*, pp. 69–90; Beloch, *G.G.* III. 94, pp. 234–6; G. Busolt, 'Der zweite Athenische Bund und die auf der Autonomie beruhende Hellenische Politik von der Schlacht bei Knidos bis zum Frieden des Eubulos', *Jahrbücher für Philologie und Paedagogik*, Supplementband 7 (1873–5), 641–866; E. Meyer, *Geschichte des Alterthums*, v. 924–7, p. 373–80; E. Fabricius, 'Die Befreiung Thebens', *Rh. Mus.* 48 (1893), 448–71; S. Accame, *La lega ateniense*, pp. 18–25; H. Bengtson, *Griechische Geschichte*, pp. 264–71; J. B. Bury, *A History of Greece* (London 1951), 3rd ed., pp. 561–3; W. Judeich, 'Athen und Theben vom Königsfrieden bis zur Schlacht bei Leuktra', *Rh. Mus.* 76 (1927), 171–97; V. Ehrenberg, 'Zum Zweiten Athenischen Bund', *Hermes* 64 (1929), 325ff.; F. H. Marshall, *The Second Athenian Confederacy* (Cambridge 1905), chapter 2; A. P. Burnett, 'Thebes and the Second Athenian Confederacy'. None of these scholars has seen the order of events and the political structure underlying those events correctly. More useful, though not completely accurate remarks can be found in R. E. Smith,

reliability of our sources. Xenophon blames the Thebans for instigating the Sphodrias affair: 'The Thebans feared that they alone, unaided by any others, would make war upon the Lacedaemonians. Therefore they devised the following scheme.' According to him it was they who persuaded Sphodrias, 'by bribery, so goes the story', to attack Athens in order to embroil the Athenians in a war with Sparta. The plan Sphodrias adopted was to launch a surprise attack on the Peiraeus, 'since it had no gates', hoping to get there before dawn.[47]

It is hard to imagine that even Xenophon could have believed such a tale. He is plainly attempting to exculpate the Spartans and free them from the disgrace which attached to the shameful action of Sphodrias. The charge of bribery does lend a veneer of plausibility to the tale, for Spartan commanders in the field had been known to succumb to the lure of gold in the past. Sphodrias does not seem to have been in need of such enticement, given the sum of money left in his hands by Cleombrotus. It seems quite unlikely that Sphodrias would in any case have gambled so much and in fact challenged the policy of Agesilaus, without the support, not of Theban gold, but of powerful friends in Sparta.

Diodorus' account is more plausible and must certainly be right.

> 'The truce which the Lacedaemonians and Athenians had concluded in the earlier period remained unshaken up to this time. But now Sphodriades the Spartan, who had been placed in command and was by nature flighty and precipitate, was prevailed upon by Cleombrotus, the king of the Lacedaemonians, without the consent of the ephors, to occupy the Peiraeus'.[48]

There can be no doubt that Cleombrotus was the author of the expedition. Plutarch informs us that Sphodrias belonged to a

---

'Opposition To Agesilaus' Foreign Policy', *Historia* 11 (1953–4), 280; see also H. W. Parke, 'The Development of the Second Spartan Empire', *JHS* 1 (1930), 37–79. See also the articles of Buckler and MacDonald as mentioned in note 2.

47. Xenophon, *Hellenica* 5. 4. 20. My translation. Plutarch supports this account; see *Pelopidas* 14 and *Agesilaus* 24.

48. Diodorus 15. 29. 5–6. Sphodriades is an alternative spelling for Sphodrias. The same person is meant.

faction opposed to Agesilaus.[49] The actions of Sphodrias make it clear that he could not be a member of the conservative faction which opposed adventures outside the Peloponnese. Since he was an opponent of Agesilaus, he must have belonged to still a third group, probably associated with the friends of the old Spartan admiral, Lysander.[50]

What then of Cleombrotus? What was his attitude towards Spartan foreign policy? The young king was certainly heir to the allegiance of those Spartans who had supported his brother Agesipolis and his father Pausanias. His policy in Boeotia had been directly in the tradition of their policies: to install governments in allied states who were indebted and friendly to themselves and to permit these states a high degree of autonomy so long as they remained loyal to Sparta. Had Cleombrotus been successful in Boeotia, he would have gained influence and power at the expense of Agesilaus. But he had failed. A new plan was needed. It is easy to believe that the idea of a surprise attack against the Peiraeus was born in this moment of desperation. Had the plan succeeded, Athens would have been at the mercy of Sparta, and useless as a potential ally to Thebes. The great menace presented to Sparta of a Theban–Athenian alliance would be removed, and Cleombrotus would now return to Sparta in triumph, having put Agesilaus in the shade. No doubt Phoebias' seizure of the Cadmeia provided an example and helped stimulate his imagination. The fate of Phoebidas, which was far from disastrous, might give Cleombrotus confidence that his catspaw would suffer no worse fate than had the instrument of Agesilaus.[51]

49. Plutarch, *Agesilaus* 24. 3.

50. For a fuller discussion of the friends of Lysander, see the material referred to in note 32. This faction would no doubt have been in eclipse since the Peace of Antalcidas, which would check their pretensions in the Aegean and Asia Minor. Since they did not, so far as we can tell, have a leader who could successfully challenge Agesilaus, they would of course have been eager to attract the young king Cleombrotus. The marriage of expediency would have appealed to both sides.

51. The story of Phoebidas is told in Xenophon, *Hellenica* 5. 2. 24–33. Phoebidas might have been condemned as a violator of the Peace of Antalcidas, but Agesilaus asked the infamous question as to whether he had done something good or bad for the state. Agesilaus was followed by Leontiades, who proclaimed that the action of Phoebidas helped to ensure that Thebes would be Sparta's loyal ally for the future. The appeal to utility was more than enough to outweigh legal or moral niceties, and Phoebidas went unpunished. Cleombrotus may

Cleombrotus must have given some thought to the effect this *démarche* could have on the political scene in Sparta. His own partisans, the conservative stay-at-home group, would be shocked, but not likely to turn against the man who was their most prestigious leader, the son of Pausanias. Agesilaus' group would of course be angered, but it would be difficult for them to criticize a successful *coup* which was simply a copy of their action at Thebes. If they put the same question to Sphodrias as had been put to Phoebidas, 'was his action harmful to Sparta', the answer would have to be negative. Best of all, a successful attack on the Athenians would be most attractive to the supporters of Lysander's policy, who had been leaderless since Lysander's death in 395. Their policy of exerting Spartan power in the Aegean and beyond required the neutralization of Athens. Thus with one successful stroke Cleombrotus could hope to save himself from disgrace, win the support of a new faction, gain control over the board of ephors by seeing that his partisans replaced Agesilaus', and thus gain a position of supremacy in Sparta which his brother, and even his father, had not attained. This would certainly be heady wine for the young king, and Sphodrias was just the willing tool needed.

The attack of Sphodrias was, therefore, not a foolish gamble, but a calculated stratagem with important political overtones. Some scholars have doubted that the plan was possible,[52] but Xenophon makes it quite clear that Sphodrias took special measures to make the plan work.[53] The fact that the plan failed, because the march

well have imagined that the same thing would happen with Sphodrias, though it would be Cleombrotus who was asking the very same question.

52. For example, Burnett, 'Thebes and the Second Athenian Confederacy', p. 2, n. 3 believes that if the event is to be dated in March, as Judeich, for example, dates it, the weather would have made the march impossible. For a more favorable view, see Grote, *History of Greece*, vol. vii, p. 86 and notes.

53. Xenophon, *Hellenica* 5. 4. 20–1. Translation mine.

> 'And Sphodrias listened to the Thebans. He boasted that he would capture Peiraeus, since it had no gates. He therefore led his troops from Thespiae, after they had eaten an early dinner, saying that he would reach the Peiraeus before dawn.'

I am pleased to note that Professor MacDonald agrees with the idea that Cleombrotus is responsible for the raid on the Peiraeus. His article came into my hands only after this paper was written. I would hope that my arguments about the political pressures on Cleombrotus in Sparta might offer good reasons why he would support Sphodrias' actions.

took longer than planned, is not evidence that the plan was ill-conceived. The attack took place probably in early March, and some winter storm or other unanticipated hindrance may have interfered. This would hardly be the only military expedition in history which failed to carry out a mission which it was possible to accomplish.

Sphodrias led out his forces in early evening, and attempted to reach the Peiraeus before dawn. He was not able to march further than Thria.[54] He did some damage to the homes and cattle in the vicinity but, since daybreak had revealed his army to the Athenians, he retreated without doing further harm.

A most revealing part of the story is told us by Xenophon, who remarks that Spartan ambassadors were present in Athens:

> 'Now it chanced also that there were ambassadors of the Lacedaemonians in Athens at the house of Callias, their *proxenos*. These men were named Etymocles, Aristolochus and Ocyllus. When the invasion was reported, the Athenians arrested these men in the belief that they were in on the plot.

54. Burnett, 'Thebes and the Second Athenian Confederacy', p. 2, n. 3 remarks

> 'This event is sometimes placed as early as March (see W. Judeich, 'Athen u. Theben vom Königsfrieden bis zur Schlacht bei Leuctra', *Rh. Mus.* 76, pp. 127, 177), but the passes of Parnes and Kithairon are often still snowy in that month, and it is hard to believe that Sphodrias' party could have gotten even to the Thriasian plain in one March night. The fact that an early dawn surprised the invaders suggests late spring. The raid occurred during the visit of the Spartan ambassadors in Athens; this much is certain. Thus it must have come after Sparta had learned of the organization of the new allied council, in other words, in May.'

The event should be placed in March. Whether the passes were snowy or not is not a very helpful argument. If they were, then that might very well explain why Sphodrias didn't reach his goal by dawn. If they weren't, then Sphodrias' army (presumably a hoplite force) might not have been able to march as quickly over mountainous terrain as, for example, Athenian peltasts. Professor Burnett seems to mistranslate the Greek, which does not say that Spodrias was surprised by an early dawn, but that 'when dawn came upon Sphodrias, he was still at Thria' – Θριᾶσι δ' αὐτῷ ἡμέρα ἐπεγένετο (Xenophon, *Hellenica* 5. 4. 21). No word as to Sphodrias' mental state or emotional reactions at the time. The march was most probably feasible in one night, given an all-out effort and good fortune, but Sphodrias must have received neither. As argued above, the Spartan ambassadors were in Athens to see about the trial of the generals, which was probably not formed until the summer of 378 anyway.

The ambassadors were shaken by this turn of events and
pleaded in their defense that if they had known of the plan,
they would never have come to Athens and risked being
arrested. Least of all would they have stopped at their
proxenos' house, which would be the first place the Athenians
would look for them. They went on saying that the Athenians
would soon know that the Lacedaemonian government was
not a party to the plot. Sphodrias would be put to death, they
said, and the Athenians would hear about it. The Athenians
judged that they were innocent and let them go.'[55]

Etymocles was one of the friends of Agesilaus.[56] No doubt he and
his comrades had been sent under Agesilaus' influence to Athens,
and probably to secure a gesture of Athenian goodwill and to
express a continued desire to be friendly to Athens. The trial of the
generals, which had just taken place, was the Athenian response to
their mission.[57] It is understandable that the ambassadors would
be surprised, for they had not expected that Cleombrotus or any
of his friends would try to undermine Agesilaus' policy. The
Athenians were angry, and it was only by promise of a speedy condemnation of Sphodrias that the ambassadors were released. At
this point the Athenians would still listen to explanations, but
their confidence in Sparta was shaken deeply.

The ephors, as Xenophon tells us, recalled Sphodrias for trial,
and on the outcome of the trial depended many things: which
faction would control Athens, the victory of Agesilaus or of
Cleombrotus in Sparta, war or peace.[58]

VI. The Athenian reaction

The sneak attack of Sphodrias could not fail to alarm and
infuriate the Athenians. Not only was Athens at peace with Sparta
and as yet unallied to Thebes or any other Spartan enemy, but it

55. Xenophon, *Hellenica* 5. 4. 22–3. My translation.
56. For Etymocles, see Xenophon, *Hellenica* 5. 4. 22; 5. 4. 31–2.
57. Busolt, 'Der zweite Athenische Bund', p. 681 believes that the 'democrats' were in control before the raid of Sphodrias. I can find no evidence to
support this, and Xenophon clearly contradicts this opinion in *Hellenica* 5. 4. 34.
58. Xenophon, *Hellenica* 5. 4. 24.

had just given tangible proof of its fidelity, not to say subservience, by condemning two of its highest elected officials to appease Spartan irritation. It must have taken no little effort by Callistratus and the conservative faction to convince the Athenians that they ought to take such an embarrassing action. The unprovoked, unjustifiable assault by Sphodrias directed against the Peiraeus threatened to put an end to the dominance of Callistratus and to turn the Athenians away from his pro-Spartan policy.

In his defense Callistratus might argue that it was too early to turn against Sparta. Sphodrias' actions could not have been sanctioned by the Spartan government. No doubt he would shortly be repudiated by the Spartans, just as the Athenians had repudiated their miscreants. It would therefore be a mistake, as his opponents argued, to make an alliance with Thebes, which would guarantee a war with Sparta. The best course was to wait for the conclusion of Sphodrias' trial. If he were convicted, the credibility of Sparta's pledges in the peace treaty would be vindicated. If he were acquitted, then the Athenians could deliberate further.

Callistratus, probably reassured by the Spartan ambassadors who had just left, had every reason to believe that Sphodrias, a political opponent and enemy of Agesilaus, would certainly be condemned. He no doubt was able to persuade the Athenians to await the outcome of Sphodrias' trial.

VII. The Spartan reaction

When the news of Sphodrias' raid on the Peiraeus reached Sparta, the board of ephors recalled him for trial and pressed capital charges against him.[59] Sphodrias however did not present himself for trial, no doubt because he feared for his life.[60] The source of that fear was certainly Agesilaus, whose diplomacy he had undercut, but probably also the conservatives, who did not welcome foreign, extra-Peloponnesian adventures which only stirred up war. Agesilaus had the deciding vote as to Sphodrias' fate.

Xenophon relates in some detail the charming story of Cleony-

59. *Ibid.*
60. Xenophon, *Hellenica* 5. 4. 24–5. Plutarch, *Agesilaus* 24. 3 clearly identifies Sphodrias as a member of the party opposed to Agesilaus.

mus, the son of Sphodrias, who persuaded Archidamus, the son of Agesilaus, to intercede with the king on his father's behalf.

> 'Sphodrias had a son Cleonymus, who was at the age just following boyhood and was, besides, the handsomest and most highly regarded of all the youths of his years. And Archidamus, the son of Agesilaus, chanced to be extremely fond of him. Now the friends of Cleombrotus were political associates of Sphodrias and were therefore inclined to acquit him, but they feared Agesilaus and his friends, and likewise those who stood between the two parties; for it seemed that he had done a dreadful deed.'[61]

Xenophon continues by telling us that Cleonymus was able to persuade Archidamus to intercede with his father. The passage above, however, is very clear evidence for the existence of three factions in Sparta at this point. Their foreign policies seem clear as well: those who stood between were the conservatives who had supported Agesipolis and Pausanias, and who wished to confine Spartan resources to the Peloponnese; Agesilaus and his friends wanted to dominate the Greek mainland, but were eager to maintain the neutrality of Athens. This policy of course precluded Spartan interest in the Aegean. Cleombrotus and his faction, after the attack on Athens, could contemplate a return to the discarded policy of Lysander, and hoped to play a role in the Aegean, while leaving the affairs of central Greece to its inhabitants. It would not be surprising if the majority of support for Cleombrotus and Sphodrias came from the old Lysandrians. These are the very policies which had divided Sparta since 404,[62] subject to the usual qualification that whenever a leader died, his faction was helpless until it either joined with another faction or found a new leader. The Cleombrotus faction now expected the Agesilaus faction to adopt a hard line in dealing with Sphodrias.

Xenophon continues by telling us how involved a task it was for Archidamus to put the question to his father.

> 'At that time, accordingly, he went from the public mess-room to his home and retired to rest; then he arose at dawn

61. Xenophon, *Hellenica* 5. 4. 25–7.
62. See the material mentioned in note 32.

and kept watch, so that his father should not leave the house without his notice. But when he saw him going out, in the first place, if anyone among the citizens was present, he gave way to allow them to converse with Agesilaus,... Finally, however, Archidamas gathered courage to approach Agesilaus and say "Father, Cleonymus bids me request you to save his father; and I make the same request of you, if it is possible." And Agesilaus answered: "For myself I grant you pardon; but how could I obtain my own pardon from the state if I failed to pronounce guilty of wrongdoing a man who made traffic for himself to the hurt of the state, I do not see."'[63]

At this point, then, Agesilaus planned to punish Sphodrias severely, just as Cleombrotus' faction feared. Xenophon continues:

'Now at the time Archidamus said nothing in reply to these words, but yielding to the justice of them, went away. Afterwards, however, whether because he had conceived the idea himself or because it had been suggested to him by someone else, he went to Agesilaus and said: "Father, I know that if Sphodrias had done no wrong, you would have acquitted him; but as it is, if he has done something wrong, let him for our sakes obtain pardon at your hands." And Agesilaus said: "Well, if this should be honorable for us, it shall be so." Upon hearing these words Archidamus went away in great despondency. Now one of the friends of Sphodrias in conversation with Etymocles, said to him: "I suppose that you, the friends of Agesilaus, are all for putting Sphodrias to death." And Etymocles replied: "By Zeus, then we shall not be following the same course as Agesilaus, for he says to all with whom he has conversed the same thing, that it is impossible that Sphodrias is not guilty of wrongdoing; but that when, as child, boy, and young man, one has continually performed all the duties of a Spartan, it is a hard thing to put such a man to death; for Sparta has need of such soldiers."'[64]

It is not difficult to see through the ingenuous tale of Xenophon and the rationalizations of Agesilaus. It is plain that at first

63. Xenophon, *Hellenica* 5. 4. 28–30.
64. Xenophon, *Hellenica* 5. 4. 31–3.

Agesilaus meant to convict Sphodrias, but changed his mind later. Why?

The answer may again be found in the relations between Spartan factions and their reactions to developments in foreign affairs. Agesilaus first planned to deal harshly with Sphodrias, believing that by this action he could regain favor at Athens. The rough treatment that Sparta's ambassadors in Athens had received gave some indication that Athenian confidence in Sparta might be hard to win back in any case. The fact that the Athenians expected Sphodrias to be condemned as the guarantee of their future cooperation might strike Agesilaus as an excessively high-handed demand, even though he himself had just recently demanded just such a concession from Athens. It was acceptable for Sparta to demand such concessions from others; for others to do the same might establish a precedent which could threaten Sparta's domination of her neighbors. It might seem to Agesilaus to be too risky to alienate the faction of Cleombrotus certainly in exchange for the less certain hope that Athens would be so completely assuaged by the condemnation of Sphodrias that she would be content with the *status quo ante* for the future. Even though the trustworthy faction of Callistratus had not yet been overthrown by the Athenians, there was no guarantee that they could maintain themselves in the face of popular anger, either immediately or thereafter.

At home Agesilaus was not in a comfortable position. His policy of harsh treatment for Thebes had proved a failure. He no doubt feared that since war with both Athens and Thebes was imminent, Sparta might turn to his rival, Cleombrotus, for leadership. Agesilaus also had to take the conservative faction into account. These Spartans had always been opposed to foreign entanglements, and, if war was now necessary, they might equally turn against him, who had handled Spartan affairs since the Peace of Antalcidas, and who had gotten them into this position, as against Cleombrotus, who was only the proximate cause of their potential difficulties with Athens. The supporters of Cleombrotus, on the other hand, who had thus far not attacked the king, would certainly join the conservatives in such an attack, if he convicted Sphodrias. If both the conservatives and Cleombrotus' faction united in opposition to him, he was finished. By acquitting Sphodrias, Agesilaus no doubt hoped to divide the Cleombrotus faction, and thus develop sufficient support for his leadership. Thus he would be able to continue hostilities against Thebes, and ensure that the other king would not take a leading role in the war. Apparently Agesilaus was successful, for Xenophon tells us that

> 'The Lacedaemonians on their side called out the ban against the Thebans, and believing that Agesilaus would lead them with more judgment than Cleombrotus, requested him to act as commander of the army. And he, saying that he would offer no objections to whatever the state thought best, made his preparations for the campaign.'[65]

Sparta therefore voted for war on two fronts, against Thebes and Athens, and gave Agesilaus a renewed mandate for conducting Spartan affairs. The shrewd king's political maneuvers had once again brought him to a dominant position in Sparta. But in satisfying their king's ambitions, and in voting for war, the Spartans had also voted for an end to the Peace of Antalcidas.

VIII. The Athenian reaction to Sphodrias' acquittal

Any possibility that Callistratus and the pro-Spartan conservatives may have had of restraining the Athenians from going to war with Sparta was crushed by the acquittal of Sphodrias. The Athenians were furious at this latest example of Spartan insolence and injustice, particularly since this time it was directed against them. They voted to go to war. It is at this point that the pro-Theban imperialists took a dominant position in the government, their as Xenophon demonstrates:

> 'As for the Athenians, those among them who favored the Boeotians pointed out to the people that the Lacedaemonians had not only not punished Sphodrias, but even commended him, for plotting against Athens. Therefore the Athenians furnished Peiraeus with gates, set about building ships, and gave aid to the Boeotians with all zeal.'[66]

It is the pro-Theban faction which takes charge of the war measures, and it is the pro-Spartan faction which is discredited.

65. Xenophon, *Hellenica* 5. 4. 35.
66. Xenophon, *Hellenica* 5. 4. 34.

Now that the gloves were off, the Athenians could take war measures and support Thebes actively. It is at this point that Diodorus' account of the expedition of Demophon should be placed:

> 'The Athenian people heard the ambassadors through to the end and voted to dispatch immediately as large a force as possible for the liberation of Thebes, thus repaying their obligations for the former service and at the same time moved by a desire to win the Boeotians to their side and to have in them a powerful partner in the contest against the superiority of the Lacedaemonians...Finally Demophon, who had been made general, and had immediately raised a levy of five thousand hoplites and five hundred horse, on the following day at dawn led forth his troops from the city, and pressed on in an effort to outstrip the Lacedaemonians.'[67]

Diodorus has made a mistake in his chronology. He knew that the Athenians ultimately supported Thebes officially, and did so both to return Theban courtesy in sheltering Thrasybulus and his friends during the period of the Thirty in Athens, and because Athens judged that Theban support was crucial in any sort of land campaign against Sparta and also for defensive purposes. The Peloponnesian War might not have been a defeat for Athens had Thebes supported her rather than Sparta. Diodorus judged that the most logical time for the Athenians to manifest this support was immediately after the seizure of the Cadmeia. As we have seen above, however, there is reason to believe that the Athenians moved much more slowly than Diodorus imagined, and that it was only after the acquittal of Sphodrias that the pro-Theban faction in the city was in a position to carry such a measure through the assembly.

In Diodorus' account, after the seizure of the Cadmeia, he discusses the formation of the Second Delian League. If we accept the error of chronology regarding the timing of Demophon's expedition, it is easy to see that the Athenians, once having decided

67. Diodorus 15. 26. 1–4. Burnett, 'Thebes and the Second Athenian Confederacy', p. 16, ignoring the evidence of Xenophon and the political infighting which helps to clarify the course of events, places the expedition of Demophon in the summer of 378 (which is not too far off), but after *IG* ii², pp. 40 and 43 (which is wrong).

to support Thebes and oppose Sparta, would seek additional allies as quickly as possible, and seek to enroll both old and new friends in an organization that could co-ordinate opposition to Sparta. It is at this point, in the spring of 378, that Athens began those series of steps which resulted in the charter of the Second Confederacy (*IG* II² 43).

Another decree logically falls into this same period. It is an Athenian decree, *IG* II² 40, which deals with several embassies, including a Theban one, which came to Athens in 378. The crucial point of this decree, however, is the distinction made between Thebes and the other allies of Athens. The Athenians decree that the Thebans should be invited to dinner, and describe this invitation as ξενία. The other allies are also to be invited to dinner, but the word used is δεῖπνον.[68] The distinction of terms is significant. The Thebans are not yet on the same footing as the other allies. To be sure, the Thebans must be an ally of Athens, for the expedition of Demophon implies this. Yet she was apparently not yet a member of the Athenian confederacy which was then being formed.[69] The language of the decree leads one to believe that the Athenians have invited the Thebans to Athens along with some of the other allies in the hope of persuading them to join the League. The Thebans could hardly have been eager to join, for they had always been landlubbers and were hardly interested in beginning a naval career when they were fighting for their very survival against Sparta. Perhaps also memories of the Athenian Empire of the fifth century made them cautious. The Athenians, on the other hand, since they were prepared to fight Thebes' battle against Sparta, would have liked Theban assistance in the Aegean as a *quid pro quo*. Since Athens was already connected to Thebes by virtue of Agesilaus' expedition, she must be the suitor in the new alliance. The wooing was ultimately successful, and Thebes became a member of the Second Athenian Confederacy.

Diodorus describes the League as follows:

> 'The Athenians sent their most respected citizens as ambassadors to the cities which were subject to the Lacedaemonians,

68. See *IG* II², p. 40, particularly lines 3 and 10.
69. Diodorus 15. 29. 7–8 makes it plain that Thebes was only admitted to the συνέδριον κοινόν late, after the Aegean states had been enrolled. This seems the most likely order of events.

urging them to adhere to the common cause of liberty. For the Lacedaemonians, relying on the size of the force at their disposal, ruled their subject people inconsiderately and severely, and consequently many of those who belonged to the Spartan sphere of influence fell away to the Athenians. The first to respond to the plea to secede were the peoples of Chios and Byzantium; they were followed by the peoples of Rhodes and Mytilene and certain others of the islanders; and as the movement steadily gathered force throughout Greece, many cities attached themselves to the Athenians. The democracy, elated by the loyalty of the cities, established a common council of all the allies and appointed representatives of each state. It was agreed by common consent that, while the council should hold its sessions in Athens, every city great and small should be on an equal basis and enjoy but one vote, and that all should continue independent, accepting the Athenians as leaders.'[70]

Diodorus tells us that the Sphodrias affair was the catalyst that caused war between Athens and Sparta. In this he is correct, though because of the chronological error he puts the formation of the league too early. No league would be possible without Thebes, which could keep Sparta occupied on land. Diodorus tells us that

'(the Athenians) decided to make war on them and chose three of their most distinguished citizens as generals, Timotheus, Chabrias, and Callistratus. They voted to levy twenty thousand hoplites and five hundred cavalry, and to man two hundred ships. They likewise admitted the Thebans into the common council on terms equal in all respects. They voted also to restore the land settled by cleruchs to its former owners and passed a law that no Athenian should cultivate lands outside of Attica. By this generous act they recovered the goodwill of the Greeks and made their own leadership secure.'[71]

Again it is easy to reconcile the accounts, if we admit that Diodorus has the right facts in basically the right order, but out of place. He

70. Diodorus 15. 28. 1–5.
71. Diodorus 15. 29. 7–15. 30. 2.

knew that Sphodrias was important for beginning the war, but because he had tied the foundation of the League to the restoration of the exiles, he missed the significance of the Sphodrias affair for both Athenian and Spartan politics. In Athens the party of Callistratus had been removed from power by the pro-Theban forces in the city, which were helped to victory in Athens by Agesilaus' machinations in Sparta. Callistratus was general for the year 378/7, it is true, but his influence was now confined to finances, not policy.[72] Athens was now committed to new adventures, which had as their focus the crushing of Spartan pretensions as *hegemon* of Greece. The Peace of Antalcidas was no more, and Sparta was again faced by a potentially long and costly war to preserve her dominance. Ultimately it would finish Sparta as a major power in Greece.

Chronological appendix

The following table will compare the order of events as arranged by Diodorus, Xenophon, and Mrs Anne Pippin Burnett. I will add my own arrangement.

1. Diodorus

1. Return of the exiles with official support of Athens (15. 25. 1).
2. Spartan garrison in Thebes seeks help from Sparta (15. 25. 3).
3. Thebans seek help from Athens. Athens votes the expedition of Demophon (15. 25. 4–15. 26. 3).
4. Allied army besieges the Cadmeia (15. 26. 4).
5. Spartan garrison retreats; the relieving army from Sparta arrives, attacks Thebes, fails, and retreats (15. 27. 1–3).
6. Athenians retreat (15. 27. 4).
7. Athenians form the Second Delian League (15. 28. 1–5).
8. The attack and acquittal of Sphodrias (15. 29. 5–6).
9. The Athenians declare war, admit the Thebans to the League (15. 29. 7–8).

---

72. Callistratus is mentioned by Theopompus as being responsible for finances and for calling the new taxes 'contribution' rather than 'tribute'. See 115 Theopompos F 98 in F. Jacoby, *Die Fragmente der griechischen Historiker*, II.

ɪɪ. Xenophon

1. Return of exiles (*Hellenica* 5. 4. 1–9).
2. Athenian troops, under two generals, come to their aid unofficially (*Hellenica* 15. 4. 9).
3. The Spartan garrison seeks aid from Plataea and Thespiae (*Hellenica* 5. 4. 10).
4. The Thebans defeat the relief force (*Hellenica* 5. 4. 10).
5. The Spartan garrison surrenders (*Hellenica* 5. 4. 11 12).
6. The Athenians try to prevent a massacre (*Hellenica* 5. 4. 12).
7. Sparta deliberates about war against Thebes. Agesilaus refuses the command. Cleombrotus is chosen general (*Hellenica* 5. 4. 13–14).
8. Cleombrotus advances into Boeotia, dallies, retreats. He leaves Sphodrias at Thespiae (*Hellenica* 5. 4. 14–18).
9. The Athenians are frightened by Spartan actions and repudiate the two generals (*Hellenica* 5. 4. 19).
10. The Thebans bribe Sphodrias to attack the Peiraeus (*Hellenica* 5. 4. 20–1).
11. The Athenians are angry with Sparta, question the Spartan ambassadors in Athens, but let them go (*Hellenica* 5. 4. 22–3).
12. The Spartan ephors recall Sphodrias for trial; he does not obey, yet nevertheless is acquitted (*Hellenica* 5. 4. 24–33).
13. The pro-Theban faction in Athens persuades the Athenians to declare war (*Hellenica* 5. 4. 34).

ɪɪɪ. Recently Mrs Burnett has attempted to present a chronology which makes use of the epigraphical evidence. The following represents the conclusion of her article in *Historia* as noted above in note 39.

December 379 Return of Theban exiles; unofficial aid from Athenian border garrisons.

January 378 Thebans fail to come to terms with Sparta (Isoc. 14. 29); Athenians panic at news of Cleombrotus' advance, send Chabrias to protect Eleutherae, and try to placate Sparta with prosecution of the generals active at the recapture of the Cadmeia.

February 378   Cleombrotus establishes Sphodrias and with-
draws from Boeotia.

March   Pro-Spartan party at Athens embarrassed by
poor show of Cleombrotus, discredited by hasty
conviction of the strategoi, further weakened by
optimism over Aegean diplomatic successes;
first Theban treaty signed.

April   Organization of Aegean synedrion; Spartan
preparations for war in Boeotia make Theban
alliance unpopular at Athens.

May/June   Raid and acquittal of Sphodrias; Athenian
preparation for war; invasion of Agesilaus;
psephisma of Cephalus.

This chronology is unimpressive because it follows the account of
Diodorus without attempting to reconcile it with that of Xenophon, and because it is based on a superficial understanding of the
events, which ignores political realities.

iv. The chronology which follows is explained by the arguments in
the preceding chapter.

December 379   Return of exiles to Thebes (*Hellenica* 5. 4. 1–12).
or early   Athenian unofficial assistance (*Hellenica* 5. 4.
January 378   9).

January 378   Thebans send embassy to Sparta and it returns
(Isocrates, *Plataicus* 29). Sparta calls out the ban
and attacks Thebes (*Hellenica* 5. 4. 13–14).

February 378   Cleombrotus on the march. Lingers at Plataea,
Thespiae, and for sixteen days at Cynoscepha-
lae (*Hellenica* 5. 4. 14–18).

21 February–   Election of new Athenian generals. No change
7 March 378   in Athenian factions (see note 40 above).

March 378   Arrival of Spartan ambassadors (*Hellenica* 5. 4.
19, 22–3). Trial of two Athenian generals
(*Hellenica* 5. 4. 19). Raid of Sphodrias (*Hellenica*
5. 4. 20–1; Diodorus 15. 29. 5–6).

March/April   Sphodrias is acquitted (*Hellenica* 5. 4. 20–1;
378   Diodorus 15. 29. 5–6; *Hellenica* 5. 4. 24–33).

April 378   Pro-Theban faction takes power in Athens, and

	declares war against Sparta (*Hellenica* 5. 4. 34). The Athenians vote an alliance with Thebes and dispatch the expedition of Demophon (Diodorus 15. 25. 4–15. 26. 3).
Spring/ Summer 378	Athenians form the Second Athenian League. The Aegean states are first enrolled (Diodorus 15. 28. 1–5). Athenians persuade Thebans to join the League (*IG* II² 40; Diodorus 15. 29. 7–8).
February/ March 377	Charter of the League (*IG* II² 43).[73]

73. A recent article by G. L. Cawkwell, 'The Foundation of the Second Athenian Confederacy', *CQ* 68 (23) 1 (May 1973), 47–60, appeared only after my discussion was already in proof. While I admire his usual industry and ingenuity, I am unpersuaded by his analysis.

Aristotle's *Athenaion Politeia* and the establishment of the Thirty Tyrants

W. JAMES McCOY

EVER SINCE the publication of Kenyon's *editio princeps* of Aristotle's *Athenaion Politeia* in 1891, students of Athenian history have been forced to reckon with its contents. There is some measure of agreement that the latter portion of this document (i.e. chapters 42–69) is of greater historical value in that Aristotle is presenting a more detailed and contemporary account of the fourth-century Athenian government and constitution. The credibility of the earlier chapters, on the other hand, has suffered from the censor's knife. Some criticisms, to be sure, are justifiable,[1] but to dismiss in a casual manner the entire narrative of chapters 1–41, principally on the grounds of error and distortion in Aristotle's sources, is a serious mistake.[2] This is especially true where Aristotle furnishes information not found in other extant sources. An example is his relatively detailed history of the period between 413 and 403 B.C. (chapters 29–41), which, as Sandys correctly noted, held 'the writer's evident interest'.[3] Here Aristotle describes the activities of the commission of thirty *syngrapheis*,[4] presents the tantalizing constitutional documents of the 400 and the 5000,[5] and

---

1. See, e.g., K. von Fritz and E. Kapp, *Aristotle's Constitution of Athens and Related Texts* (New York 1950), pp. 7ff., esp. pp. 11–12.

2. See, e.g., C. Hignett, *A History of the Athenian Constitution* (Oxford 1952), pp. 27ff.; A. W. Gomme, *A Historical Commentary on Thucydides*, vol. 1 (Oxford 1959), p. 42 and n. 5. T. W. Africa, *Science and the State in Greece and Rome* (New York 1968), p. 99, refers to the *Athenaion Politeia* as 'a farrago of misinformation and doctrinaire distortions'.

3. J. Sandys, *Aristotle's Constitution of Athens* (London 1893), p. lviii.

4. *Ath. Pol.* 29. Hignett (*Athenian Constitution*, p. 356) and E. Meyer, *Forschungen zur alten Geschichte*, vol. II (Halle 1899) pp. 416ff., for example, contend that Aristotle is here talking about the same commission which Thucydides mentions in 8. 67. 1. But cf. especially M. Lang, 'The Revolution of the 400', *AJP* 69 (1948), 272–81; see also W. J. McCoy, 'The Non-Speeches of Pisander in Thucydides, Book Eight' in *The Speeches in Thucydides* (Chapel Hill 1973), pp. 78–89.   5. *Ath. Pol.* 30–1.

introduces other material (particularly post-Thucydidean) which
is neglected by, or contradicts, the testimonies of Xenophon,
Diodorus, Lysias, Plutarch and others. One of the most interesting
and controversial developments treated within these chapters is the
establishment of the Thirty Tyrants in 404 B.C. Since no one source
relates the whole story, it is necessary to reconstruct the situation
piecemeal. It is my purpose to show that *Athenaion Politeia* 34. 2–3
is indispensable for this reconstruction.

As a preliminary to the inquiry, we must first consider the
sources of the *Athenaion Politeia*, an aspect of the work which has
often been discussed by critics. Two sources can be identified with
a degree of certainty: the poems of Solon and a list(s) of archons.
It is also likely that Aristotle made some use of public and/or
private archives and that he had access to the works of fifth- and
fourth-century historians and atthidographers, especially Androtion.[6] Beyond this, however, conjecture reaches ridiculous propor-
tion, heightened, of course, by Aristotle's obvious partisanship in
praise of Thucydides son of Melesias, Nicias, and Theramenes.[7]
Hignett, for example, argues that because Aristotle relied on
oligarchic pamphlets for his view of Athenian history at the end of
the fifth century (or, for that matter, Athenian history from Solon
to Theramenes), political bias discolors his entire testimony.[8]
Other scholars have been even more hypothetical, conjuring up an
'Anonymous of 392',[9] an 'Anonymous of ca. 380',[10] and a partisan

6. See U. von Wilamowitz-Moellendorff, *Aristoteles und Athen* (Berlin 1893),
vol. I, pp. 260–90; F. Jacoby, *Atthis* (Oxford 1949), *passim*; von Fritz and Kapp,
Aristotle's Constitution of Athens, pp. 12ff. See also H. Bloch, 'Historical Literature
of the Fourth Century' in *Athenian Studies Presented to William Scott Ferguson,
H.S.C.P.*, suppl. vol. I (1940), 341–55. Many detractors of the worth of the
Athenaion Politeia underscore Aristotle's use of Androtion not only because of
the latter's political bias but also because of his family and personal connections.
Androtion was the son of Andron (a colleague of Theramenes in the Four
Hundred and the mover of the condemnatory boulê decree against Antiphon)
and a pupil of Isocrates (who was generally favorable to conservative poli-
ticians). Consequently they contend that Aristotle was totally captivated by the
political views of Androtion's *Atthis*; cf., however, von Fritz and Kapp,
Aristotle's Constitution of Athens, p. 13, n. 11.

7. *Ath. Pol.* 28, 32, 36.

8. Hignett, *Athenian Constitution*, pp. 28ff.

9. O. Seeck, 'Quellenstudien zu des Aristoteles Verfassungsgeschichte
Athens', *Klio* 4 (1904), 282ff.

10. Wilamowitz-Moellendorf, *Aristoteles*, vol. I, p. 286.

of Theramenes, yea, even Theramenes himself, as the author of a pamphlet used by Aristotle.[11] But none of these so-called pamphlets or anonymous writers can be substantiated, and even if they could we need not think that Aristotle was a slavish copier. His ideas and praise for a certain kind of politician are likely to have been his own. Moreover, to contend that such subjectivity interfered with his recording of factual data is as futile an argument as asserting the contrary. Unless we can prove differently, what Aristotle says ought to be taken seriously.

Besides the *Athenaion Politeia*, several ancient sources provide information pertaining to the establishment of the Thirty: Xenophon (*Hellenica* 2. 2. 10–2. 3. 3), Diodorus (13. 107; 14. 3–4), Lysias (especially 12. 62ff. and 13. 5ff.), Andocides (especially 3. 11–12), and Plutarch (*Lysander* 14–15). Taken as a whole they seem to present a more or less consistent narrative with two important exceptions, both of which emanate from Aristotle.[12] Aristotle says that there was a clause making a return to the *patrios politeia* a condition for peace in the treaty negotiated between Athens and Sparta in April of 404;[13] he also absolves Theramenes from complicity with Lysander in proposing the appointment of the Thirty. In addition, Aristotle is the only source with any insight into the tripartite division of contemporary Athenian politics.

The critics of the *Athenaion Politeia*, more recently A. Fuks,[14] contend that Aristotle's variations from the other testimonies are the result of statements in his sources: in particular, the histories of the Athenian atthidographers. Fuks argues that Aristotle is here following a pro-Theramenean source and so fabricates an apologetic version of late fifth-century Athenian history. In contrast, he asserts that the other sources collectively present a more detailed account of the peace treaty between Athens and Sparta and are to be believed when they omit any mention of a clause dealing with the *patrios politeia*. Fuks admits, however, that the *patrios politeia* was

---

11. A. von Mess, 'Die Hellenika von Oxyrhynchos', *Rh. Mus.* 63 (1908), 381–4; 'Aristoteles AΘHNAIΩN ΠOΛITEIA und die politische Schriftstellerei Athens', *Rh. Mus.* 66 (1911), 356–92; G. Busolt, *Griechische Geschichte*, III. 2, pp. 607ff.; Wilamowitz-Moellendorff, *Aristoteles*, vol. I, p. 166.

12. Diodorus 14. 3–4 conforms with the *Athenaion Politeia* in both cases.

13. I accept Fuks' dating throughout this paper (see note 14); cf. Hignett, *Athenian Constitution*, pp. 378–83.

14. A. Fuks, *The Ancestral Constitution* (London 1953), esp. pp. 52–83.

an important political issue in Athens, but that it only became one after the conclusion of the peace treaty.[15] He also maintains that the other sources are more reliable when they name Theramenes as the mover and originator of the government of the Thirty.

Fuks' study of the 'ancestral constitution' is intelligent and informative, but his criticism of the historical relevance of the *Athenaion Politeia* rests on at least two weak foundations. First, as noted above, we are unable to confirm definitely the identity of Aristotle's source(s) for the closing years of the fifth century. What might seem an excellent hypothesis is still only conjecture;[16] as such it can neither eliminate embarrassing information nor invalidate an otherwise uncontested statement. Secondly, Fuks is inconsistent when it comes to his evaluation of sources. While he is ready to sympathize with a biased stand or dismiss a lapse on the part of Xenophon, Ephorus, Diodorus, and Lysias, he seems reluctant to afford the same leniency and dispensation to the *Athenaion Politeia*. Consequently he is willing to entertain the evidence of members of the former group at the expense of Aristotle. But the *Athenaion Politeia* is relevant and must be taken seriously; without it the internal history of Athens during the critical months from April to September 404 B.C. is incomplete.

Let us now examine in greater detail the major phases of our problem: first, the peace treaty between Athens and Sparta and its immediate aftermath; then, the meeting of the Athenian assembly that voted the Thirty into office.

After their crushing defeat at Aegospotami, the Athenians found themselves in a most unpromising position. Their city was besieged by land and sea; they had no fleet, no allies, and little food. Yet they continued to hold out, fearful that if they surrendered they

---

15. Fuks (*ibid.*, p. 61), nevertheless, admits that
   'such an expression as *kata ta patria, autonomous kata ta patria*, or even *ten patrion politeian* might have occurred in the final draft of the treaty of 404. If it did occur, it must have been the normal guarantee on the part of Sparta not to interfere in Athens' domestic affairs; it was not an instruction to adopt any definite constitution, as it appears in *Ath. Pol.* and Ephorus.'
Fuks seems to be hedging and weakening his stand. To the mass of Athenians such a phrase would mean 'democracy' (see below, pp. 140–1).

16. See, e.g., G. Busolt ('Aristoteles oder Xenophon?', *Hermes* 33 (1898), esp. 75ff.) who contends that both Aristotle and Diodorus 14 (via Ephorus) are closely adhering to the *Atthis* of Androtion in matters relating to the Thirty.

would suffer the same punishments which they had earlier meted out to members of the Spartan alliance. Although they restored civic rights to the disfranchised, they refused to talk peace, even though many were dying of starvation. Finally, when the supply of food was exhausted, they sent an embassy to the Spartan king, Agis, at Decelea and said that they were willing to join the Spartan alliance on the condition that their Long Walls and the Piraeus remain intact. Agis told them that he himself had no authority to negotiate and referred them to Sparta. The Spartan ephors, however, stopped the embassy at Sellasia and sent it back to Athens to obtain more realistic proposals. Still the Athenians were unwilling to consider the destruction of their walls and even passed a decree forbidding anyone to make such a motion.[17]

Theramenes took a different view of the situation. Xenophon says that he made a speech before the assembly and persuaded the Athenians to send him to Lysander to inquire why Sparta insisted on the demolition of the Long Walls.[18] He stayed with Lysander more than three months and returned to Athens only when he was confident that the effects of famine would force the Athenians to yield to any terms whatsoever. He reported to the assembly that Lysander had detained him all this time and finally told him to go to Sparta, since only the ephors could supply the information he desired. Accordingly the Athenians appointed Theramenes and nine others as ambassadors to Sparta with plenary power.[19] They returned to Athens with the following terms for peace: the destruction of the Long Walls and the fortifications at the Piraeus, the surrender of the fleet, save twelve ships (Diodorus says ten); the recall of all exiles; the dissolution of the empire and the loss of foreign possessions; a commitment to follow Spartan leadership in any expedition by land or sea and to have the same enemies and

17. Xen., *Hell.* 2. 2. 10–15; also Lys. 13. 5–8.
18. Xen., *Hell.* 2. 2. 16. Lysias (13. 9) gives a slightly different version. He says that Theramenes told the Athenians that if they appointed him an ambassador to negotiate a peace with Sparta he would see to it that Athens' walls remained secure. Theramenes was in no position to make such a promise; the account of Xenophon, therefore, seems more probable.
19. Xen., *Hell.* 2. 2. 16–17; also Lys. 13. 11–12. Lysias (12. 71) puts the entire blame for the final peace on Theramenes' shoulders, but as G. Grote rightly comments (*History of Greece*, vol. VI (London 1872), p. 450, n. 1): ' (Theramenes) plainly ought not to be required to bear it.'

friends as Sparta.[20] In addition to these terms, Aristotle and
Diodorus state that the treaty included a stipulation that Athens
was to be governed according to the *patrios politeia*.[21] Theramenes
spoke in favor of accepting these conditions, and despite some
opposition the majority of Athenians agreed with him and voted
to accept the peace.

If Aristotle and Diodorus are correct concerning the *patrios
politeia* clause (and there is no compelling reason to doubt their
testimony),[22] we must first offer some explanation why the other
sources may have omitted it, and then attempt to justify its inclusion in the peace treaty.

Xenophon is a poor witness for Athenian politics and nowhere
refers to the *patrios politeia*, even though it was an important contemporary issue.[23] In addition, his philo-Laconian sentiments are
well attested. Had he mentioned the *patrios politeia* he would have
shown the Spartans to be faithless negotiators. Instead, he excul-
pates them, especially Lysander, from any direct involvement in
Athenian politics by attributing the creation of the Thirty solely to
a decision of the Athenian assembly.[24] Lysias is a deeply partisan
observer of these events. He was violently bitter against Theramenes and held him almost personally responsible for his family's

20. Xen., *Hell.* 2. 2. 20; Diod. 13. 107. 4; Plut., *Lys.* 14. 4; Andoc. 3. 11–12,
39; Lys. 13. 14.

21. *Ath. Pol.* 34. 3; Diod. 14. 3. 2.

22. Many take a contrary stand, claiming that discussion about the government did not commence until *after* the ratification of the peace treaty: e.g.,
J. Beloch, *Griechische Geschichte*, II. 1, pp. 428–9, n. 3; E. Meyer, *Geschichte des
Alterthums*[4], IV. 2, pp. 365–6, n. 1; Fuks, *Ancestral Constitution*, pp. 61, 65. W. S.
Ferguson (*Cambridge Ancient History*, vol. v (Cambridge 1926), pp. 364–6; see
also Busolt, *G.G.*, III. 2, pp. 1635–6, n. 1) believes that Sparta concluded a
separate alliance with Athens in addition to the formal peace (as happened in
421) which gave the Athenians self-government 'as of old'; he suggests that the
patrios politeia was 'alluded to doubtless, but not actually prescribed, in the
treaty of alliance with Sparta, as the concomitant of autonomy'. This seems to
me an ingenious yet unnecessary invention. J. A. R. Munro ('Theramenes
against Lysander', *C.Q.* 32 (1938), 19) comments: 'there was no injunction
about the constitution beyond the stereotyped provision in the treaty that it
should be *kata ta patria*, and this could be diversely interpreted and be regarded
as a guarantee rather than an instruction'. See also above, n. 15.

23. Xenophon's silence is regrettable, especially if he was an eye-witness to
some or all of these events. See E. Delebecque, *Essai sur la vie de Xénophon* (Paris
1957), p. 61, also pp. 29–39.

24. Xen., *Hell.* 2. 3. 2.

misfortunes. A blackening of Theramenes' reputation was required for successful prosecution against both Eratosthenes and Agoratus (orations 12 and 13).[25] Andocides, as even Fuks admits, 'does not propose to quote the treaty in full but only what was relevant to his immediate purpose'.[26] Diodorus does not mention the *patrios politeia* in 13. 107; perhaps here he was following a source which omitted this clause.[27] Plutarch presents a major obstacle. He claims access to an actual decree of the Spartan ephors which does not include the *patrios politeia*. Certainly this enhances the value of Plutarch's evidence, but the 'dogma of the ephors' would not necessarily correspond to the final version of the peace treaty.[28] All these explanations, to be sure, are conjectural, but so are those which attempt to eradicate the *patrios politeia* clause.

Since this line of argument leads to stalemate we must seek more convincing justification for the clause providing for the *patrios politeia*. This may be found, in part, in what happened during Theramenes' stay with Lysander. We do not know the details of their conversations, but it is reasonable to assume that among the topics discussed was the future government of Athens, all the more so since the Athenians were passionately devoted to the integrity of their democracy. Theramenes wanted to conclude a peace with Sparta. He was doubtless ready to concede the destruction of the Long Walls and the fortifications at the Piraeus, the return of exiles, the loss of empire, and Athens' general subservience to Sparta – he had little choice. Yet, in light of his mandate, he must have insisted upon the continuation of self-government in Athens, perhaps along the lines of his ideal 'moderate democracy'. He was surely opposed to the establishment of a permanent and narrow oligarchy, for he had opposed it in 411 and probably believed that

25. Certain critics of the *patrios politeia* clause (e.g., Fuks, *Ancestral Constitution*, p. 72; Meyer, *G.d.A.*[4], v, pp. 13–14, n. 1) contend that Lysias' testimony (especially 12. 70ff.) could not have been fraudulent. But as I will attempt to point out Lysias was manipulating and not telling the whole story.

26. Fuks, *Ancestral Constitution*, pp. 55–6, 58. Andocides even refers to a stele (3. 11) presumably inscribed with the terms of the treaty.

27. Diodorus is often careless and inconsistent; see, however, Fuks, *Ancestral Constitution*, pp. 56, 58.

28. Fuks (*ibid.*, p. 55) says: 'the dogma states the Spartan conditions only', i.e., *sine quibus non*, 'it does not give the final peace treaty'.

the institution of a limited democracy would be sufficient safeguard to check the excesses of the radicals.

We may wonder why Lysander, with total victory in sight, should have been willing to make any concessions whatsoever. The answer, I think, lies in the one bargaining point which Theramenes had. Theramenes was a shrewd politician who knew enough about the internal politics of Sparta to realize that Lysander's position there was tenuous. At the moment Lysander was a hero and enjoyed the full support of the ephors and people, but he still had to contend with the two kings whose jealousy could turn against him. His foreign policy, moreover, ran counter to that of King Pausanias. Pausanias was a leader of the conservative, traditional faction within the Spartan state, which rejected the idea of imperial expansion and viewed with increasing suspicion and alarm the ambitious and adventurous policies which Lysander pursued.[29] After all, it was Lysander's scheme to establish in each state he conquered a government which was loyal not so much to Sparta as to himself. In particular, he usually established a decarchy,[30] a board of ten native collaborators subservient to him and aided by a Spartan garrison under a harmost appointed by him.[31] In many instances Lysander was careless in not seeing to it that his ruling groups included men of broad popular support,[32] but the cities of Asia Minor were of less importance than Athens where Lysander had to exercise greater restraint. If chaotic *stasis* broke out in Athens (which could readily occur under a narrow oligarchy) his enemies in Sparta were sure to take advantage of the situation to his detriment.

29. See C. D. Hamilton, 'Spartan Politics and Policy, 405–01 B.C.', *A.J.P.* 91 (1970), 294–314. Hamilton convincingly discusses a tripartite division of Spartan political factions at this time. He is careful to point out, however, that the first sign of open cleavage between Lysander and his political opponents did not occur until the summer of 404. Nevertheless, Pausanias could still harbor resentment towards Lysander which the latter duly recognized.

30. Plutarch (*Lys.* 14) says that Lysander had already started this process among the Greek cities of Asia.

31. See H. W. Parke, 'The Development of the Second Spartan Empire', *J.H.S.* 50 (1930), 37–78. Parke (p. 77) says: 'The fact is that the Spartan empire as founded by Lysander was an anomaly when joined with the Peloponnesian League and the Spartan constitution. It is possible that Lysander would have modified the constitution to match the empire, but he was prevented from doing this.'

32. Plut., *Lys.* 13. 3–5.

Since Theramenes at this time had considerable public support, Lysander realized that a satisfactory peace was now possible, especially if he and Sparta submitted to Theramenes' demand for the *patrios politeia*. Lysander, to be sure, would have preferred a strict oligarchy, but he could willingly agree, if only temporarily, to such a vague term as *patrios politeia* even if Theramenes made him see clearly that he intended by it a moderate democracy. Once a peace treaty was signed, Athens reduced to complete impotence, and the many oligarchic exiles restored, Lysander would find it easier to ignore his agreement and perhaps impose his will upon Athens. In fact, he could have anticipated heated political debate within Athens on the *patrios politeia* issue which would afford him a future excuse to intervene. For the moment, however, he did not want an enemy in Theramenes, nor did he want to create unnecessary friction between himself and his opponents in Sparta.

The existing board of ephors supported the actions of Lysander, who had informed them of the nature of his conversations with Theramenes before the appearance of the official Athenian embassy.[33] That some clause mentioning the *patrios politeia* was included in the peace treaty seems more than probable, because this more than any other issue is debated in Athens during the interval between the acceptance of the peace treaty and the establishment of the Thirty.[34]

---

33. Xen., *Hell.* 2. 2. 18.

34. Fuks (*Ancestral Constitution*, pp. 58–60, 76–8) and Meyer (*G.d.A.*[4] v, pp. 13–14, n. 1), for example, contend that Aristotle and Diodorus (14. 3) are following a pro-Theramenean source which apologetically pre-dates the political schism between Theramenes and the more reactionary members of the Thirty. They deny such a break until after the establishment of that body (following Xen., *Hell.* 2. 3. 15). Overt differences, of course, did not erupt until this time, but it is ridiculous to suppose that Theramenes and Critias had the same political goals for Athens. Theramenes was always his own man. As a master politician he never exposed himself in a reckless manner, especially when his so-called political colleagues were supported by armed power. He had bided his time as a member of the Four Hundred thinking that this body would accomplish its temporary function and then dissolve itself when the Five Thousand came into being. When this did not happen he made no attempt to undermine the oligarchy until assured of some 'moral' support from Alcibiades and the Athenian fleet on Samos. Only then did he encourage his fellow moderates (who were a numerical majority of the Four Hundred) to intrigue against the oligarchic extremists (see Thuc. 8. 89ff.). In like manner, Theramenes was willing to wait patiently and test his new colleagues in the Thirty. When they

The *patrios politeia* was a vague and ambiguous term which certainly had different levels of meaning depending on one's political sympathies.[35] The Athenians tried to resolve the issue, but it proved too controversial. In the end, this unstable state of affairs led directly to the creation of the Thirty. As Xenophon is silent about these turbulent months, we must turn to Lysias, Diodorus, and especially Aristotle to appreciate the substance of this controversy.

Aristotle says that after the conclusion of the peace treaty based on the *patrios politeia* the popular faction (οἱ δημοτικοί) tried to preserve the democracy (τὸν δῆμον), that both the nobles (who were members of hetairies) and the returning exiles were eager for oligarchy (ὀλιγαρχίας ἐπεθύμουν), and that those who did not belong to hetairies but who were otherwise considered as belonging to the best classes (including Theramenes, Archinus, Anytus, Cleitophon, and Phormisius)[36] desired the *patrios politeia*.[37] Diodorus is less definite and describes only a dual division in the controversy, one between oligarchs and democrats: the former

refused to comply with their assigned task to frame the laws for a new constitution (Xen., *Hell.* 2. 3. 11) and instead occupied themselves in brutal political prosecutions, Theramenes challenged them and died a martyr.

Lysias also implicates Theramenes in a conspiracy to suborn the Athenian democracy even before the ratification of the peace treaty with Sparta, in particular by intriguing against certain Athenian generals and taxiarchs who were unwilling to abide by the terms of the peace (Lys. 13. 5ff., 13ff.). As a result the latter were arrested and imprisoned. But Theramenes' membership in the Thirty, at least in the eyes of Lysias, made him culpable for any and all atrocities against the democracy and local democrats. Theramenes, therefore, became a victim of guilt by association. It is interesting to note that some of those implicated in the activities of the Thirty (e.g., Eratosthenes) defended themselves on the grounds that they had been supporters of Theramenes, and such a defense seems to have been effective under the restored democracy.

35. See M. I. Finley, *The Ancestral Constitution* (Cambridge 1971). Finley presents an interesting study of the use of the 'ancestral constitution' theme in different historical settings, both ancient and modern.

36. Meyer (*G.d.A.*[4], v, p. 14, n. 1) is puzzled by Aristotle's list: 'Das hat schwerlich irgendwelche Gewähr; und jedenfalls stand keiner dieser Männer dem Theramenes besonders nahe, da keiner von ihnen unter den Dreissig ist.' But Aristotle merely says that all these men were of the same opinion regarding the *patrios politeia* and that Theramenes was the leading 'whip' for this cause. This does not necessarily imply intimate political association or the mandatory inclusion of any or all of these men among Theramenes' appointees to the Thirty.

37. *Ath. Pol.* 34. 3.

wanting to revive the ancient state of affairs (τὴν παλαιὰν κατάστασιν) where the few would predominate; the latter, who constituted a majority, preferring the *patrios politeia* which by common consent was democracy (δημοκρατίαν).[38] Lysias furnishes additional information concerning the political milieu at Athens.[39] He says that sometime between Aegospotami and the establishment of the Thirty (δημοκρατίας ἔτι οὔσης) members of the Athenian hetairies appointed five overseers (called *ephors*) to organize and initiate a campaign of fear and conspiracy against the democracy, while at the same time they themselves manipulated the appointments of phylarchs and other magistrates and predetermined the passage of necessary measures. In this context Lysias is doubtless referring to the subversive activities of the same group which Aristotle categorizes as desiring oligarchy.

The crux of this political division was the 'abstract' *patrios politeia*, which could be construed as a slogan or platform for any faction. The radical democrats wanted to preserve the existing democracy; their concept of *patrios politeia* was probably very similar to that espoused in 411 by Thrasybulus and the Athenian fleet on Samos.[40] The oligarchs, by advocating a return to ancestral conditions, probably looked upon the *patrios politeia* as pre-Solonian. The moderates, however, in keeping with their aspirations of 411 (when apparently the *patrios politeia* was also publicly used as a catch-all phrase of propaganda)[41] promoted the establishment of a limited or restricted democracy with Solonic and/or Cleisthenic overtones.

Although the *patrios politeia* at this or any time cannot be precisely defined, it is best associated with democratic propaganda, whether moderate or radical. Aristotle strictly confines his association of the term with Theramenes and his associates, probably because Theramenes was chiefly responsible for the terms of the peace treaty. But the majority of Athenians must also have been of a similar opinion that the *patrios politeia* was democratic (following Diodorus); otherwise the oligarchs would not have found themselves so hard pressed to recall Lysander.

Diodorus and Lysias are the only sources which discuss the assembly that voted on the appointment of the Thirty. The

38. Diod. 14. 3. 3.   39. Lys. 12. 43–4.
40. See Thuc. 8. 76. 6.   41. See *Ath. Pol.* 29.

Athenaion Politeia does not furnish direct testimony. Aristotle merely says that Lysander forced the issue and intimidated the Athenians into accepting the oligarchy proposed by the motion of Dracontides.[42] Nevertheless, since Diodorus contends that the *patrios politeia* was crucial to this assembly and since both Diodorus and Aristotle agree on the *patrios politeia* issue, the events fall within the scope of our investigation.

Diodorus says that Lysander was summoned from Samos by the oligarchs of Athens to settle the governmental controversy. When he arrived he assembled the Athenians and advised them to choose thirty men to head the government and manage all the affairs of state. Theramenes immediately rose in opposition and referred to the peace treaty which stated that Athens was to be governed according to the *patrios politeia*. Lysander countered this affront by asserting that the terms of the peace were no longer valid since the Athenians had not demolished their Long Walls on schedule, and then threatened Theramenes with death if he continued to interfere. Theramenes and the Athenians were so terrified that they voted to dissolve the democracy and elect the Thirty.[43]

Lysias, however, accuses Theramenes of direct complicity with Lysander. His account runs as follows. Theramenes not only sent for Lysander's ships from Samos and prevented the assembly from meeting until Lysander reached Athens, but during the debate on the constitution he also encouraged the Athenians to entrust the affairs of state to the Thirty and to adhere to the government proposed by a decree of Dracontides. When the assembly voiced its disapproval, Theramenes disregarded the uproar, 'since he knew that many Athenians were engaged in similar activities and that he spoke of matters that had the approval of Lysander and the Lacedaemonians'. Lysander then told the Athenians that they were guilty of breaking the truce and emphasized that it was a question of their lives and not just of the Athenian constitution if they refused to listen to Theramenes. At this point the 'good citizens' either remained silent or departed, whereas the 'bad citizens' formally voted the appointment of the Thirty.[44]

The accounts of Diodorus and Lysias seem at first sight to

---

42. *Ath. Pol.* 34. 3; see also Plut., *Lys.* 15. Xenophon (*Hell.* 2. 3. 2) abstains from citing any name in connection with the creation of the Thirty.

43. Diod. 14. 3. 4–7.   44. Lys. 12. 71–5.

present conflicting testimony, but, as P. Salmon has suggested, a careful examination will show that they are in fact reconcilable and that each author is reporting different parts of the same assembly.[45] We will never know who was really responsible for the reappearance of Lysander, yet it is interesting to note that Lysander was approached directly and not through the Spartan board of ephors. If, in fact, the Spartan ephors had already agreed to a *patrios politeia* clause, it is easy to see why the oligarchs should go directly to Lysander who had already begun to set up his system of oligarchic decarchies.[46] As to the assembly itself, the following sequence of events seems likely.

Since Lysias (12. 71–2) states that Lysander dictated the time of the assembly, it is reasonable to assume that he was among the first speakers and perhaps even introduced the matter of the Thirty. When he had finished, Theramenes spoke out against his proposition, reading aloud the terms of the peace which provided for the *patrios politeia* and declaring, 'it would be a terrible thing if the Athenians should be robbed of their freedom contrary to the oaths'. Lysander retorted that Athens had failed to comply with the terms of the treaty and threatened Theramenes with death 'if he did not stop opposing the Lacedaemonians' (following Diodorus). Is it stretching a point to suppose that Theramenes then became highly emotional and for the moment too terrified to challenge Lysander any further? I think not. Perhaps it was during this temporary lapse that one of his associates, a certain Dracontides, proposed the decree which called for the creation of the Thirty. When Theramenes had regained his composure, he surely realized that there was no alternative (especially with the presence of Spartan soldiers). He then persuaded the assembly, despite strong opposition, to vote for this arrangement (following Lysias).

45. P. Salmon, 'L'Établissement des Trente à Athènes', *L'Antiquité Classique* 38 (1969), 497–500. Meyer (*G.d.A.*[4], v, pp. 16–17 and n. 3), Beloch (*G.G.*, ii. 1, pp. 430–1), Ferguson (*C.A.H.*, v, p. 366), and G. Glotz and R. Cohen (*Histoire grecque*, vol. ii (Paris 1931), p. 51) all prefer the text of Lysias (hostile to Theramenes) to that of Diodorus (favorable to Theramenes). Munro (*C.Q.* 32 (1938), 23–4), on the other hand, prefers Diodorus, although he recognizes in this source a certain apologetic character (as he does in *Ath. Pol.* 34. 3) which looks to justify the conduct of Theramenes.

46. It is interesting to note that in 397/6 the Spartan ephors dissolved the decarchies of Lysander and decreed that each city should return to its respective *patrios politeia* (Xen., *Hell.* 3. 4. 2; Plut., *Ages.* 6).

The Athenians continued to trust him, 'observing his fairness and thinking that his nobility would check the ambition of the leaders to some degree', and elected him one of the Thirty[47] (following Diodorus).

Lysander knew that Theramenes was the most influential democrat in Athens; at the same time he must have realized the inherent danger of excluding him from the new government. He did not object, therefore, to Theramenes' membership in the oligarchy and even allowed him to appoint ten members of the Thirty.[48] After all, the participation of moderates and the façade of a coalition government might help to reconcile the partisans of democracy. Lysander was also reluctant to risk unnecessary trouble by remaining in Athens, and since he had now, in effect, violated the peace treaty without reference to the Spartan ephors he probably thought it prudent to leave Athens without interfering further in Athenian affairs. Yet his goal had been accomplished: Athens was ruled by a narrow oligarchy, and the dominant voice in that oligarchy belonged to men who owed their position not so much to Sparta but to Lysander himself.

Theramenes' political struggle with his colleagues among the Thirty eventually resulted in his prosecution and death. But perhaps 'his' *patrios politeia* was somewhat realized when the Spartan king, Pausanias, supplanted Lysander and negotiated a final peace treaty which guaranteed the Athenians a democratic form of government.[49] The reorganized democracy was at first very careful not to indulge in former excesses and to follow the leadership of moderate politicians who sought to restore its

47. Munro (*C.Q.* 32 (1938), 26) suggests that the Thirty was actually a political victory for Theramenes over Lysander, who wanted a decarchy in Athens. This is true in the sense that Theramenes continued to participate actively in the political arena, but against overwhelming odds.

48. Lys. 12. 76. The five Athenian ephors also appointed ten members of the Thirty, and those present at the assembly another ten. Fuks (*Ancestral Constitution*, p. 73) thinks that the ten chosen ἐκ τῶν παρόντων 'were all meant to represent the less intransigent...democrats', which in effect gave Theramenes two-thirds control of the Thirty. But F. D. Smith's contention (*Athenian Political Commissions* (Chicago 1920), p. 81) that they were 'anti-democratic' seems more probable in view of what happened.

49. As part of the reform program of 403, the Athenians took up the task of recodifying the laws initiated back in 410. According to Andocides (1. 83), the decree for this program began: 'The Athenians shall be governed in the ancestral way (*kata ta patria*)...'

stability. Theramenes, I think, would have been pleased with this arrangement.

Our investigation of the events leading to the establishment of the Thirty has shown, I trust, that we cannot dismiss the historical testimony of the early chapters of the *Athenaion Politeia* without careful scrutiny. In certain cases (such as the one in point) it provides essential evidence for reconstructing the history of the Athenian state.[50]

50. I should like to express my gratitude to Professors D. Kagan and F. O. Behrends for their helpful suggestions and criticisms during the preliminary stages of this paper.

Nearchus the Cretan[1]

E. BADIAN

Κρῆτες ἀεὶ ψευσταί

THE REPUTATION of Nearchus, the Cretan from Amphipolis, shines like a good deed in the admittedly naughty world of Alexander historians.[2] A loyal friend of Alexander's since youth, he was among those banished as a result of the Pixodarus affair,[3] and he retained an honest and sincere admiration for the king,[4] yet without indulging in reprehensible flattery.[5] An eminent historian, known chiefly for topographical and military researches, waxes rhetorical:[6]

'The description going back to him of his reunion with Alexander the Great after his voyage over the Indian Ocean is a unique pearl of world literature, which in loyalty and depth of penetration into a human personality (here that of Alexander the Great) is unsurpassed by any other description surviving from antiquity, and which can be compared –

1. The main sources will be cited as follows: A = Arrian, *Anabasis*; C = Curtius, *History of Alexander*; D = Diodorus Siculus, *Library*, Book 17; P = Plutarch, *Alexander*; *Ind.* = Arrian, *Indica*.

2. See the various modern judgments cited below.

3. A 3. 6. 5; P 10. 5. Cf. E. Badian, *Phoenix* 17 (1963), 245f.

4. H. Berve, *Das Alexanderreich auf prosopographischer Grundlage* (Munich 1926), vol. II, no. 544. (Henceforth cited under author's name only.)

5. W. Capelle, *RE*, s.v. 'Nearchos', col. 2153. It should be added that the standard treatment is now that of G. Wirth, 'Nearchos der Flottenchef', *Eirene* 11 (1969), 615–39 (henceforth cited under author's name only) – a major contribution to the study of Alexander's policies and administration, going well beyond the promise of the title. Occasional disagreement in detail must not obscure the fact that I have greatly profited by reading that work. What seemed to me still needed was more exhaustive study of Nearchus' character and the nature of his account.

6. C. F. Lehmann-Haupt, who insisted on writing a forty-page entry on Nearchus (in part repeating an earlier publication of his) in the work of his pupil J. Papastavru, *Amphipolis. Geschichte und Prosopographie* (*Klio*, Beiheft 37 = N.F. 24 (1936)), in order to 'do justice to the requirements of such a proso-pography' (p. vii). (This work is henceforth cited 'Lehmann-Haupt'.)

6-2

and that only at a considerable distance – to very few passages in ancient literature.'

Nearchus the writer is matched by Nearchus the great man: he is the only one of Alexander's subordinates who has any major achievement of his own to show, and who, 'as it were, provides a complement by sea to the conqueror of the earth'.[7] It is rare to find the mild protests of a perceptive scholar like Truesdell S. Brown: 'A more careful examination shows that...Nearchus was not exclusively concerned with painting an accurate picture of events, particularly events in which he had himself played a part.'[8] Lionel Pearson studied Nearchus against his literary background,[9] showing not only the obvious imitation of Herodotus, but the more surprising epic elements borrowed from the *Odyssey*. It should not be necessary, by now, to demonstrate that Nearchus was not a detached scientist trying to present an objective record of the results of his voyage of exploration for the instruction of his readers. Not only was he, as even Berve had to acknowledge,[10] insufficiently critical of the *mirabilia* that he heard from local sources: we know that he reported his own wonders where he must have known better, to impress rather than to instruct; thus the whale 90 cubits long that was measured by his own men,[11] or the skins of large ants of which he personally saw a considerable number brought into the Macedonian camp,[12] or the savages with hair all over their bodies and claws like beasts', who dressed in the skins of fishes,[13] or shadows falling towards the south at a time well after the autumn equinox.[14]

7. Thus Berve, quoted approvingly by Lehmann-Haupt, p. 98.

8. T. S. Brown, *Onesicritus* (Berkeley and Los Angeles 1949), p. 105. (Henceforth cited under author's name only.) Brown tries to give Onesicritus his due, against the attacks on him that ultimately go back to Nearchus. He perhaps still does not do full justice to Onesicritus' real nautical talents and responsibilities (see below).

9. L. Pearson, *The Lost Histories of Alexander the Great* (Cleveland 1960), chapter 5. (Henceforth cited under author's name only.) See pp. 134f. for imitation of the *Odyssey* in several passages, and comparison with Herodotus throughout.   10. Berve (n. 4).

11. *Ind.* 39. 4. Brown (p. 121) mistakenly reports it as 50 cubits and calls even this 'fantastic'.

12. *Ind.* 15. 4.   13. *Ind.* 24. 9.

14. *Ind.* 25. 4 (also some very odd statements about stars). For the time of year see 21. 1 (20 Boedromion: departure from Pattala) and 21. 13 (a stay of

The fanciful travelers' tales may be forgiven: they were expected by the public, and duly provided for its delectation. What will interest us here is the image of himself and, in particular, of his relations with Alexander that Nearchus builds up, and his remarks on his rivals, particularly Onesicritus.

The fact of Nearchus' close and early connection with Alexander is clear. He belonged to the select group of Alexander's friends exiled after the Pixodarus affair,[15] and he was one of the first of that group to receive his reward and his chance to prove himself, when he was put in charge of a greatly enlarged Lycia as his satrapy.[16] We next find him, unaccountably, at Bactra-Zariaspa. There the king spent part of a winter and dealt with various administrative matters, in ways unfortunately not clear from our sources. He was met there by various satraps and commanders, among them Nearchus, who brought him a force of Greek mercenaries, we do not know from where.[17] After this he again disappears from historical record for about two years. We do not know either the reason for his recall from Lycia or the way or ways (if any) in which Alexander employed him after that recall. His satrapy seems to have been joined to Antigonus' Phrygia, and it has even been argued that the need for a separate Phrygian province

twenty-four days in a fortified camp a few days later). For the involutions and complexities of attempts to acquit Nearchus of this startling tale, cf. Lehmann-Haupt, pp. 133f. (with references). Pearson rightly stresses the imperfects and iterative optatives in the account as we have it in Arrian – claiming far more than a single experience. There is no reason to think that Arrian himself consistently introduced this element. That Nearchus thought he had seen no shadow at noon may just possibly be believed. *Pace* Pearson, it does not imply that he claimed to have crossed the equator. Shadows are hard to see within several degrees of the sun. What arouses suspicion, of course, is the time of year: since we appear to be dealing with a time about October at the very earliest, he would have had to be some distance south of the equator if there were really no shadows at noon.

15. See n. 3 above.

16. A 3. 6. 6. The term 'satrapy' may be an anticipation of later usage, but is in any case convenient.

17. A 4. 7. 1–2. Arrian is at his worst and vaguest at this kind of report. Asander, son of Philotas, who brought Alexander some Greek mercenaries at the same time, had probably commanded all the mercenaries at the time of the invasion (D 17. 4, with Berve's note under no. 138), had then become the first satrap of Lydia after its conquest (A 1. 17. 7), and is next heard of (whether still in that capacity we are not told) taking part in the capture of Halicarnassus (A 2. 5. 7).

disappeared with the dissolution of the Persian fleet.[18] Yet it remains puzzling that Antigonus, whose task in his own province was by no means an easy one, should have been burdened with an area known throughout antiquity for its warlike mountain tribes: one must suspect that Nearchus had not proved up to expectation in his arduous assignment.[19] If he got another command – a question we cannot answer – it was at any rate not a major one: had he played an important part in Alexander's vicinity, as he does just before the king's death, we could not have failed to hear. For an ex-satrap it must in any case have been demotion. Nothing prepares us for the later appearance of Nearchus in command of a fleet.

In fact, the next occasion on which we meet him, in Assacenia, is one where he commands land forces on reconnaissance. We are suddenly informed that Nearchus and Antiochus, chiliarchs of the hypaspists, were entrusted with this mission, the latter taking three regiments of hypaspists, the former the Agrianes and the light-armed.[20] Whether Nearchus at the time really held this lowly officer's rank – Antiochus is otherwise quite unknown – must remain somewhat doubtful. It would be a unique appointment for a man of Greek birth; and it must be noted that on the actual occasion he does not, like his colleague, command hypaspists or any other Macedonian troops. Nor do we ever, during the rest of his service under Alexander, find him doing so. The fact that he takes temporary charge of the Agrianes – one of Alexander's favorite units[21] – would not of itself mark him out as more than one of the *hetairoi*, available for temporary commands whenever Alexander required them.[22] It must be suggested (though it cannot

18. Wirth, pp. 620f.

19. On Antigonus see Berve, no. 87; Wirth, p. 621, n. 49. Wirth's conjecture that Nearchus had already settled all the tribes by force or conciliation during his short tenure seems over-optimistic. The fact (cited in support) that we do not hear anything about them in the following years can be amply paralleled all over Alexander's empire and is entirely due to the quality and interests of our sources. Where we do hear of events remote from Alexander's person and not requiring his intervention, it is not usually in the Alexander tradition at all. That Nearchus' recall – to no occupation known to us – should be understood as a mark of honour and a sign of his success in his post (thus Wirth) would need evidence to make it credible.

20. A 4. 30. 6.

21. Rightly noted by Wirth (p. 616) as perhaps a point in Nearchus' favor.

22. See Berve, *Das Alexanderreich*, vol. 1, p. 34.

be proved) that Arrian, unsatisfactory as so often, has misunderstood his source, and that the description he applies to both commanders rightly belonged only to the second, Antiochus, who is found actually commanding hypaspists on this occasion.[23]

Whatever he had been doing since his recall from Lycia, nothing (as we noted) prepares us for the very next occasion on which we hear about him: his appointment to command the fleet that was to sail down to the Indus and then to the sea.[24] There is no good reason to think that the plan of sailing down to the sea in ships was ever thought of before Alexander was forced by his men to turn back at the Hyphasis: not a mention of it in the better sources, nor – in the light of Alexander's attested and incompatible desire to penetrate much further east – the slightest historical plausibility.[25] Diodorus (17. 89. 4f.) and Curtius (9. 1. 3) ascribe to him both a desire to conquer all of India and a plan to sail down the Indus to the Ocean, and they claim this as his motive for allegedly building a fleet on the Hydaspes after his victory over Porus. Strabo (15. 1. 29) mentions the building of a Hydaspes fleet without specifying the time, but makes it clear that it took place 'near the cities he had founded (ἐκτισμέναις ὑπ' αὐτοῦ) on either side of the river'. Thus Strabo puts the building at a time when the cities had already been founded, i.e. after Alexander's return to the Hydaspes from the Hyphasis, just where Arrian also reports it, and where

23. Wirth (*ibid.*) notes difficulties in the passage, but makes no positive suggestion. W. W. Tarn's assertion (*Alexander the Great* (Cambridge 1948), vol. II, p. 150) that Nearchus was holding 'an interim command' of a chiliarchy only explains *ignotum per ignotius* and leaves confusion worse confounded.

24. A 6. 2. 3; *Ind.* 18. 10. (Also as a trierarch: *Ind.* 18. 4.)

25. Wirth (p. 629, n. 89), improving on the 'Vulgate' sources, regards the plan as a fully formed 'bereits bei Betreten Indiens', on the strength of 4. 30. 9 and 5. 35, which show that Alexander gave orders to build a bridge and some boats as he approached the Indus. Indeed, he regards this supposed plan as showing 'die Zielsetzung von Alexanders Indienpolitik' (p. 630). But in fact these small boats (only two thirty-oared boats got there) are in both passages closely connected with the bridge and were clearly meant to speed the crossing of a major river, by a large force and its supply train. Arrian suggests (plausibly enough, in view of parallel instances) that the bridge itself was a bridge of boats; though he found no explicit evidence (5. 7). In any case, these little boats have nothing to do with the later Hydaspes fleet. To explain the later decision to start his voyage on the Hydaspes, Wirth conjectures that the Hydaspes in the end proved more favorable for such a plan 'schon wegen vorhandener Anlagen'. But of those there appears to be no trace in the sources, any more than of any change of plan, or indeed of any earlier plan for sailing down to the sea.

alone it makes historical sense. The source, in both cases, may be Aristobulus, and since both the attestation and the plausibility are superior to the other version, this one ought to be believed. The variant in Curtius and Diodorus may be due to mere confusion in their source, but also possibly to a desire (which is clear in Curtius, but may, of course, be his own contribution) to illustrate the boundless ambition that Alexander had by this time developed. In any case, it does not belong to history.

It follows that one cannot logically expect Alexander to have started training Nearchus for his future naval responsibilities before the thought of those responsibilities had itself entered his mind.[26] We are compelled to assume that that decision was almost as sudden as it appears in our sources. The reasons for it cannot be known. But as we have seen, there is no sign of Nearchus' having distinguished himself in his military assignments up to this point. This new task was largely an organizing assignment, requiring no fighting ability: the fighting was to be done by Alexander himself and a few trusted Macedonian commanders, with the land forces. As regards knowledge of ships, the Cretan may be presumed to have had some early connection with ships. Perhaps Alexander wanted to give an old friend, of whose loyalty there was no doubt, but for whom no niche had so far been found, a chance in another sphere.

In any case, one must not exaggerate the responsibilities *ex post facto* – nor the success. Alexander was never far away and kept tight control, and his personal intervention was necessary to salvage what he could after a far from brilliant performance (for which the commander of the fleet must surely bear the blame) at the junction of the Hydaspes and the Acesines.[27] Alexander now took good care to arrange that the next likely trouble-spot – the junction of the Acesines and the Hydraotes – should not be nego-

---

26. Wirth (p. 631) suggests that the command of the Agrianes may be a preparation for the naval command: 'stellten Leichtbewaffnete doch die zu Landungsunternehmen eingesetzte Besatzung seines Flottenverbandes dar'. Despite the reference to *Ind.* 24. 4f. (where Nearchus selects light-armed men to swim ashore and mount an attack), this seems far-fetched. Besides, the theory falls together with that of Alexander's long-range plan for sailing down the Indus, which is its prerequisite and for which there is no acceptable evidence to be seen (cf. last note).

27. A 6. 4–5. The theme is variously embroidered in the 'Vulgate' sources.

tiated until he was himself present to take command (and, we may add, though no one bothers to mention it, until his own pilot Onesicritus could take charge of the actual navigation).[28] While Alexander was recovering from his dangerous wound, we duly find the fleet and the army waiting at the junction,[29] which they passed only when he was fit to take personal charge.[30] It is clear that Nearchus had again failed to distinguish himself, and that Alexander was aware of it. His organizing ability may have been irreproachable, but his actual navigational control had been less successful; while military action had – perhaps fortunately – not been needed.

This must be borne in mind when we next consider the famous scene in which Nearchus describes how he suggested himself as commander for the voyage of exploration along the southern coast. It is, of course, this story of his which has contributed much to the common view of his naive loyalty.[31] That the king was by now hoping such an expedition would prove possible may be accepted; also that Nearchus, after his command of the Indus fleet, was the obvious candidate. But that is not all.

It must first be noted that there is a chronological puzzle regarding this conversation, which might seem to throw immediate doubt

28. A 6. 5. 5–7. Note ἐνταῦθα δὴ (at the junction) τούς τε φθάνοντας ὑπομένειν ἐκέλευσεν ἔστ' ἂν ἥκῃ αὐτός (Onesicritus: *Ind.* 18. 9.).

29. A 6. 13. 1.

30. A 6. 14. 4. Alexander decided to start his own journey on the Hydraotes and to sail down the Hydraotes into the Acesines himself, no doubt to test the junction with his own ship and steersman before the fleet passed through. (The fleet was on the Acesines, which it had entered at that ill-fated junction with the Hydaspes.) The fact that he did not simply take his place at the head of the fleet on the Acesines shows his careful attention to the problem of navigating major river junctions, which had now been discovered.

31. *Ind.* 20. See, e.g., Berve, p. 270: 'In seiner männlich-einfachen Art hat N. selbst die Szene dieser Ernennung in ihren Einzelheiten prachtvoll dargestellt.' Cf. Lehmann-Haupt, p. 106: 'In schlichter, aber um so lebendigerer und eindrucksvollerer Art...' Wirth (p. 632) is rightly more critical, recognizing Nearchus' self-assertion. But this is to some extent merely the necessary consequence of his view that Alexander had been grooming Nearchus for this command over a long time (see notes 25 and 26 above), so that the appointment was in fact a prearranged certainty. His criticism of Nearchus is here, therefore, based on false premises. I cannot find any evidence for his statement (*ibid.*) that Nearchus was the most important man in the army during the second half of 326 and until autumn 325 – a time during much of which we hear nothing about him, while during the rest he merely has a routine post with the fleet, and the really important events are taking place elsewhere.

on Nearchus' veracity. Arrian's summary of Nearchus in the *Indica* (20. 1) starts at this point and gives no precise chronological setting. At the end of his account, one of the reasons Nearchus gives for the troops' confidence over the outcome of the expedition is that Alexander had explored the mouths of the Indus and had offered sacrifice to Poseidon and to other gods. This ought to mean that the appointment came after the king's return from that expedition. In *Anabasis* 6. 18f. the exploration of the Indus mouths is told in great detail, and in 19. 5 we hear that Alexander sacrificed to Poseidon on behalf of the safety of the expedition which he was proposing (ὅντινα ἐπενόει) to send under Nearchus. This account (not from Nearchus) ties the sacrifice to the proposed expedition under Nearchus, which the account in the *Indica* does not do, and implies that the appointment had already been made, i.e. it puts the appointment (on a reasonable interpretation) before the exploration of the Indus mouths and appears to contradict Nearchus. And though it must be noted that the relative clause giving Nearchus' name is an addition by Arrian himself (as is clear from the imperfect), and that its subject-matter may not have come from the source, the basic facts as recorded in this fuller account should be accepted. The expedition was not officially constituted – and thus sacrifices on its behalf were impossible – until Nearchus had been appointed to command it; and though the abbreviated account in the *Indica* does not actually say so, it should be understood that the sacrifices there referred to were indeed those on behalf of the expedition, which Nearchus himself must also have put after his own appointment. The appointment therefore preceded the voyage to the mouths of the Indus, and both sources must have agreed on this. It is perhaps only the nature of Arrian's brief summary in the *Indica* that creates an appearance of contradiction. Nearchus himself must have made the distinction in time between the two reasons for the men's confidence much clearer: first, immediately after his appointment, the fact of the appointment itself; then, after Alexander's exploration of the mouths of the Indus, his sacrifices there, on behalf of the expedition. Here, at any rate, there is no good reason to doubt Nearchus, or, for that matter, to accuse the source of the account in the *Anabasis* of error.

But the part of the dialogue between Alexander and Nearchus, in which the king makes a candid survey of various (unnamed) commanders who might be considered for the appointment, needs further scrutiny. With the possible exception of the steersman of his own ship, no other commander could surely have been seriously considered for the task, since none of them had anything like the requisite experience. Indeed, in part the passage must be read as depreciation of Onesicritus, whose name would at once come to mind. That he was considered and rejected may well be believed. It is clear that Alexander had confidence in him as a navigator: he must have saved the remnants of the fleet after its narrow escape from disaster, and he must have helped to prevent the recurrence of such a disaster, especially (as we saw) at the next river junction. But his undoubted merits were those of a technician: he had, as far as we know, no experience of high command or major organization, and a task such as the expedition along the coast would be beyond any merits he had shown. What is more interesting, perhaps, is how Nearchus cleverly uses his account of the conversation to imply rejection, on various specified grounds, of numerous other leaders, who must have been of some eminence. Yet a conversation such as he describes – Alexander mentions various leaders and, one by one, charges them with lack of loyalty or lack of courage! – is surely remote from any probability. Who, after all, *were* all these great men whom Alexander would consider for this major responsibility, but whom he found lacking in one of these essential qualities? And would he really confide his thoughts of that nature to Nearchus? Finally (as we know) the solution appears: Nearchus offers his own services, and Alexander, after long hesitation because he does not want to expose one of his own friends to such dangers, at last accepts the offer and appoints Nearchus to the command of the fleet. Again, obviously there is a kernel of truth. But we must note the elaboration. Had none of the numerous leaders previously mentioned and rejected as unsuitable been friends of Alexander's? It is surely as strange that the supposed confidential discussion should have included only men *not* among his friends as we found the idea of the discussion as a whole, and the grounds allegedly given for their rejection.

What Alexander's real worry was is in fact casually mentioned by Nearchus a little earlier: he was afraid of losing the whole expedition – not so much because of the large loss of human life involved, although Nearchus seems to imply this too in a rhetorical repetition of this idea on the occasion of his pathetic reunion with the king,[32] as for the more characteristic reason that the effect of his victories would be wiped out by such a major disaster (κηλὶς αὕτη τοῖς ἔργοισιν αὐτοῦ τοῖσι μεγάλοισι ἐπιγενομένη τὴν πᾶσαν εὐτυχίην αὐτῷ ἀφανίσῃ). Alexander always thought heroically. It is very likely that, when speaking to Nearchus about his own candidacy, Alexander politely disguised his fear and his reason for hesitation. But that the real reason was doubt of Nearchus' adequacy for such a major operation is to some extent implied even in the tactful wrapping of fear over his personal safety, and must have been as obvious to Nearchus – who cannot have been unaware of the lack of brilliant success in his career up to that point – as it seems to us. He tells us that it took much insistence on his part to persuade Alexander to accept his offer and to take the risk, for the sake of his great idea. That will be true enough, even though the nature of the risk is somewhat disguised.

To complete the tale, his status as the one beloved friend has to be stressed once more at the end: the fleet took courage at the appointment, chiefly because the men thought that Alexander would never have exposed his friend Nearchus to manifest danger (κίνδυνον καταφανέα) – as he had, of course, so many times exposed men like Craterus and Perdiccas, and even his dearest friend Hephaestion, as unhesitatingly as he exposed himself. With skilful rewriting, Nearchus has changed an incident which may even have been somewhat embarrassing to him – Alexander's hesitation in accepting his services – into a resounding declaration of Alexander's unique attachment to him, and confidence in him, above all the other great men close to the king; and he has casually conveyed the impression that this special relationship in which he stood to the king was universally known throughout the army. Nothing in any other source we have tends to support the story.

Nearchus' famous account of his appointment emerges as a typical piece of 'memoirs' writing: true facts are used as a framework for apologia and self-glorification. With our suspicions aroused, we are next led to investigate the actual position to which he was appointed and the authority he was given. It will be necessary to approach the problem with an open mind.

32. *Ind.* 20. 2; cf. 35, especially s. 8.

The chief point here is the position of Onesicritus and his relations with Nearchus. T. S. Brown has amply shown that the traditional view that Nearchus' account was in part written to contradict that of Onesicritus is correct, but that this is not sufficient reason for inevitably preferring it. The actual position of Onesicritus does not by any means emerge clearly from our sources.[33] That he was the steersman of Alexander's ship on the voyage to, and on, the Indus may be regarded as certain: it is reported in the *Indica*, i.e. admitted by Nearchus himself. We have seen that he probably served in that capacity with some distinction, and it is clear that Alexander attached him to the new expedition for that reason, i.e. in part precisely to supply the technical skill in which Nearchus had not excelled. His exact status in that fleet is, however, somewhat debated. Arrian (6. 2. 3), though he never explicitly tells us Onesicritus' rank on that voyage, implies the same rank as before: he charges him with having called himself ναύαρχος when in fact he was only a steersman;[34] and although that remark is connected with his appointment to the king's ship in the Indus fleet, he again describes him as steersman in *Anabasis* 7. 10. 9, an account taken from Nearchus and describing a difference between the two during the *paraplous*. Finally, he again refers to him as 'steersman of the king's ship' on the occasion of his decoration at Susa.

The rest of our evidence is radically different, and concordant. Plutarch and Strabo both call Onesicritus ἀρχικυβερνήτης, and Plutarch further defines this as ἄρχοντα τῶν κυβερνητῶν, which at least shows how he understood the word. Pliny, who uses Onesicritus' work extensively (whether or not he knew it at first hand) in the *Natural History*, calls him *dux* (2. 185) and, more explicitly, *classis praefectus* (6. 81) – clearly the title ναύαρχος quoted by Arrian as usurped by him. The latter may be discarded as (at least) *suggestio falsi* on Onesicritus' part, as is generally

33. The evidence is collected by F. Jacoby, *Die Fragmente der griechischen Historiker*, no. 134, pp. 723–5, where the passages I cite will be found.

34. Oddly enough Suidas picked up that remark and referred it to Nearchus (*ibid*. 133 T 1). It should be noted that the word ναύαρχος, at least in Hellenistic Greek, does not necessarily mean 'commander of a fleet'. See, e.g., Polyb. 1. 21. 4, where it seems to refer to commanders of individual ships and is certainly *contrasted* with the commander-in-chief. Onesicritus probably chose it precisely because it was a vague word, claiming much without being strictly a lie.

recognized. What rank Nearchus assigned to his enemy, we cannot
tell with certainty. If Arrian's references cited above are taken
directly from Nearchus, then he merely described him as 'steersman'. If, as is at least equally possible, Arrian added the rank out
of his own recollection, then Nearchus may have omitted all
reference to his rank, preferring this to recording his promotion.[35]
For there cannot be any real doubt that his title was
ἀρχικυβερνήτης. Strabo's testimony is decisive. For Strabo, though
he read and used both Nearchus and Onesicritus, obviously did not
find this title in either of them, since one claimed more, the other
either less or nothing. Strabo's source, therefore, must be his other
major Alexander source, Aristobulus; and Aristobulus had no axe
to grind and can hardly have got it wrong.

    What an ἀρχικυβερνήτης did and how much authority he had is
hard to disengage on our very meagre evidence. Plutarch's explanation is probably no more than his own interpretation, which
may or may not be correct. Modern assessments appear to have
been similarly *a priori* and conjectural; yet some are more reasonable than others. Beloch regarded Onesicritus as 'den seemänni-
schen Leiter' of the expedition, without committing himself on his
precise relationship to the authority of Nearchus; Berve accepted
the interpretation and thought that Onesicritus had the nautical
and Nearchus the strategic command.[36] Jacoby thundered against
this view:[37] 'Berve's annahme...nach Beloch...ist – von ihrer
inneren unglaublichkeit abgesehen – ein beim stande der über-
lieferung unzulässiges kompromiß.' (He does not further define
what he finds 'internally incredible', or which part of the view he
objects to.) As for the title given by Strabo and Plutarch, he
describes it as 'kein offizieller titel'. In fact, although information
on the title is very scarce in our literary sources, we know enough

35. In view of Arrian's description of him at Susa in terms of his earlier
service on the Indus (7. 5. 6: 'steersman of the king's ship'), it is quite likely
that he in fact did not find any precise attribution of rank in Nearchus, for the
period of the *paraplous*.
    36. K. J. Beloch, *Griechische Geschichte*[2], III. 2, p. 36; Berve, p. 289.
    37. *F. gr. Hist.* III D, pp. 469f. Brown (pp. 8f.) is vague and unsatisfactory,
rejecting Berve, but coming to no real conclusion himself. J. R. Hamilton,
Plutarch, Alexander. A Commentary (Oxford 1969), p. 183, hesitantly accepts the
attested title ('may have been'), but has no discussion on the duties and rank
of that officer.

to be quite sure that there *was* such an official title. The only literary reference to the office, apart from those concerning Onesicritus, appears to be that in Diodorus 20. 50. 4 to a Pleistias of Cos, who, ἀρχικυβερνήτης ὢν τοῦ σύμπαντος στόλου, shared command of Demetrius' right wing in the battle of Salamis in 306 B.C.[38] We may deduce from that passage (which must be taken as coming from Hieronymus of Cardia) both that the officer concerned was of reasonably high rank and that he did not need to exercise his normal functions (which are clearly irreconcilable with a command of the sort he was given) during an actual naval battle, so that he was available for a limited tactical command in it. This not only refutes Jacoby, but adds strong support to a view such as Beloch's, already probable on linguistic grounds – provided one defines the meaning a little more closely: the ἀρχικυβερνήτης must be the officer in charge of navigation for the whole fleet, just as the κυβερνήτης was for the individual ship. This would both agree with the etymology of the word and fully explain the Diodorus passage. It must be presumed that the office as such was quite common, at least in Hellenistic fleets, even though we do not hear much of it; and the reason for the silence is precisely that the officer as such had no duties in battle, which is what chiefly interests our sources. The office clearly shows Alexander's confidence in the navigational skill of the man who had served as his own steersman.

Having clarified this, we can also be somewhat clearer about the official relationship between Nearchus and Onesicritus. There can be no question of equality, as Berve tried to make out and Beloch possibly believed. Nearchus was in overall command ('strategic' command – to that extent Berve's formulation is acceptable), Onesicritus in charge of navigation. I.e., it would be Nearchus' job to decide where the expedition was going and Onesicritus' to see that it got there. This helps to explain the conflict between the two men that is reported to us and to put it in its proper light (32. 9f.). When the fleet sighted the cape called Maceta (apparently some part of the Oman peninsula), Onesicritus proposed to set a

---

38. I found the reference in Stephanus' *Thesaurus*. Strangely enough, it is not in LSJ nor in Barber's *Supplement*. How many other literary references may have been missed is therefore impossible to say. (LSJ gives a reference to a papyrus of the fifth century A.D., not relevant here.)

course for it as their next stage (ἐπέχοντας ἐπ' αὐτὴν πλώειν ἐκέλευεν), as he had a right to do as a matter of routine. Nearchus then overrode the order, saying that this was not a mere matter of navigation, but a decision of principle concerning the overall purpose of the expedition, and he rebuked Onesicritus rather sharply for having regarded it as a routine matter. (He goes on to say, in his own version, that as a purely routine decision it was also not a very good one.) What was no doubt a legitimate difference of opinion, bound to arise at times, is reported by Nearchus in such a way as to make his enemy appear a naive fool (νήπιον). When Nearchus next tells us that his decision was accepted, this is no reason to think (as Berve did) that that implies equality between the two men. First, the word ἐνίκα may not be Nearchus' own, but Arrian's, especially as Arrian here at once goes on to give what is explicitly his own view.[39] What word Nearchus used we have no means of telling.[40] Secondly, although Nearchus' authority was superior, the 'consent of the governed' was worth obtaining, as is clear on many occasions in Greek history: a man like the Macedonian Archias, although he never appears as Nearchus' hierarchic equal, could not be ignored – especially if, as might always happen, things went wrong and one needed justification. The persistent need to obtain consent is often misunderstood, and this has led to some strange misconceptions about the concept of *hegemonia* or chief command in Greek forces.

It follows that Nearchus, in this case, was quite right to describe himself as superior to Onesicritus; one can blame him only for failing to give Onesicritus his due – and of that we shall have more to say in another connection. We must now look at the great story of the meeting of Alexander and Nearchus in Carmania.

As we have it in the *Indica*, it deserves all the praise that has been showered upon it as literature. As romantic and pathetic writing, it is superb. The crews weeping with joy at hearing Greek spoken again; the failure of the search party to recognize those they had

---

39. ταῦτα ἐνίκα, καί μοι δοκέει... For students of Arrian's method it is interesting to note that his assertion of independent and concurrent judgment is refuted by A 7. 20. 10, which shows that he is merely repeating (in parts verbatim) the substance of what Nearchus had written. (The words used at 7. 20. 9 are also indecisive.)

40. The word νικᾶν is often used in this way in Herodotus; e.g. 8. 9 (Artemisium – where, of course, the Greeks also had a commander-in-chief).

been sent to search for, on account of the changes that hardship
and suffering had wrought in their appearance; Alexander's
weeping over the fate of his fleet under the strange misapprehen-
sion that it had been lost, and the sudden change to rejoicing as he
is informed of the truth; finally the *paradoxon* of the man (a
hyparchos in our story, to increase the pathos) who rushes to bring
good news in hopes of a reward, only to be put in prison[41] – all
these incidents, most of them modeled on much literary precedent,
show great skill at literary embroidery. To what extent they are
true is another question, in most cases unanswerable. But the
paradoxon, at least, is hard to believe as it stands: the tale
of the poor man, previously arrested, suddenly seeing Nearchus
and falling at his feet to plead for his intervention, then
securing his freedom through that intervention as if he were
really a criminal to be pardoned – that tale raises all sorts of
questions in the mind of one misguided enough to weigh its
claims to acceptance as fact.

The touches of conventional pathetic fiction are obvious, and
forgivable, just like the *mirabilia* included for the delectation of the
reader. The story of the hardships on the way back to the coast –
another *paradoxon*, since we are specifically told Alexander had
expected the way to be easy – perhaps has a similar claim to our
toleration; the natives, of whom we had heard no word when
Nearchus, with six or seven companions, was making his way up
through unknown country in search of the king, are suddenly
discovered in possession of all the fortified posts in Carmania and
attack Nearchus and his escort two or three times a day, until they
at last fight their way through to the coast. The man of sorrows
must not have an easy passage even at this stage.[42] As Pearson saw
(but few others have seen it), we must not take this narrative as
simple and unadorned fact. Curtius and Plutarch report the

41. *Ind.* 33. 5; 34. 6–12; 35. 2–5; 34. 1–5 with 36. 1–2.
42. τῷ δὲ οὐδὲ τὰ τῆς ὁδοῦ τῆς ἐπὶ θάλασσαν ἔξω πόνου ἐγένετο (36. 8).
The events surrounding the execution of Astaspes, the satrap of Carmania,
whose death provides a gruesome and effective climax to Alexander's Bacchic
rout and thereby to Curtius' ninth book (C 9. 10. 21; cf. 29), and the appointment of Tlepolemus to the satrapy cannot be disentangled with sufficient
certainty to provide a check on Nearchus. If Arrian is right, Nearchus is
mistaken in his report of the change of governor in Carmania; and the execution of Astaspes is not mentioned by any other source.

meeting with Alexander without any pathetic coloring.[43] Similarly, whereas Nearchus himself rather tediously repeats the scene of his first appointment when it comes to the question of continuing his journey (Alexander does not want to expose him to further danger, but Nearchus again insists until he gains permission), Curtius simply reports that the king, eager to collect more knowledge, ordered Nearchus to resume the *paraplous* as far as the mouth of the Euphrates (as indeed we find him doing). Diodorus, who reports the same order, adds some drama to the meeting (as we shall see); but he sets the scene at the coastal city of 'Salmous' and omits the whole story of the march up country in search of Alexander and the march back to the coast. The question is: is he perhaps right? Is the whole story of that painful journey perhaps pure fiction, as some of the details so obviously are? The question must at least be asked and an answer sought.

Unfortunately the other sources do not help, as they report the meeting in the simplest terms and do not provide a setting. It is usual to reject Diodorus without investigation, and at most to puzzle over how his error could have arisen.[44] This attitude is perhaps not unreasonable, given Diodorus' record; but it is better to shed all prejudice and to approach the problem on its own terms.

According to Arrian, citing Aristobulus (and not Nearchus) in *Anabasis* 6. 28. 3, Alexander in Carmania brought thanks-offerings and held ἀγῶνα μουσικόν τε καὶ γυμνικόν to celebrate both the conquest of India and the escape of the army from the Gedrosian desert – events no doubt all the more calling for celebration since each had been only a very limited success. In this account Nearchus receives no mention. In Diodorus we hear of the Bacchic revel after the escape from the desert, then – after an inserted passage on the punishment of the wicked satraps – we are told that Alexander celebrated σκηνικοὺς ἀγῶνας at Salmous: he was just engaged upon this, when a fleet sailed into the harbor and Nearchus and his officers came into the theater, where they received a splendid welcome from the whole army present at the games. This account is very different from Nearchus' own (*Indica* 36. 3): here, after

43. C 10. 1. 10; P 68. 1.
44. Thus, e.g., C. B. Welles in his Loeb edition of Diodorus vol. 8, p. 429, n. 2 and p. 431, n. 3.

Nearchus' arrival, Alexander sacrifices to various gods in gratitude for the safety of Nearchus and the fleet, and then holds ἀγῶνα γυμνικόν τε καὶ μουσικόν, as well as a πομπή, in which Nearchus joins him ἐν πρώτοισιν.

Let us start with Aristobulus. Once more there is no reason to think that he had any axe to grind, any animosity against Nearchus. Indeed, dubious apologist though he is where the king is concerned, he surely deserves all the credit that Arrian attaches to him in a case such as this. Nor can we easily accept *another* round of games, in Carmania, on behalf of Nearchus and his fleet, just after those on behalf of the main army. (Sacrifices might be duplicated, and are not worth arguing about.) We are forced to reject Nearchus' account and explanation of these celebrations in favor of Aristobulus'.

Next, the Bacchic rout. Both in Curtius and in Diodorus it precedes the arrival of Nearchus, and in Diodorus (Curtius does not mention them) the games. Similarly in Plutarch: the Bacchic rout is followed by games (67) – ἀγῶνες χορῶν happen to be specified, as a background to the story of Bagoas' victory with a chorus and Alexander's congratulatory kiss, but we must surely assume general ἀγῶνες μουσικοί (to use the term common to Aristobulus and Nearchus), of which Diodorus' σκηνικοί would also be part. In Plutarch, Nearchus again arrives after the account of the games. It is noteworthy that the details in Curtius, Diodorus and Plutarch are here so different that they cannot be presumed to derive from the same immediate source. Curtius connects the Bacchic procession with the death of Astaspes, not mentioned by any other surviving source; he omits the games, even though on an earlier occasion he features the infamous Bagoas.[45] He reports Nearchus' arrival a little later. Diodorus, as we saw, has both the procession and the games (σκηνικοί), and during the latter Nearchus arrives; he does not mention Bagoas. Plutarch, finally, has the procession, immediately followed by the games (choral games) with the Bagoas story, and then Nearchus' arrival.

From these sources, so different in detail, a common outline of events emerges: first a procession (which, with literary exaggeration, has become the Bacchic revel), then the games, then

---

45. See E. Badian, *CQ* 52 = N.S. 8 (1958), 150f.

Nearchus' arrival. The procession and the games (preceded no doubt by the sacrifices which we find in Aristobulus and in which the other sources were simply not interested) celebrate events concerning the main army, not Nearchus and the fleet. It is only Diodorus who gives any connection between any of those events and Nearchus, and that is an accidental one: Nearchus arrives in the middle of the games. Let us note that he does not depend on a source biased against Nearchus: quite the contrary. For he stresses the joy of the whole army at the arrival of the fleet. Should we accept the fortunate coincidence? Perhaps we should, for the silence of the other sources on this point is, at any rate, no argument against: Curtius was not interested in the games at all, while Plutarch tells Nearchus' arrival after the games, but may well have chosen not to associate them precisely because he wanted to make the Bagoas story the climax of the games, for reasons of character-painting. In other words, they simply did not choose to tell us what, for their various purposes, did not particularly interest them. And we have already had occasion to notice that, apart from Nearchus himself, the sources do not show very great interest in the adventures of the fleet. Of course, we can always take refuge in that *Quellenforscher*'s phantom, the original source (which we could call Cleitarchus), from which the immediate sources (Curtius, Diodorus and Plutarch) are descended by a series of intermediate selections and embroideries and which simply made up the whole story. But it is surely more reasonable to derive the similarity in structure from a common background of *fact* (by whomever reported).

And here we may again consider Aristobulus, who mentions games, but neither the Bacchic revel nor (at least in connection with the games) Nearchus. That he does not mention the Bacchic rout is not surprising, in one who is known as an apologist.[46] For that matter, he does not mention the Bagoas story, but that is no reason for disbelieving it.[47] But he at least authenticates the games as such, and that lends credibility to the accounts in the other sources.

46. He was regarded even in antiquity as a typical *kolax* (see *F. gr. Hist.* 139 T 5), and the judgment can be confirmed. (See E. Badian, *CW* 65 (1971), 37ff.)

47. See the discussion in *CQ* 52 = N.S. 8 (1958) (cited n. 45 above).

In view of the overwhelming agreement among the other sources, we must conclude that Nearchus has simply annexed to himself the games which Alexander celebrated – without any obvious worry about the fate of the fleet, let us observe – in connection with the army. (He may also have annexed the sacrifices reported by Aristobulus.) If we believe Diodorus' version – and we have seen that this is at least legitimate – his arrival in the midst of that celebration must have given him the idea: it would not look too good in his story to have Alexander (supposedly frantic over the fate of his best friend and the fleet) celebrating games on behalf of the army just as that friend at last safely arrived – and to have no equivalent celebration for that arrival. A small shift in chronology – only a day or two – and a little reinterpretation could produce the desired effect. As for the Bacchic procession: since it had just preceded the games and must (even allowing for exaggeration) have been quite a colorful affair, he must surely have heard about it at once. We note that a slight shift in chronology would again improve upon the facts. Nearchus knows of a πομπή which no other source relates: this one comes *after* the games, and Nearchus himself is in it – ἐν πρώτοισιν, of course. The man who, as we have observed, had skilfully rewritten the account of his first appointment would not find it difficult.

So far, at least in outline, the conclusion seems firm enough. Diodorus' story has proved worth investigating. Shall we follow him the rest of the way and accept his setting on the coast, in the city of Salmous? Unfortunately we do not know where that city is: if we did, it would settle the question. But we must realize that, if we accept this setting, the consequences are even more serious: nothing less than that the whole of Nearchus' pathetic account of the march up country and down again is fiction. Of course, that is by no means impossible. We have seen enough of Nearchus' methods, and enough to doubt in that very account, to make it conceivable. Yet Diodorus, even where in general correct, is unfortunately quite capable of adding misunderstanding of his own and inserting it in a basically true story. The picture of the fleet sailing into the harbor, and the whole seaside setting, may conceivably be no more than his own elaboration of the fact that the officers of the fleet so dramatically arrived in the theater during the performance. Here we must simply keep an open mind, recognizing that we must choose between two sources that are, for different reasons, quite unreliable.[48]

Finally, the rewards after the completion of the voyage. Once more we find Nearchus twisting the facts to put himself in the centre of the stage and to deny others – and in particular his enemy Onesicritus – their deserts. In the *Anabasis* Arrian tells us that at Susa both Nearchus and Onesicritus received gold crowns in the grand prizegiving;[49] as did several others, all distinguished men, including all the Bodyguards. This account, independent of Nearchus, no doubt comes from Ptolemy, who can hardly have omitted the scene. There is no reason to doubt any part of it. Nearchus' account, as we have it in the *Indica*, however, is very different. There (42. 5f.) the fleet sails 150 stadia up the Pasitigris (Karun) and the men spend some time in celebration, while waiting for Alexander and the army to arrive. After they hear precise details of his route, they sail further up the river (no distance is given) and meet him at the bridge when he is about to take the army across to Susa. This must be near Ahwaz, on the old route which Alexander had taken, in an easterly direction, in 331: it would certainly not be much higher up (i.e. nearer Susa), since he would then have had to cross the Dez as well, and we have no record of his doing so (quite apart from the fact that it would be an unnecessary complication). There, according to Nearchus, Alexander again sacrificed and held games in gratitude for the safe arrival of the fleet (no other source mentions games or a celebration at this stage), and Nearchus himself was fêted by the whole army. There also (ἔνθα καί), we are explicitly told, Nearchus and Leonnatus received gold crowns, Nearchus for the *paraplous*, Leonnatus for the victory over the Oreitae, which (we must remember) had greatly helped the fleet.[50]

Here again we must regretfully doubt the whole celebration. Forewarned by what we found in connection with the previous occasion, we shall not find it difficult to recognize the method. The great victory celebration at Susa has been transformed into a

48. A 6. 28. 5 might tip the balance in Nearchus' favor, if we could be sure that Arrian is not here too drawing on Nearchus, to whom he refers by name straight after.

49. A 7. 5. 4f. Jacoby's attempt to deny Onesicritus his crown on *a priori* grounds is rightly rejected by scholars (see, e.g., Pearson, p. 84).

50. *Ind.* 23. 4f.

special local celebration near Ahwaz. The crowns given to many prominent leaders for their various exploits have become awards to Nearchus and his friend Leonnatus, who had protected him and assured his passage. Most significant of all: even from the narrow point of view of the fleet and its concerns, we note the absence of any mention of the gold crown given to Onesicritus, for his part in assuring the success of that venture.

The fact of Nearchus' successful completion of his venture stands on record. So does his major reward: his marriage, at Susa, to a woman of royal Achaemenid blood, a daughter of one who had been Alexander's mistress.[51] This, for normal purposes, would sufficiently show Alexander's regard for him. His appointment to an important command in the planned Arabian expedition may be accepted as almost inevitable, even though the only reference we have is vague and unilluminating, in Arrian's worst manner:[52] the appointments are taken as already known, though neither Arrian nor any other surviving source reports them, and Alexander merely explains his plans to his officers, of whom Nearchus is one. We are not told that he was to be in charge; and though this is usually assumed in modern accounts, it is technically impossible, since Alexander himself intended to be there. Moreover, the account comes from the *Ephemerides*, which also report that Alexander, when already close to death, had parts of Nearchus' account of his expedition read to him.[53] It is probably that same source that reports the onset of the king's fatal illness after he had given a banquet for Nearchus.[54] The nature of the *Ephemerides* is by no means certain: what is clear is merely that they are not the basic and utterly trustworthy source they were once believed to be.[55] Whether they are gossip or forgery, the possibility that Nearchus – who was, of course, present at Babylon and was a friend of the Royal Chancellor Eumenes – had some hand in their compilation is not to be excluded; though, of course, here he could

51. On the relationship between Alexander and Barsine, I (like most scholars) see no reason to accept Tarn's arguments (last *Alexander the Great*, vol. 2, pp. 330f.) against its existence.

52. A 7. 25. 4, misrepresented as a positive report of his appointment to the command by Berve, Lehmann-Haupt and others.

53. P 76. 1f. (20 Daesius: he died on the 28th).

54. P 75. 4f.; cf. A 7. 24. 4 (Nearchus not named); 25. 1.

55. See *CW* 65 (1971), 50f.; A. B. Bosworth, *CQ* 65 = N.S. 21 (1971), 117ff.

not have things all his own way, and his prominence in the final
scenes has to be shared with others.[56]

There can be no doubt that Nearchus played an important part
in the last months of Alexander's life. Boyhood friendship had, after
some years of at least relative failure, been reinforced by success.
Nearchus' ambition was kindled and he must have hoped for a
future among the leaders of the new empire. Alexander's death
was a cruel blow to him. The lack of interest in his person and his
achievements, which we find in our tradition apart from the
influence of his own work, probably gives us a fair indication of the
view that was generally taken of him. While Eumenes, the only
other Greek of real prominence, had a central post that gave him
power and (inevitably) political allies, Nearchus was attached
solely to Alexander's person. His successes were marginal to the
interests of the Macedonian commanders, and he had no military
force of his own or (beyond that personal attachment to the king)
political leverage. With Alexander's death he had no prospects but
an immediate return to obscurity. There was one weapon he still
had – uncertain, but worth trying. At Susa, as we saw, he had
married a daughter of Barsine, and had thus become the son-in-
law of Alexander's mistress. When the barons and the army met
at Babylon, after the king's death, to consider the future, Nearchus
played his one card. Relying on loyalty to the dead king, he proposed that the son of Alexander and Barsine (whom Alexander had
apparently never recognized as a legitimate prince) should be
proclaimed king, since he was the only living offspring of Alexander: it was no use waiting for Roxana to give birth (whether to a
boy, no one could tell), and it was clear that the army was in fact
not willing to do so. Unfortunately, Nearchus' proposal, which
would have given him a truly dominating role at the new court,
was also obviously unacceptable. The army, reluctant even to wait

56. Eumenes: *F. gr. Hist.* 113 T 13*b*. The report that it was Nearchus who
passed the Chaldaeans' warning to Alexander not to enter Babylon on to the
king (P 73. 1; D 112, 3f.) suggests some interesting possibilities, unfortunately
beyond serious investigation. It could itself come from the *Ephemerides* (on any
interpretation of their nature), since the event concerns both the king and
Babylon. Whether or not it does, it may show a connection between Nearchus
and the Babylonian priests, which – in so far as the *Ephemerides* might be based
on a document compiled by them: see A. E. Samuel, *Historia* 14 (1965),
1f. – could help to account for his prominence in that account.

for the legitimate offspring of Alexander's marriage to an Oriental princess, was by no means willing to consider the succession of a semi-Oriental bastard. The nobles for their part, while happy enough (as became clear) to have a weak monarchy, could not admit a situation that would have left the central power *de facto* in the hands of a Greek. 'Nulli placebat oratio.'[57] It was Nearchus' last hope, his only bid for power. Henceforth he had to reconcile himself to subsiding into the subordinate position that befitted a Greek, in a world ruled by Macedonian barons with the support of Macedonian armies.[58]

It was thus that his frustrated ambition was transmuted into the retrospective cloudcuckooland of the writer of memoirs. His report on his travels, which he must have submitted to Alexander, made a convenient framework. He depicted himself as the one true friend of the king, loyal and in turn trusted, nearer and dearer to the king than all his Macedonians – the only man whose fate could move the king to Homeric tears or to Homeric celebration. His rejection by Alexander's heirs at Babylon thus stood out in all its shocking horror: by casting him out, they had betrayed the true heritage of Alexander. The king had been right, in that famous confidential conversation, to doubt either their courage or their loyalty. The most shocking thing of all, of course, was the betrayal by another Greek, a man whom Nearchus, in his moment of power, had unfortunately offended: Onesicritus had published his own account, and we may conjecture that Nearchus did not appear in it as he wished to see himself and as he hoped posterity would see him. Vindication and counter-attack became the keynotes of Nearchus' memoirs.

It is truly strange that this impassioned personal and political *Tendenzschrift*, the product of ambition frustrated by a combination of fate and personal inadequacy, has imposed itself on traditional Alexander scholarship as a 'schlichte Schilderung',[59]

57. C 10. 6. 10f.

58. Justin 13. 4. 14f. is the only source reporting that he received a satrapy (Lycia) in the first distribution at Babylon. This must be rejected as an error based on his first appointment under Alexander, as is generally recognized. Jacoby, *F. gr. Hist.* II D, p. 448, collects massive evidence disproving it (though he then inclines to accept it!). On Polyaen. 5. 35, sometimes used in support (thus Jacoby), see Lehmann-Haupt, p. 137.

59. Lehmann-Haupt, p. 116 (presumably taken from Capelle, *RE*, s.v. 'Nearchos', col. 2152: 'schlichte Darstellung'; cf. col. 2153).

in which the author completely obscures his own person;[60] as 'einfach, besonnen und glaubwürdig'.[61] In the light of this, it may, however, seem less strange to find historians no less ingenuously taken in by the self-advertised virtues of contemporary politicians.[62]

60. Capelle, *ibid.*: 'Es tritt aber der Autor und damit der Mensch N. ... durchaus hinter seinem Gegenstand zurück.'

61. Berve, p. 272.

62. It is my sad duty to dedicate this little study to the memory of a scholar who (I hope) would have been pleased to read it.

Myth and *archaeologia* in Italy and Sicily—Timaeus and his predecessors

LIONEL PEARSON

THUCYDIDES GIVES only a very brief account of early Sicilian history, so that we remain uncertain how accurate and well-founded his chronological details are and how much more he could have told us if he had wished to do so. Without any doubt he could have told some interesting things about Hiero and his contemporaries, if he had thought it relevant to his theme. But could he have added much to his summary account of the colonial settlements or given any substantial history of the development of these colonies in the seventh and sixth centuries? If he had made inquiries, in the Herodotean manner, in Syracuse or Gela or Acragas, or in Taras or Posidonia (it seems anachronistic to use the Latin names), would people have been able to provide him with the same generous measure of local history and myth and τὸ μυθῶδες that he could have collected in Thebes or Argos, Miletus or Samos? It might be easier to answer the question if we had some of the text of Antiochus of Syracuse or Hippys of Rhegium, or more substantial portions of the poetry of Stesichorus. But as things are, we can only wonder if Greeks in Italy and Sicily knew much more about their early history than we do.[1]

It has always been convenient to suppose that Thucydides had read the history of Antiochus.[2] But there is no indication that other

1. It is useless to pretend that we know much about it. 'Everyone in Magna Graecia before the reign of Hiero moves in a cloud of legend' (M. L. West, 'Stesichorus', *CQ* N.S. 21 (1971), 302).

2. For a good and careful discussion see A. W. Gomme, K. J. Dover and Antony Andrewes, *Historical Commentary to Thucydides*, vol. IV (Oxford 1970), pp. 198–210. Thucydides gives a chronological outline of colonial history without any supporting argument. That need not mean that he was unfamiliar with reasons for accepting the dates that he gives. It is possible that Antiochus calculated the various dates by using a generation count of thirty-five years, as is maintained by R. van Compernolle, *Étude de chronologie et d'historiographie siciliotes* (Brussels–Rome 1960). But it is hard for me to believe that the man who wrote the severe sentences of 1. 20 would have been content with that sort

students of history from the Greek mainland in the fifth and fourth centuries paid any attention to this writer, except for Ephorus, whose fragments reveal a concern for the history of the Greek West that seems not to have been shared by his contemporaries. All kinds of people, no doubt, were interested personally or politically in the Greek West. But as time went on did they acquire much knowledge of its history, or were they still as ignorant as Thucydides says the Athenians were in his day?[3] Were the histories written by Italian and Sicilian Greeks available to them to read? The fact seems to be that no Greek writer of prose from the West, who was not a sophist or a philosopher, made much of an impression in Aegean Greece until Timaeus came to Athens and spent most of his life there.[4] It is unlikely that many copies of his predecessors' books ever found their way to Athens or Corinth or Miletus.

Timaeus, however, seems to have become a recognized standard historian within a century after his death. Polybius takes it for granted that his work is well known, and his angry and bitter criticism must be explained in part by Timaeus' popularity.[5] Nor does Polybius succeed in discrediting him. The name of Timaeus appears in lists of the standard Greek historians in Cicero and writers of the early empire, and critics who complain of the 'lies' told by Greek historians are as likely to mention his name as that of Ephorus or Cleitarchus.[6] For Plutarch, Diodorus, and Dionysius

of calculation or accepted the bare statement of a Syracusan writer. This leaves us a choice between two alternatives. Either (1) Antiochus gave reasons for his conclusions, with references to local records and monuments, perhaps using a generation count as a subsidiary argument, and Thucydides was satisfied with his reasoning, or (2) Antiochus presented the results of his generation count without any further argument, in which case Thucydides must have found information in some other quarter, which confirmed his figures, perhaps as the result of inquiry in the cities of Sicily.

3. ἄπειροι οἱ πολλοὶ ὄντες τοῦ μεγέθους τῆς νήσου καὶ τῶν ἐνοικούντων τοῦ πλήθους (6. 1. 1). Thucydides helps the ill-informed reader not merely with measurements and numbers, but with a brief historical outline.

4. Polyb. 12. 25d. 1.

5. Polybius (12. 25c) can hardly be fair in finding the secret of his popularity in his abusive style; but, like Thucydides, he expresses contempt for historians who strive only to give pleasure for the moment.

6. Cf. F. Jacoby, *Die Fragmente der griechischen Historiker*, IIIB, p. 566, T 20, 21, 29 – Cic. *De Orat.* 2. 58, *Brut.* 325, *Ad Att.* 6. 1. 18 (he is sure that Atticus 'knows his Timaeus', just as Caelius 'knows his Cleitarchus', *Ad Fam.* 2. 10. 3).

of Halicarnassus he is a familiar author, whose work they certainly know at first hand.[7] When Strabo is writing about Italy, in Books 5 and 6, he cites Timaeus, and also Antiochus, on a number of occasions; but it is not necessary to believe that he consulted their actual texts. His principal sources in these books, as can easily be shown, are Polybius, Posidonius, and Artemidorus of Ephesus, all of whom he mentions quite frequently. It is likely that his quotations from Timaeus are taken from Artemidorus, and that Artemidorus found the references to Antiochus in Timaeus.[8]

If we knew more about the book trade in Greek times, we might perhaps be able to say with greater confidence what sort of book was likely to travel eastward from Sicily to Athens and other centers of the older Greek world. But we can at least be fairly sure that poetry and philosophy 'traveled' more freely than history. When Pindar speaks of his songs 'traveling on every ship',[9] he

---

Cf. T. 28, 30, 31 – Scymnus 125–6, Vitruvius, *De Arch.* 8. 3. 27, Pliny, *N.H.* 1. 4, 1. 6. Josephus considers him a notorious liar, T. 17 – *C. Apionem* 1. 16, and Polybius is full of indignation at his 'deliberate falsehoods' – 12. 3. 6; 4. 4; 4d. 4; 7. 6; 10. 6; 11. 3–5; 12. 4–7; 13. 1–3. Cf. T. 15a – Clem. Alex., *Strom.* 1. 1. 2.

7. Cf. e.g. T. 11 – Diod. 5. 1. 3; T. 22 – Dion. Hal. *De Din.* 8; T. 23 – *De Sublim.* 4; T. 18 – Plut. *Nic.* 1.

8. For the most recent discussion see F. Lasserre, *Strabon* (Budé ed.), vol. III (Paris 1967), pp. 4–25. W. Aly, *Strabonis Geographica*, Band 4 (Bonn 1957) (*Antiquitas* I, 5), pp. 211–79, discusses the sources of Books 5 and 6, but he is more interested in strictly geographical matters than mythological detail. Like Lasserre he is fully aware that matters mentioned by Timaeus can have reached Strabo through other channels besides Artemidorus. Since, however, Strabo has no occasion to be concerned with mythology except in connection with particular places or areas, the geographer Artemidorus is generally a more likely source of the tales that he records than a historian like Polybius or Posidonius. Among useful earlier studies cited by Lasserre the following may be noted: G. Hunrath, *Über die Quellen Strabos im sechsten Buch* (Diss. Marburg, 1879); R. Daebritz, *De Artemidoro Strabonis auctore* (Diss. Leipzig 1905); O. Steinbrück, *Die Quellen des Strabo im fünften Buch* (Diss. Halle 1909); F. Sollima, *Le Fonti di Strabone nella geografia della Sicilia* (Messina 1897); J. Beloch 'Le Fonti di Strabone nella descrizione della Campania', *Mem. accad. Lincei, Classe di sc. morali,* serie 3, 10 (1882).

G. Hagenow, *Untersuchungen zu Artemidors Geographie des Westens* (Göttingen 1932) is not convincing in his attempt to prove that Artemidorus restricted himself to geographical description (cf. Lasserre, *Strabon*, p. 9).

9.   ἀλλ᾽ ἐπὶ πάσας ὁλκάδος ἔν τ᾽ ἀκάτῳ, γλυκεῖ᾽ ἀοιδά,
σteῖχ᾽ ἀπ᾽ Αἰγίνας, διαγγέλλοισ᾽ ὅτι
Λάμπωνος υἱὸς Πυθέας εὐρυσθενὴς
νίκη Νεμείοις παγκρατίου στέφανον (*Nem.* 5. 3–5).

does not mean that copies of the text were to be found on board, but that the fame of each performance spread. His songs were sung in various cities of the Greek world; and any lyric or dramatic poet, who had become famous, was likely to travel himself, responding to invitations from distant cities to direct performances of his works. The western tours of Pindar and Aeschylus are well attested, though we may be a little less certain about the travels of Ibycus and Arion.[10] Plato tells us of various philosophers and sophists who came from the West, and his own journey to Syracuse is fully documented. A philosopher's reputation was made more by his teaching than by his books, and he might undertake a lecture tour and attract large audiences in places where few had read his books. Historians could hardly expect this kind of enthusiastic welcome; we must not generalize from the tale of the extravagant fee paid to Herodotus for his lecture in Athens.[11]

In the case of Timaeus the question of his manuscript traveling is hardly relevant, since he is said to have lived for about fifty years in Athens (Polyb. 12. 25d), and so presumably made his reputation there. But the Alexandrian poets Lycophron and Apollonius make it clear at once that his work attracted plenty of attention. Lycophron's *Alexandra* shows heroes of Greek mythology meeting with adventures in Italy that are almost completely unknown in earlier literature, and the scholiasts identify many details as taken from Timaeus.[12] The scholiasts do not reveal the full

10. The poem of Ibycus dedicated to the tyrant Polycrates (*P. Oxy.* 1790; Denys L. Page (ed.), *Lyrica Graeca Selecta* (Oxford 1968), no. 263) seems to prove that he went from Rhegium to Samos and was well received there, thus confirming the statement in Suda *s.v.* Ἴβυκος. For Arion the romantic tale of his rescue by the dolphin (Hdt. 1. 23–4) can hardly be called evidence.

11. Plut. *De mal. Hdt.* 862B. One need not take very seriously the portrait of a traveling lecturer given by Lucian, *Herodotus*, or the story of his unsuccessful attempt to demand a large fee from the Corinthians, as told by Dio Chrysostom, 37. 7. The tale of a golden crown given to the Attic historian Cleidemus is hard to evaluate, as the text of Tertullian which records it is corrupt – *dum ob historici stili praestantiam auro coronatŭr* is a far from certain emendation (*De Anima* 52 – *F. gr. Hist.* III B, 323 T. 2).

12. Schol. Lyc. 615, 1137 – F. 53, 55 (the story of Diomede in Italy, Daunus and the Daunians); 633 – F. 66 (the Gymnesiae islands, colonized by Boeotians); 732 – F. 98 (an Athenian general sacrifices to Parthenope at Neapolis); 1017 – F. 78 (the Argyrini in Epirus); 1050 – F. 56 (the River Althaenus and an etymology of the name, in typical Timaean style, cf. below p. 180); 1142, 1155 – F. 146 (the girls sent by the Locrians to work as servants of Athena of Ilium).

extent of his debt to Timaeus, as one easily sees by comparing his text with the numerous passages in Strabo's account of Italy where the mythological associations of various places are mentioned. The correspondence in numerous details is remarkable, and even when Lycophron's scholia offer no help Strabo's dependence on Timaeus as an ultimate source (with Artemidorus as intermediary) is not difficult to establish. The passages in Strabo and Lycophron must be compared with the account of early times in Italy and Sicily given by Diodorus in Books 4 and 5, where he names Timaeus as a principal source of information.[13] The correspondence is equally remarkable. Johannes Geffcken, in his masterly monograph, *Timaios' Geographie des Westens*,[14] was able to show in convincing fashion not only the large amount of mythological detail that is common to all three authors, but also how much 'Timaean material' can be identified in other writers. The *thaumata* often attracted the attention of collectors of 'strange tales', like the author of *Thaumasia Akousmata* (*De Mirabilibus Auscultatibus*), whose work is preserved in the Aristotelian corpus,[15] and Antigonus of Carystus;[16] and not only Antoninus Liberalis,

13. Diodorus cites him in 4. 21 – F. 89; 4. 22 – F. 90; 4. 56 – F. 85; 5. 1. 3 – T. 11; 5. 6 – F. 38. See also Jacoby's note on F. 164.

14. Philologische Untersuchungen 13 (Berlin 1892). See also the important pioneer work of Karl Müllenhoff, *Deutsche Altertumskunde* (Berlin 1870), vol. 1, 426–80, and cf. Paul Günther, *De ea quae inter Timaeum et Lycophronem intercedit ratione* (Diss. Leipzig 1889), Wilamowitz, *Hellenistische Dichtung* (Berlin 1924), vol. II, pp. 143–64, and the good summary in Jacoby, *F. gr. Hist.* III B, pp. 526–8.

15. E.g. *Mir. Ausc.* 78 (strange drugs from plants on Monte Circeo); 79 (metamorphosis of Diomede's men into birds, cf. Lyc. 592–602; Strabo 5. 1. 9; 6. 3. 9); 81 (Phaethon and Daedalus); 82 (rape of Persephone at Enna, cf. Diod. 5. 3. 1–3); 85 (causeway built by Heracles in Italy, cf. Lyc. 697; Strabo 5. 4. 6); 88 (Gymnesiae islands, cf. note 12 above); 95 (cave of the Sybil); 100 (settlement of Sardinia by the Thespiadae, cf. Diod. 4. 29–30; 5. 15; Strabo 5. 2. 7); 102 (the 'birdless' Lake Avernus); 105 (Jason's visit to Elba, cf. below p. 180); 107 (Philoctetes' death in Italy, after founding cities there, cf. Strabo 6. 1. 3; Lyc. 927–9); 108 (tools of Epeius in temple near Metapontum, cf. Lyc. 930–2; Strabo 6. 1. 14). This list is not intended to be exhaustive. This collection of 'strange tales' can be dated to the third century B.C., as no writer later than Timaeus is cited, except in the closing sections, which were evidently added later, with borrowings from later Greek authors.

16. Antigonus of Carystus quotes Timaeus in 1 (the cicadas at Locri and Rhegium, cf. Strabo 6. 1. 9); 140 (the tale of Arethusa, cf. Polyb. 12. 4d), and refers more frequently to Lycus (*F. gr. Hist.* III B, 570), another writer on early Italian history, said to be father or adoptive father of Lycophron. Note

but Ovid also found some good instances of *metamorphosis* among
these Italian tales;[17] and some of the stories found their way into
the *Aeneid*.[18] It is not important to the present argument whether
Virgil and Ovid learnt about them directly from Timaeus or
Lycophron or through some Latin antiquary like Varro or Cato.
What matters is that they can be traced back to Timaeus. The
same details, and others which resemble them, appear in more
prosaic Latin works, in Justin's Epitome of Pompeius Trogus and
in Pliny's *Natural History*.[19] Pliny mentions Artemidorus as well
as Timaeus among his sources,[20] and here too, as with Strabo,
it is easy to see when his ultimate source is almost certainly
Timaeus.

One must not expect every detail to appear in all these authors,
and it is no reason for surprise if there are notable differences in
the form that a story takes if it is repeated in two or three different
places. Anyone who thought a story was worth repeating might
want to alter it or improve it, if he felt so disposed. But once it is
recognized that certain versions of mythology, which can definitely
be traced back to Timaeus, find their way into these works, one
can go a step further and think it highly likely that any mythological episode with an Italian or Sicilian setting that appears in more
than one of these works will have been taken ultimately from
Timaeus. One can also be more confident about identifying
'Timaean material' once it becomes clear that there are some
characteristics that are common to these stories, *semeia*, if not

also 152 (Lake Avernus) and 172 (metamorphosis of Diomede's men, cf.
preceding note).

Antigonus' book seems to have been written about 240 B.C. Cf. Wilamowitz,
Antigonos von Karystos, Philologische Untersuchungen 4 (Berlin 1881), p. 22.

17. Ant. Lib. *Met.* 37 (Diomede's men, see notes 15 and 16 above); 31 (an
Apulian metamorphosis, cf. Ovid *Met.* 14. 512–26, after his account of
Diomede's men in 14. 483–511).

18. Virg. *Aen.* 1. 242–4 (Antenor in the country of the Veneti, cf. Livy 1. 1);
8. 9; 10. 28–9; 11. 226, 243–50, 271–7 (Diomede in Italy). Virgil is naturally
more directly concerned with traces left by the Trojans than with Greek heroes.

19. Cf. esp. Justin 20. 1. 6–20. 2. 7, where he lists the Italian cities supposed
to have been founded by Greeks in the heroic age, and Pliny, *N.H.* 3. 59
(etymology of Formiae, cf. p. 180 below); 3. 70 (temple of Hera near Paestum
founded by Jason, cf. Strabo 6. 1. 1); 3. 120 (Spina founded by Diomede, cf.
Strabo 5. 1. 7); 3. 130 (Trojan origin of Veneti, cf. Strabo 5. 1. 4); 10. 126–7
(Diomede's men); 15. 119 (Circe).

20. *N.H.* 1. 4; 1. 6; 1. 33; 1. 34; 1. 37; cf. *F. gr. Hist.*, Timaeus T. 31.

actually *tekmeria*, that Timaeus has had a hand in fashioning them or adapting them for his purpose.[21]

The mythological range of Apollonius is more narrowly limited than that of Lycophron. He brings new interest to the return voyage of the Argonauts by bringing them into the Adriatic down the Eridanus (the Po), which is supposed to be a branch of the Danube; and he makes them go further westwards (by an inland waterway) into the Tyrrhenian Sea, to consult Circe; this gives them the chance to leave behind them numerous traces of their voyage along the shores of Italy. Like Lycophron Apollonius is a bookish poet, with access to a good library, and he likes to introduce curious details of bizarre or antique geography, that he has found in old writers, like Hecataeus of Miletus,[22] as well as novelties from the more modern and more popular Timaeus. It is not important for readers of the *Argonautica* to identify all his sources; the scholiasts perform some notable feats of bibliography, but the poem can be appreciated without the degree of learning that Lycophron demands of his readers. Lycophron, however, must surely hope to give his properly qualified readers some pleasure, not merely to baffle them. In many instances they will have been able to interpret his 'clues' if they had read their Timaeus. Like makers of the more difficult kind of crossword puzzle Lycophron expects his readers to solve the problems that he sets them if they have done enough reading and if they have certain books available in the house. He doesn't expect them to make a series of trips to the library at Alexandria, to consult a rare manuscript (like the *Periegesis* of Hecataeus).

Timaeus' history found many other readers besides poets and collectors of local legends. It dealt with the history of the Greeks in the West from early times until his own day, and he was outspoken in expressing his opinions, especially his disapproval, so that he

21. Cf. Geffcken, *Timaios' Geographie* (see n. 14 above), p. 3. Strictly one should always say 'Timaeus or one of his predecessors' (cf. Jacoby, *F. gr. Hist.* IIIB, p. 528), but one may be reasonably sure that Timaeus knew the work of earlier historians of the West, and repeated (or contradicted) items from their books as he thought it worth while. Wilamowitz, *Antigonos v. Karystos* (see n. 16 above), p. 4, justifies this method of reconstruction if the author is one 'für den es hinreichende Charakterismen gibt'.

22. Cf. L. Pearson, 'Apollonius of Rhodes and the old geographers', *AJP* 59 (1938), 443–59.

earned the nickname of 'Επιτίμαιος, the Fault-finder. But for the
present our concern is with his treatment of mythology and the
pre-history of the West, and we must ask how he came upon those
new unfamiliar stories. Did he find them by ὄψις and ἱστορίη in
the manner of Herodotus, traveling through the different areas of
Italy and Sicily and making inquiries about local traditions and
cults of local heroes? Polybius thinks he should have made much
more extensive inquiries, and berates him severely for not doing
so (12. 4c). The ill-tempered criticisms of Polybius are not always
a safe guide, but the stories often betray themselves as more
sophisticated inventions than one expects in genuine local
traditions; they often betray the work of a literary or academic
mind, of a man who has read widely and is borrowing or adapting
what he has read and who wants his stories to serve some purpose.
The Latin poets may do their best to present mythical episodes in
Italy as authentic legend, treating them as though they were part
of traditional Greek mythology and had been narrated by Greek
poets of an earlier period (though they will have learnt about them
from some Hellenistic source). We should not allow them to mislead us; we must recognize the difference between legends that
seem to go back to a time of simple faith and stories that have been
created in a more sophisticated age.

What evidence can in fact be claimed for the early emergence of
Greek myths in an Italian setting? Many episodes in the *Odyssey*
probably go back to very early times indeed, to a period older than
that of any written text of Homer. But at what date approximately
are we to suppose that Scylla and Charybdis were identified with
their traditional sites on the strait of Messina or the Cyclopes given
their home on the slopes of Mount Etna? and when was the island
of Circe first identified with the peninsula of Circeo, which looks
like an island? Not before Greeks knew something about the coast-
line, not before Greek ships had penetrated these waters, hardly
before the later years of the eighth century when the earliest Greek
colonies were founded in the West.

It may be argued that the tale of Odysseus' travels first took
shape in earlier centuries when Mycenaean and Minoan ships had
sailed the Western Mediterranean, before darkness descended in
the twelfth or eleventh century and blocked the way. But when
people of the tenth or ninth century listened to the bards, their

geographical knowledge would not extend as far as Italy, they would hardly expect or care to know where precisely Odysseus had landed. Only the most incurable romantic will maintain that a kind of folk-memory retained knowledge of these coasts all through an illiterate age. Curiosity about geographical detail is not likely to have been roused until the sea-lanes opened again and people started looking for Homeric sites in the West, expecting perhaps that they might not be more difficult to identify than Troy or Tiryns.

How soon can we positively say that identifications were made? Since the great mass of post-Homeric epic is lost and the Hesiodic corpus survives for the most part only in fragments, without a clear date-label on each fragment, we can trace only a few of the early attempts at identification. Hesiod in the *Theogony* says that Circe bore Odysseus three sons, Agrios, Latinos, and Telegonos, and that 'in a remote place, far from the Sacred Islands, they ruled over all the Etruscans' (1011–16). These lines seem to guide us towards Circeo, an 'out-of-the-way' place in Latium, which was beyond the range of Greek colonization and within the bounds of Etruscan territory until the sixth century. Does this mean that the identification was made in Cumae and that the report came back to Hesiod's father in Aeolian Cyme, and that he told his son about it?[23] There is in fact no identification of Circeo as Circe's island in extant literature before Theophrastus, who adds that the local inhabitants 'point out the tomb of Elpenor'.[24] If we want to see what Timaeus added by way of proving the identification, we can turn to Strabo, who remarks that the place looks like an island and adds: 'They say it is very rich in roots, so as to fit in with the tale of Circe. It has a little town, a sanctuary of Circe, and an altar of Athena; and a so-called cup of Odysseus is said to be on show there' (5. 3. 6).[25] None of this would surprise Strabo's readers, at a time when Greek *paideia* had made great progress in Latium, and it would confer distinction on the little town if it could claim to be a place mentioned in the *Odyssey*. But in Timaeus' day the initiative

23. *Works and Days* 633/6. The question of course disappears if one believes that the closing portion of the *Theogony* is a later addition and not 'genuine' Hesiod.

24. *Hist. Plant.* 5. 8. 3.

25. A story is told in *Mir. Ausc.* 78 of a particularly deadly drug supposed to be produced there. Cf. Pliny, *N.H.* 15. 119; 25. 11.

in making the identification would have to come from Greeks. It is designed to please Greeks; a temple of Athena so-called (whatever its real origin) in a place never colonized by Greeks is intended as proof that Greeks must have been there once. Like so many of the tales told by Timaeus, this is a tale that turns a part of Italy into a Greek land, where Greeks have an ancestral right to take possession – just as good as Athenians in Attica. Whether it was Timaeus or one of his predecessors or some Greeks from Cumae who identified this old building as a temple of Athena, they were serving a Greek purpose.

Attempts to find Greek etymologies for non-Greek place names (however absurd they may seem to modern scholars) are part of the same design; they are supposed to prove that Greeks were there in very early times. The Argonauts in their search for Circe's island might be supposed to land at Formiae or Gaeta; Timaeus derives the name Formiae from Ὁρμιαί (because it was a good anchorage), suggests a Laconian word καιάτας, meaning bay, as the etymology of Gaeta and also, as an alternative, that the name was derived from Aietes, that Medea named the place after her father.[26] On the isle of Elba the best harbor had a name that could be explained as meaning 'Port Argo' (λιμὴν Ἀργῷος). This was taken as proof that the Argonauts had been there in search of Circe's island; and the bright pebbles on the beach were supposed to be their ἀποστλεγγίσματα, the lumps of oily mud that they scraped off their bodies after athletic exercise (like the soldiers of Alexander the Great the Argonauts are represented as arranging athletic contests, when they are fortunate enough to stay longer than a day or two in one place). Diodorus makes it quite clear that the story

26. The derivation of the name from Aeneas' nurse Caieta is not found before Virgil, *Aen.* 7. 1–4. The Gaeta–Aietes etymology is mentioned by Diodorus in telling the tale of the Argonauts' voyage, for which he cites Timaeus as his source (F. 85 – Diod. 4. 56. 6). The other two etymologies are in Strabo 5. 3. 6 (cf. Pliny, *N.H.* 3. 57) and must certainly be attributed to Artemidorus–Timaeus. It is likely that Timaeus gave both the Gaeta etymologies. Lycophron (or 'the author of 1226–80') carefully combines them both:

Ἀργοῦς τε κλεινὸν ὅρμον Αἰήτην μέγαν (1274)

while working them into the story of Aeneas' voyage.

One cannot always be sure that an etymology is an invention of Hellenistic times; the derivation of the Palici from πάλιν ἱκέσθαι comes from Aeschylus, *Aetnaeae* (Fr. 27, Mette).

was in Timaeus (F. 85 – Diod. 4. 56). Apollonius picked up the theme, and so did Strabo and the author of *Thaumasia Akousmata*.[27]

Elba is far beyond the limits of Greek colonization, and it is a mistake to use the word 'tradition' in speaking of tales like the Argonauts' landing there. It is evidently a Greek invention, because it is not a story which the Etruscans would have invented or cherished for themselves. The Greek legends illustrated in Etruscan art have no special connection with Italy. Even on the Ficoroni cista, which illustrates episodes of the Argonaut story,[28] none of the incidents occur which are set in Italy by Hellenistic writers. There is nothing in Etruscan art, early or late, which suggests that the Etruscans wanted their country to play its part in Greek legend. It is the Greeks, not the Etruscans or the Italic peoples who want to show that Italy is Greek territory, that Greeks were there before Etruscans or Samnites or Apulians.

One cannot suppose that Samnites would want to regard themselves as partly Spartan by descent. Only a Greek would want to devise such a theory, and Strabo is not convinced by it: 'Some people actually say that Spartan colonists joined with the Samnites in their settlement of the country (which explains their philhellenic character) and that some of the population in fact are called Pitanatae; but this appears to be a Tarentine fiction,

27. Strabo 5. 2. 6; *Mir Ausc.* 105, where the story is said to be told by 'the Greeks living on Elba'. Can Timaeus have said that there was a Greek settlement on the island? Apollonius (4. 654-8) mentions the λιμὴν ᾿Αργῷος and says that the heroes 'wiped away the sweat with pebbles after their exercise' and that the pebbles are still lying on the beach. The *textus receptus* offers some difficulty, and Fränkel in the *OCT* suggests that a line may be missing in which the pebbles were compared to στλεγγίσματα φωτῶν.

Lycophron (874-6) mentions a beach in Western Sicily where oily pebbles, which the sea never washes clean, bear witness to the στλεγγίσματα of the Argonauts. This raises the question whether Timaeus told the story of Sicily as well as Elba (which is not impossible); or has Lycophron transferred the scene to Sicily, since no hero's *Nostos* included a visit to Elba? Geffcken, *Timaios' Geographie*, p. 25, refuses to believe that Lycophron is speaking of Sicily, and insists that he expects us to recall the Elba story (even though it would have no particular relevance in the Sicilian context of these lines). He is followed, however, by Jacoby (*F. gr. Hist.* IIIB, *Noten*, p. 340), who makes things unduly difficult for himself by his belief that Timaeus gave a continuous account of the Argonauts' voyage and that he took the 'branch theory' of the Danube seriously.

28. Cf. E. Pfuhl, *Malerei u. Zeichnung der Griechen* (Munich 1923), vol. III, Fig. 628.

intended to flatter and win the friendship of a powerful neighboring people' (5. 4. 12). Modern historians are equally scornful of the theory,[29] and Strabo's notion that it would please the Samnites is somewhat absurd. But by a stroke of luck we can see how it may have arisen. Coins have been found in Samnium with the legend Π[ΙΤΑ]ΝΑΤΑΝ ΠΕΡΙΠΟΛΟΝ, and they are explained as the issue of a Tarentine colony in Samnite territory, probably issued in the late fourth century,[30] so that Timaeus could very well have seen them and used them as the basis for his 'theory'. He would no doubt expect his readers to have read their Herodotus, who speaks of a Πιτανάτης λόχος at Sparta, as well as Thucydides who says that no such thing existed;[31] now they could see that Herodotus was right for once! We could hardly have a better example of an appeal to archaeological evidence (in support of an untenable theory).

This is not the only occasion where we must suspect that Timaeus is appealing to what we should call archaeological evidence. Sardinia is far beyond the limits of Greek colonization and plays no part in conventional versions of Greek mythology. But it abounds in remains of ancient buildings, the so-called *nuraghi*, which a Greek observer would at once recognize as the work of pre-historic inhabitants. Why not say they were put up by Greeks of the heroic age? There would be no archaeological experts to say that the resemblance of these buildings to Mycenaean work was misleading,[32] and few if any of Timaeus' readers were likely to visit Sardinia (it is not necessary to believe that he had gone there himself).[33] So he can say, without fear of contradiction,

29. E.g. E. T. Salmon, *Samnium and the Samnites* (Cambridge 1967), p. 30.

30. *British Museum Catalogue of Greek Coins*, Italy, p. 398, B. V. Head, *Historia Numorum*, 2nd ed. (London 1911), p. 27; Salmon, *Samnium*, p. 71, n. 6.

31. Hdt. 9. 53, Thuc. 1. 20. 3.

32. The superficial resemblances are easily observed from illustrations in archaeological handbooks. Cf. M. Guido, *Sardinia* (New York 1964), p. 109, C. Zervos, *La Civilisation de la Sardaigne* (Paris 1954), pp. 43–104. Zervos admits the likelihood of Mycenaean influence on the architecture, but one must not be misled by the curious language he uses about the story of Iolaus, as though it were authentic history, 'les historiens nous apprennent', 'nous dirons que les Thespiades régnèrent sur l'île pendant plusieurs générations' (pp. 32–3). He does not mean that these people built the towers and tombs.

33. Cf. Jacoby's skeptical remarks about his *Forschungsreisen* (*F. gr. Hist.* IIIB, pp. 532–3).

that the mountain people known as Diagesbeis were formerly called Iolaeis, after Iolaus, that Heracles sent a good number of the fifty sons borne to him by the fifty daughters of Thespius to settle the island, under the command of Iolaus, together with other Greeks and barbarians; that they established a number of cities and built gymnasia and temples and other structures; and that traces still survived of their work, to show that Hellenic civilization once flourished there, before Phoenicians or Carthaginians arrived. Strabo and Diodorus both tell the story (which certainly must not be called a 'tradition'), and it also appears in the *Thaumasia Akousmata*.[34] Diodorus even says the name Iolaeis is still used, but Strabo says this is not so (perhaps Artemidorus had corrected Timaeus on this point, or at least brought him up to date).[35] It is a story that might appeal to the Romans, when they took Sardinia from the Carthaginians after the First Punic War, but one need not suppose it was invented for their benefit. Like other stories it is designed to show that the Greek world of the heroic age was less narrow than that of later times.

Students of pre-history may want to exclaim that, if this is so, Timaeus was apparently aware of something that archaeology has re-discovered in modern times. But it is more important to remem-

34. Strabo 5. 2. 7; Diod. 4. 29–30; 5. 15; *Mir. Ausc.* 100, whose anonymous author adds the remarkable detail that Aristaeus had been a farmer and a king in Sardinia, and that before his time it had been dominated by monstrous birds. This makes Sardinia another cradle of civilization (like Sicily), and its poverty under Carthaginian rule is contrasted with its early prosperity. The right time for such a tale was certainly in the third century, about the time of the First Punic War.

35. Diod. 5. 12. 2; Strabo 5. 2. 7, καλοῦνται Διαγησβεῖς, ᾽Ιολαεῖς πρότερον ὀνομαζόμενοι. Strabo nevertheless writes as though Sardinia were not yet fully conquered and the mountaineers were still raiding the Italian mainland, οἱ δὲ πεμπόμενοι στρατηγοὶ τὰ μὲν ἀντέχουσι, πρὸς ἃ δ᾽ ἀπαυδῶσιν, ἐπειδὰν μὴ λυσιτελῇ τρέφειν συνεχῶς ἐν τόποις νοσεροῖς στρατόπεδον. He seems to be reproducing the language of a third-century text. Timaeus apparently liked to argue that 'old names still in use' provide evidence of Greek settlement in the heroic age. But his arguments do not often inspire confidence, as when he says that the people of Pisa called themselves 'Pylians' and that their city had been founded by Nestor's 'men of Pylos' and was named after Pisa in the Peloponnese. Cf. Strabo 5. 2. 5; Justin 20. 1. 11; Virg. *Aen.* 10. 179, *Alpheae ab origine Pisae.* This pretence that Pisa was of Greek origin and settled from Nestor's Pylos is treated with strange seriousness by J. Bérard, *La Colonisation grecque de l'Italie méridionale et de la Sicile*, 2nd ed. (Paris 1957), pp. 327–8.

ber that Timaeus was often able to examine archaeological remains that were subsequently buried in the ground and remained hidden until they were uncovered by excavators in the present century. Diodorus (4. 77–9), presumably following Timaeus, says that Daedalus fled from Crete to Sicily and built some remarkable structures for King Cocalos at Camici near Acragas, and that Minos came in pursuit of him, only to be murdered by Cocalos and buried in an underground chamber, with a temple on top of it. The story of Minos' death in Sicily is as old as the fifth century, known to Sophocles and Herodotus.[36] Herodotus adds the story of a subsequent Cretan expedition, which besieged Camici without success, and says the Cretans were driven ashore in Italy on their homeward voyage, and founded Hyria and other cities in Iapygia. One may suppose that he learnt of this tale in Italy after his migration to Thurii, perhaps from a literary source. Thus it seems that Timaeus is building on the work of one of his predecessors. Though the story has no value for the historian, Timaeus' observation may be accurate, since a building has been found in Crete which corresponds to the description of Minos' tomb, and a counterpart may have been reproduced by Minoan settlers in Sicily.[37] Perhaps the historian is 'using archaeological evidence', as in Sardinia, though hardly in a way that would satisfy a scientific archaeologist. There is archaeological evidence which indicates that Minoan ships and perhaps Minoan settlers came to Sicily; but the mythology presented to us by western Greek historians is not additional or supporting evidence; it merely

36. Sophocles, *Kamikoi*, Fr. 324 (Jebb–Pearson), Hdt. 7. 169–70. It has been suggested that the cauldron scene in one of the archaic metopes from the Foce del Sele temple represents not the 'boiling of Pelias' by Medea, but the death of Minos at the bath. Cf. G. Pugliese-Carratelli, 'Minos e Cocalos', *Kokalos* 2 (1956), 103, n. 35. If this is correct, it means that the story of Minos' murder in Sicily was current in the West perhaps as early as 500 B.C.

37. Cf. Sir Arthur Evans, *The Palace of Minos* (New York 1921), vol. III, pp. 959–78, Fig. 938; J. D. S. Pendlebury, *Handbook to the Palace of Minos* (London 1933, repr. 1955), pp. 70–3; *The Archaeology of Crete* (London 1939), pp. 194–5; N. Platon, *Crete* (Eng. trans., Cleveland–New York 1966), p. 164. On the other hand G. Becatti, 'La Leggenda di Dedalo', *Röm. Mitt.* 60–1 (1954–5), 31–2, denies that the Cnossos building is a temple-tomb, and is ready to believe that Timaeus' inspiration comes from more recent architecture. Cf. the cautious description of the monument in S. Hood, *The Minoans* (London 1971), p. 144, Pl. 24.

illustrates their inventive ingenuity in explaining the meaning of mute stones.[38]

Hellenistic poets loved to explain the origins of buildings and monuments and local religious customs, and to introduce mythological digressions at every opportunity. All that we learn about Timaeus suggests that he had similar tastes; so much mythological detail can be traced back to him that he may be using a pattern of exposition similar to that of the poets in his account of early times. There was no thread of unified political history, not even a story of political development or military conquest, that would give coherence to a continuous narrative. But if Timaeus took Herodotus and Ephorus for his models, it is likely that he started out by trying to give a geographical description of Italy and Sicily, perhaps with special emphasis on less familiar areas, and taking frequent opportunities for mythological and aetiological digressions.[39] And unless our evidence is misleading, the digressions almost always led him into Greek mythology, not into Italian or Etruscan folk-lore.

Stories that are set in the South of Italy or in Sicily are likely to be of earlier origin that those set in parts of Italy beyond the area of Greek colonization. The story of Daedalus and Cocalos is certainly an older story. Indeed Diodorus (4. 79. 4) tells us that Theron, the tyrant of Acragas, 'gave back to the Cretans' the bones from the so-called tomb of Minos, thus formally recognizing a tradition that Minoans had been in Sicily. Diodorus is no doubt repeating what he found in Timaeus, but Theron's gesture will have been reported by earlier writers.

One might expect Greek art and its local adaptations to give some hint of the legends that became popular, especially the legends attached to particular places. But there is not much more

38. C. H. Oldfather in his note on Diod. 4. 79 (Loeb ed.) refers to the so-called temple tomb in Crete, and comments: 'The discovery is striking evidence for the trustworthiness of many details of the old sagas.' It is not evidence of anything of the kind, and we have no right to speak of this story as an 'old saga'. The only tholos tombs discovered near Acragas (at Sant' Angelo Muxaro, which some archaeologists would like to identify with Camici) are unfortunately too late to be of Minoan origin; but it is quite possible that Timaeus had seen these tombs. Cf. M. Guido, *Sicily, an archaeological guide* (London 1967), pp. 102–3, 129–30; L. Bernabò Brea, *Sicily before the Greeks* (New York 1957), pp. 177–8.

39. Cf. Jacoby, *F. gr. Hist.* IIIB, pp. 533, 542–3.

help to be found in coins or pottery or temple pediments or bronze and clay reliefs than in Etruscan art. The reliefs from Locri seem to tell us that the legend of the rape of Persephone had taken a special form in this colony at least as early as the fifth century.[40] But though the Latin poets have taught us to take for granted that the meadow where she was playing was the meadow of Enna,[41] there is no indication that Enna claimed that distinction (or even that the meadow was located in Sicily)[42] until Hellenistic times. There is no indication in any extant poetry until it appears in Lycophron and Callimachus.[43] The coins of Enna from earlier centuries show that the cult of Demeter and Kore was established there, but there is no illustration of Pluto or Demeter's search until later.[44] When Diodorus tells the story in detail, in Book 5 where his dependence on Timaeus is clear, he makes us suspect that Timaeus must have played a great part in popularizing the

40. H. Prückner, *Die lokrischen Tonreliefs* (Mainz 1968); P. Zancani-Montuoro, 'Il rapitore di Kore nel mito locrese', *Rend. accad. arch. Napoli* 29 (1955), 3–10.

41. Cf. Ovid, *Met.* 5. 385–408.

42. The Homeric Hymn to Demeter does not even suggest that the meadow was in the West, λειμῶν' ἄμ μαλακόν (7), Νύσιον ἄμ πεδίον (17).

43. Lycophron expects his readers to recognize the grieving Demeter when he calls her Ἐνναία... Ἕρκυνν' Ἐρινὺς Θουρία Ξιφηφόρος (152–3). Callimachus mentions Enna as a place especially dear to Demeter:

θεὰ δ' ἐπεμαίνετο χώρῳ
ὅσσον Ἐλευσῖνι, Τριόπα θ' ὅσον, ὁκκόσον Ἔννᾳ (*Hy.* 6. 29–30).

In a fragment of the Ἐκθέωσις Ἀρσινόης Philotera, the sister of Arsinoe, already dead and deified, is described as 'just leaving Enna' and 'parting from Deo' (R. Pfeiffer, *Callimachus*, vol. 1 (Oxford 1949), Fr. 228. 43). There is no mention of Enna in the lines quoted by Diodorus from the fourth-century tragic poet Carcinus, which describe the grief of Sicily at the goddess' loss (Diod. 5. 5. 1 – A. Nauck and B. Snell (eds.), *Tragicorum Graecorum Fragmenta* (Hildesheim 1964), vol. 1, pp. 213–14).

44. Cf. G. F. Hill, *Coins of Ancient Sicily* (Westminster 1903), pp. 178, 214–15. It is not until the third century that the chariot of Hades appears on coins of Enna. G. Zuntz, *Persephone* (Oxford 1971), p. 70, n. 4, maintains that an earlier coin (Hill, *Coins of Ancient Sicily*, p. 91), showing Demeter in a four-horse chariot and carrying a torch, represents her searching for her daughter, as in Hom. *Hymn.* 2. 47–8:

ἐννῆμαρ μὲν ἔπειτα κατὰ χθόνα πότνια Δηὼ
στρωφᾶτ' αἰθομένας δαΐδας μετὰ χερσὶν ἔχουσα.

Diod. 5. 4. 3 also mentions the torches in the search, but the picture of the goddess racing through the night with a torch to light her way is something quite new. Other explanations of the coin are to be preferred.

Sicilian version of the tale; Diodorus not only describes the special beauty of the fields near Enna, he also mentions an alternative version, according to which 'it was in the neighborhood of Syracuse that Pluto found Kore and carried her off' (5. 4. 2). If Timaeus gave a geographical description of Sicily, taking each area in turn, he could have found the opportunity to mention both versions, without having to reconcile them or make a choice between them.

While there is no evidence that Enna claimed to be the scene of the rape before the third century, there is clear proof that Sicily developed its special devotion to Demeter and Kore at an earlier period. Pindar leaves us in no doubt about this when he says that Zeus made a gift of the island to Persephone (*Nem.* 1. 14) and when he calls Acragas the home of Persephone (*Py.* 12. 1–2). Bacchylides (3. 1–2) makes the picture even clearer;[45] and Cicero, in the *Verrines*, insists that this dedication of Sicily to the two goddesses confers a special sanctity on it,[46] an appeal to religious feeling that he would not have made unless he thought their piety was genuine and founded on old tradition. But it is Diodorus who shows us how Timaeus (and perhaps his predecessors) used the tradition. He says that according to 'the best authorities among the historians' it was in Sicily that Demeter and Kore first made their appearance and here that the secret of grain-growing was discovered (5. 2. 4). This means that Sicily had its answer to the Athenians who prided themselves that Athena had first taught men to grow the olive in Attica; the Sicilians had just as good a claim to consider their land the cradle of Hellenic civilization as the Athenians.[47]

45.   Ἀριστοκάρπου Σικελίας κρέουσαν
             Δάματρα ἰοστέφανόν τε κούραν ὕμνει.
46. *In Verrem* II 4. 48. 106. The description that follows, of Enna and Demeter's search for the lost Persephone, may be taken straight out of the pages of Timaeus.
47. Athenians maintained, perhaps from quite early times, that Demeter had revealed to them the art of agriculture, which they then shared with others. This seems to be the meaning, in black figure painting, when Triptolemus is shown driving out into the world with an ear of grain in his hand (e.g. J. D. Beazley, *Attic Black-Figure Vase-painters* (Oxford 1956), p. 309, no. 83; E. Gerhard, *Auserlesene griechische Vasenbilder* (4 vols., Berlin 1840–58), p. 44.
According to Isocrates, *Paneg.* 28, Demeter came to Attica in her search for Persephone and gave Athenians the gift of agriculture and the mystic rite,

While Sicily declared its special devotion to Demeter and Kore, various parts of Italy and Sicily had the opportunity to show their indebtedness to Heracles. At least as early as the fifth century Heracles was represented as passing down the whole length of Italy and crossing over to Sicily with the cattle of Geryones. The fragments so far discovered of the *Geryoneis* of Stesichorus[48] give no precise location for any of his exploits on this remarkable journey, but a fragment of Hellanicus notes his difficulties in bringing the cattle through large stretches of country where no one spoke Greek, but only an Italic dialect; and Hecataeus showed him dealing firmly with a man who offered him treacherous hospitality and receiving help from a woman in tracking down some cattle thieves.[49] It is interesting to see how these two writers anticipated the etymological devices of Timaeus. The etymology of *Italia* from *vitulus* became widely accepted in later times, but in Hellanicus' version Italy is the country where Heracles made constant inquiries about a lost heifer and found that the natives always referred to it as a *vitulus*. And according to Hecataeus the city of Motya was so called after the woman who helped him to find the men who had raided his herd. These two fragments remind us that Timaeus' predecessors did much work in preparing the way for him, though there is little of their work that we can trace.

The cult of Heracles was certainly well established among the western Greeks before the fifth century, but the effort to represent him as conferring special favors on Italy and Sicily cannot be illustrated from earlier art or poetry. Exploits of Heracles may have figured prominently in the poetry of Stesichorus, but the episodes seem not to be given any particular local setting in Italy or Sicily; even if Aeschylus is following Stesichorus when he says Heracles took a bath in the hot springs of Himera,[50] it still does not tell us how or why Heracles came to Himera. Labors of Heracles are depicted in the temples of Selinus and in the metopes of the

---

'which meant that they no longer lived like animals'. Timaeus, it seems, admitted that the Athenians received the gift 'first after the people of Sicily' (Diod. 5. 4. 4).

48. *P. Oxy.* XXXII 2617. Cf. Martin Robertson, '*Geryoneis*: Stesichorus and the vase-painters', *CQ* 19 (1969), 207–21.

49. Hellanicus F. 111 (*F. gr. Hist.* 1 4) – Dion. Hal. *A.R.* 1. 45; Hecataeus F. 76, 77 (*F. gr. Hist.* 1 1) – Steph. Byz. *s.v.* Μοτύη and Σολοῦς.

50. Fr. 32 (Nauck); 64 (Mette). The bather may be Heracles or Glaucus.

temple at the mouth of the Sele, near Paestum, but (in the examples that survive) they are not the labors which brought Heracles to the West.[51]

The Greeks felt that they had a special right to be in a country if Heracles had been there before them, and it is in keeping with this feeling that the admirers of Alexander assimilated him to Heracles. Timaeus certainly took trouble to illustrate how much different areas of Italy and Sicily owed to him. This need not mean that he put together a continuous narrative of his journey through Italy with the oxen of Geryones, but that he took advantage of the opportunity to show him active in different parts of the country. Diodorus tells us that he told the story of Heracles' battle with the giants in the Phlegraean Fields (F. 89 – Diod. 4. 21). This does not mean that Timaeus invented the tale; it is likely to be older in origin, and the Greeks who settled round the bay of Naples probably knew how to exploit the portentous character of their volcanic terrain.[52] They made it the abode of the Cimmerians and the entrance to the underworld,[53] creating a legend about the 'birdless' Lake Avernus (ἄορνος), an etymology and a local 'marvel' which Timaeus preferred to reject,[54] and 'discovering'

51. Cf. C. M. Bowra, *Greek Lyric Poetry*, 2nd ed. (Oxford 1961), pp. 88–9. In explaining the attention paid to Heracles by Stesichorus, Bowra speaks of 'the large part which the hero played in the myths and cults of Magna Graecia', but he does not warn the reader that the myths are found mostly in later literature. For details of the cult of Heracles in Sicily see E. Ciaceri, *Culti e Miti nella Storia della Sicilia antica* (Catania 1911), pp. 90ff., 275–85.

52. Strabo is aware that Lake Avernus had once been an alarming place with a sense of dark foreboding, but in his time the cutting down of the forest and the development of the area, with the building boom at Baiae, had destroyed its character, so that 'all the old beliefs were exploded', ἅπαντ' ἐκεῖνα ἐφάνη μῦθος (5. 4. 5).

53. Ephorus (F. 134 – Strabo 5. 4. 5) had worked out a story of Cimmerian cave-dwellers, who lived by mining and the fees paid to their oracle, and never left their caves except at night, which explained the lack of sunlight in their lives, as in the Odyssey:

οὐδέ ποτ' αὐτοὺς
'Ηέλιος φαέθων ἐπιδέρκεται (11. 15–16).

This is exactly the kind of rationalism that one expects from Ephorus; it is probably his invention.

54. ὁ δὲ Τίμαιος τοῦτο μὲν ψεῦδος ἡγεῖται εἶναι (F. 57 – Antig. Caryst. *Mir.* 152). Cf. *Mir. Ausc.* 102 (after describing the thick forest still growing on the hills round the lake) ὅτι δὲ οὐδὲν διίπταται ὄρνεον αὐτὴν ψεῦδος. οἱ γὰρ παραγενόμενοι λέγουσι πλῆθός τι κύκνων ἐν αὐτῇ γίνεσθαι. Antigonus knows

a causeway built by Heracles along which he drove the oxen. Timaeus certainly mentioned the causeway (it appears in Lycophron as well as in Strabo and Diodorus),[55] and it is the kind of monument that he liked to identify.

One of the giants was supposed to have fled from the field of battle, only to die and sink into the earth at a point on the opposite coast between Bari and Brindisi, where a spring of evil-smelling water sprang from his ichor. This part of the shore, Strabo says (6. 3. 5), was called Lcuternia, because Leuternioi was a name given to the giants. The story is exactly in the manner of Timaeus and must certainly be attributed to him; it is recorded in the *Thaumasia Akousmata* (97) and the name Leuternia is in Lycophron (978).

We learn from Diodorus (4. 22. 6) that Timaeus described how Heracles got his herd across the strait to Sicily, 'grasping a bull by the horns' and swimming across with him. Lycophron tells us that he killed Scylla (44–9), an appropriate attempt to make the world safer for travelers, even though its results were only temporary, since Scylla was restored to life by her father. The story might be an original invention of Timaeus; if he made Heracles cross the strait safely, the conflict with Scylla was inevitable.

Timaeus or his predecessors might have represented Heracles as fighting with the Cyclopes or anticipating some of the other western adventures of Odysseus, and Lycophron lets it be understood that he shot some (not all) of the Laestrygones (662–3). But the only exploit in Sicily which later writers made famous was his victory over the boxer Eryx.[56] This story was as old as the fifth century; according to Herodotus (5. 43) an oracle supported the Spartan Dorieus in his claim that the land of Eryx belonged to the Dorians, the descendants of Heracles, 'because Heracles himself had won the place'.[57] Heracles, by 'winning' the land, made the city of

several other 'birdless' lakes (*Mir.* 122, 152), and if Timaeus had visited Avernus he would certainly not be slow to correct statements of earlier writers. He was not called *Epitimaios* for nothing. Cf. Geffcken, *Timaios' Geographie*, p. 31, who thinks he is attacking Ephorus here.

55. Lyc. 697; Strabo 5. 4. 6; Diod. 4. 22. 2.

56. Cf. Virg. *Aen.* 5. 391–420; Ap. *Bib.* 2. 5. 10; Paus. 3. 16. 4; 4. 36. 4.

57. It is possible that the story was already in Stesichorus' *Geryoneis*, but direct evidence is lacking. Cf. J. Bérard, *La colonisation grecque*, pp. 411–12 and E. Sjöqvist, 'Heracles in Sicily', *Act. Inst. Rom. R. Sueciae* 22 (1962), 117–23,

Eryx a very old Greek foundation, next in age to the supposed Minoan colonies at Heraclea Minoa and Engyon,[58] and Timaeus evidently told the story in such a way as to make it clear that Eryx had to surrender the land if he lost the fight. In the account of Diodorus Heracles sets his own terms for the contest, and when Eryx complains that the stake of Heracles (the oxen) is worth less than the stake he is putting up (the land), Heracles explains the worth of the oxen by saying that if he loses them he will lose his chance of immortality (4. 23. 2). Heracles must acquire the land formally if the Greek claim to ownership is to be complete. Another tale told by Timaeus contains this same contrast between land and loot, as rewards of victory, in the story of Diomede's adventures in Apulia, when King Daunus offers him the choice of the land or the spoils of the war that he has helped to win.[59]

Diodorus goes on to say that after his victory over Eryx Heracles made a journey through the interior of Sicily and defeated a large force of the native Sicans, killing some of their distinguished 'generals', who 'receive honors still in our own time, Leucaspis, Pediacrates, Bouphonas, and Glychatas, also Bytaias and Crytidas' (4. 23. 5). It is no surprise that Timaeus gives Greek names to Sicans, since he was so ready with Greek etymologies for names of Italian towns, but if he said that these men were honored as heroes in his own day it is unlikely that he invented the names. In fact one of the names, Leucaspis, may be read on a Syracusan coin of the fourth century, which shows a naked warrior with shield and spear, and it is a natural assumption that Leucaspis is the name of a local hero and that it will be familiar to Syracusan readers.[60] It looks as though here, too, as in Sardinia, Timaeus is 'using the evidence of art and archaeology' to prove his point, as though the coin really were evidence of the victory of Heracles. It is also interesting to note that he is careful to call the native inhabi-

who thinks 'there can be no doubt' that the story goes back to Stesichorus. Bowra, *Greek Lyric Poetry*, 2nd ed., p. 95, is more cautious: 'Stesichorus' poems about Heracles may have some connection with Sicily.'

58. Diod. 4. 79. 5.

59. Schol. Lyc. 592. Timaeus' version of the tale of Diomede and Daunus can be pieced together from passages in Lycophron and his scholiasts, when compared with Strabo 5. 1. 9; Pliny, *N.H.* 3. 103; Antonin. Lib., *Met.* 37; Ovid, *Met.* 14. 475–511, and the passages from the *Aeneid* cited in note 18 above.

60. Hill, *Coins of Ancient Sicily*, p. 109, Pl. VII 5.

tants Sicans, not Sicels; according to some authorities Sicels were supposed to have come from Sicily only after the Trojan War.[61]

Heracles is of quite special value for the purpose of establishing Greek claims to territory, since he is an earlier settler than Homeric heroes; and he has, of course, a special appeal for Dorians. It seems that Timaeus also brought the Argonauts to Western Sicily, if we can believe that Lycophron is following him when he says they built a temple there (in a place that cannot be identified from the clues that he gives) and left their *stlengismata* behind in the form of bright colored pebbles.[62] By bringing Greek heroes to the west coast Timaeus may be intending to challenge the Carthaginian claims to early settlement, and Trojan heroes would serve their purpose as well as Greek against Carthaginian claims. Virgil picked up some of the stories of Trojans who settled in Sicily, like Acestes, the supposed eponymous founder of Egesta (which the Romans called Segesta),[63] but there is no indication that Timaeus or any of his predecessors brought Aeneas to Sicily. The tale of Aeneas' visit to Rome, though well established by the time of Timaeus, did not serve any particular purpose for Greek historians of the West.

61. Cf. Thuc. 6. 2. 3 and Dion. Hal. *A.R.* 1. 22, who notes that Philistus, like Hellanicus, put the Sicel immigration eighty years before the Trojan War, while Antiochus gave no date for it. Lycophron is careful never to use the word Σικελία, but speaks of 'the land of the Sicans' (870, 951) and the 'Sican sea' (1029).

62. Lyc. 871–6. Cf. note 27 above.

63. *Aen.* 1. 549–50; 5. 30–41. Cf. Lyc. 951–67. Acestes is supposed to be the son whom a daughter of the Trojan Phoenodamas bore to the River Crimisus, who appeared to her in the form of a dog. The story is not found elsewhere in literature, except in a rationalized form in Dion. Hal. *A.R.* 1. 52, and cannot therefore be attributed to Timaeus with any certainty. Coins of Segesta represent the River Crimisus, and some show the image of a dog on the obverse, with a girl on the reverse. Cf. Hill, *Coins of Ancient Sicily*, pp. 86–7, Pl. VI 7 and 9. It has been commonly supposed that these coins (some as old as the fifth century) are alluding to the story told by Lycophron. Cf. Geffcken, *Timaios' Geographie*, p. 27; L. Pareti in L. von Matt, *Das antike Sizilien* (Würzburg, n.d.), p. 172. The interpretation is open to question, however, as Hill recognizes (*Coins of Ancient Sicily*, pp. 89, 93–4), because a similar dog appears on coins of Eryx, Motya, and Panormus. I prefer to believe that the dog has some conventional meaning, and that Timaeus invented the legend using the coin as 'evidence' (cf. the tale of Leucaspis, p. 191 above); but there is of course no way of proving any such hypothesis.

Apart from heroes of mythology the Greek writers had various things to say about the movements of Sicans and Sicels, Ausones, Iapyges, Oenotrians, and other Italic peoples. This does not mean that they knew very much about the early history of these non-Greek peoples. But they filled the gap between the supposed heroic settlers and the coming of Greek colonists or (in non-Greek Italy) the establishment of Roman and Etruscan communities.

The work of Timaeus and his predecessors in putting together the history of early times can be reconstructed from the various fragments and quasi-fragments of their work (of which only a selection has been presented here), and although there is clearly much that cannot be recovered, a remarkably consistent picture nevertheless emerges. They used mythology to show that Italy and Sicily were from a very early period Greek lands, thus providing for the Greeks of the West as good an early history and as just a claim to the country as the cities of the mainland. It should not surprise us that they took trouble over mythical detail, since interpretation of myths had occupied the attention of Greek ἱστορικοί since the beginning. But while some writers had tried to rationalize and systematize mythology, others preferred to exploit it and adapt it for their purposes.

Herodotus, for example, does not attempt to rationalize or explain the stories of his opening chapters; he tells them in order to show that the origins of the East–West conflict are ancient, but he has no intention of investigating these origins or arguing the matter at length. Thucydides disclaims any intention of busying himself with τὸ μυθῶδες, but he is quite ready to take advantage of mythology when it serves his purpose, if it 'proves' the lack of Hellenic unity in early times (1. 3. 3) or the importance of sea-power in the heroic age (1. 9. 2–3) or provides 'evidence' of the gradual silting-up of the Achelous (2. 102. 5–6). He thinks it worth while to insist that the Tereus of mythology has nothing to do with Teres, the founder of the Odrysian kingdom in Thrace (2. 29. 3). One may suspect that others had tried to bring the Odrysians 'into the mainstream of Greek mythology', as a means of proving that they were perfectly good Greeks. This would be the same technique that the Greeks of the West were using.

There is a tendency among students of early Greek history to suppose that tales about heroic times have some sort of historical value as oral tradition, but when these stories are not attested before Hellenistic times a high degree of caution and skepticism is called for. Members of city states throughout the Greek world liked to profess that their cities possessed an early history, and liked to maintain that gods or heroes had a part in the foundation of their city and in establishing their special local cults or customs. The delight in such so-called tradition became even stronger in Hellenistic times, if the characteristics of Hellenistic poetry are any guide; and the elaborate aetiology of Callimachus and Apollonius seems to have its counterpart in the prose writers, if these efforts to reconstruct the early books of Timaeus are not misleading.

It is perhaps foolish to imagine that we know much more or much less than what such writers tell us. Were Greek settlers in the West, without realizing it, following religious customs which they had taken over from pre-Greek inhabitants of the area? It has been argued, for example, that the special devotion of Sicilian Greeks to Demeter and Kore was in some degree stimulated or affected by the fertility rites which they could observe being practiced by the non-Greek inhabitants.[64] But no writer ever tells us anything of the kind or even suggests that Greek colonies had any respect for local religions or were prepared to admit non-Greek influences into their cities. It is easier to believe that the settlers brought their religious beliefs with them fully stabilized, and looked to their own mythology to create local *aetia* or to help them recognize signs of the divine presence, with learned ingenuity replacing pious credulity as time went on. It has also been suggested that there is some kind of historical meaning in the tale that Jason and Medea landed at the mouth of the Sele in Campania, near Paestum, that it is a kind of proof of early settlement there, in the eighth century, by Thessalian colonists coming from the sea, before there was any move overland from Sybaris.[65] But the tale of the Argonauts' landing is known only from Hellenistic literature, and there is nothing to suggest that it was adapted from an earlier tradition.

In fact, since Hellenistic historians certainly enjoyed writing

64. Zuntz, *Persephone*, pp. 59–178. He has many shrewd observations in these pages, but I cannot share his belief that we have evidence in classical or pre-classical Sicily for the kind of syncretism that occurs in the Hellenistic Near East.

65. P. Zancani-Montuoro–U. Zanotti Bianco, *Heraion alla Foce del Sele*, vol. 1 (Rome 1951), pp. 9–14.

fictitious or 'creative' history,[66] just as poets liked adding new
variations and details to mythology, it is neither necessary nor
reasonable to postulate early origins for tales which look more like
the work of literary imagination than of popular belief or fantasy.
Apart from their absence in earlier poetry, the failure of these
stories to make any recognizable appearance in art is a strong
indication that they are of later origin. And when they seem
peculiarly well devised to serve the purpose of an historian's
archaeologia, it is hard to believe they were collected by conscien-
tious traveling folklorists, who wanted to preserve and record
local folk-tales.

66. For the writers who 'created' the early history of Messenia, cf. L.
Pearson, 'The Pseudo-History of Messenia and its authors', *Historia* 11 (1962),
397–426.

Symploke: its role in Polybius' Histories

F. W. WALBANK

POLYBIUS WAS not the first historian who claimed to write 'universal' history, as he admits;[1] but the only one of his predecessors whose claim he concedes is Ephorus, and Ephorus in fact did not produce a history of the whole world, but merely combined a number of separate accounts of the Greek states in a single work.[2] Polybius' *Histories* were universal in a different sense, for they dealt with a period in which (he tells us) events themselves had begun to interlock; and in his discussion of that process a great part is played by the concept of συμπλοκή. It is this concept and its relevance to Polybius' idea of universal history that I want to examine here. I do so in the hope that the subject may seem not inappropriate as a tribute to Adam Parry, whose keen interest in problems of literary composition was well known, and who had recently turned his attention to the field of Greek history.

I

Clearly Polybius attached great importance to the idea of συμπλοκή. 'It is only from the interconnection of all the events one with another and from their comparison (συμπλοκῆς καὶ παραθέσεως), and from their resemblances and differences, that a man can obtain his object and, thanks to a clear view of these matters, can derive both profit and pleasure from history.'[3] This συμπλοκή, this linking together of events throughout the inhabited world, is not something available to all historians at will. On the contrary, it is characteristic only of a particular period, that with which Polybius is himself concerned. Previously the doings of the

---

1. Cf. 5. 33. 2: several other writers have boasted that they have written τὰ καθόλου, and on a vaster scale than anyone else.
2. See on this E. Mioni, *Polibio* (Padua 1949), p. 23.
3. 1. 4. 11; as Schweighaeuser points out, κατοπτεύσας, 'getting a clear view', is probably to be taken with the 'resemblances and differences'.

world had been, as it were, scattered;[4] but from the 140th Olympiad onwards the affairs of Italy and Africa were joined together (συμπλέκεσθαι) with those of Greece and Asia, all leading to a single end (πρὸς ἓν γίνεσθαι τέλος τὴν ἀναφορὰν ἁπάντων).[5] The First Illyrian War (229/8) might seem to have been an anticipation of this; but no, that was only an ἐπιπλοκή, a contact, not a genuine involvement.[6] But from the 140th Olympiad (220/16) history had become a unified whole (σωματοειδής).[7]

At first sight the metaphors contained in the words συμπλοκή and σωματοειδής may seem incompatible; but I doubt if this is really so. It has been argued by Pédech that Polybius uses the word συμπλοκή because of its 'philosophical implications'.[8] As he points out, it forms part of the vocabulary of Leucippus and Democritus, who use it to describe the conjunction of the first elements.[9] But this is a secondary, derived meaning of a word which in its primary sense means 'a weaving or plaiting together'; and it is probably this meaning, frequently to be found in Plato in a metaphorical sense,[10] that Polybius intends here. The συμπλοκή of events is thought of as being like the weaving of a fabric; and inasmuch as the historian in his narrative produces a 'universal history' which copies the macrocosm of real events,[11] it is perhaps not too imaginative to detect a resemblance between the movement of the shuttle as it passes backwards and forwards across the warp and

4. 1. 3. 3: this passage is unfortunately marred by a lacuna, which has, however, been convincingly restored by J. M. Moore, who reads (CQ 16 (1966), 245–7), διὰ δὲ | ⟨τοῦ⟩το καὶ τὰς ἐπιβολὰς | ⟨αὐτῶν ἔτι⟩ δὲ συντελείας | αὐτ⟨οτελεῖς εἶναι,⟩ καὶ κα|τὰ το⟨ῦτο δὴ διαφέρ⟩ειν ἕ|καστα ⟨τῶν πεπραγμ⟩ένων. This indicates that prior to the 140th Olympiad events throughout the *oecumene*, being scattered, were linked together neither in their beginnings nor in their outcome.

5. 1. 3. 4.

6. 2. 12. 7.

7. See F. W. Walbank, *Polybius* (Berkeley–Los Angeles 1972), pp. 67–8. K. Lorenz, *Untersuchungen zum Geschichtswerk des Polybios* (Stuttgart 1931), pp. 17–18, compares the terminology in which Polybius describes the conditions of early human society, in which scattered individuals combine to form social units (6. 5); the comparison seems to me forced and unconvincing.

8. P. Pédech, *La Méthode historique de Polybe* (Paris 1964), p. 507.

9. Cf. H. Diels, *Die Fragmente der Vorsokratiker*[7], vol. II, p. 70n. (Simplicius, *In Aristot. phys.* p. 446, ed. Diels); 74 (Hippolyt. *Refut. omn. haeres.* 1. 12); 75 (Aristot. *Cael.* 3. 4. 303a 7); see Pédech, *Méthode de Polybe* (n. 8), n. 66.

10. See for instance *Polit.* 281a, 306 etc.

11. The weaver is presumably *Tyche*.

the historian's pen as he passes from area to area, describing the events of one year after another, and so composing the fabric of his written history.[12] Alternatively the stress of the metaphor may be not so much on the process of weaving as on the finished fabric. Or is it perhaps concerned with both? For it is after all the process of narration which produces the finished *Histories*. Whatever the exact nuance, this interpretation of συμπλοκή as referring to the interweaving of threads finds some support in a passage of book 3,[13] in which Polybius speaks of his finished work in forty books as easy to acquire and read, since they are 'as it were woven together in an unbroken series'.[14]

σωματοειδής, on the other hand, though it can indicate what is corporeal as opposed to what is unsubstantial – for example, an epiphany of Apollo[15] – is clearly used by Polybius as a technical term taken from Hellenistic literary theory and derived ultimately from the Platonic and Aristotelian concept of the unity of a literary work;[16] it means 'forming a unified whole', and since, as I have just pointed out, a literary work can be envisaged by Polybius as (metaphorically) woven,[17] there is no inconsistency between σωματοειδής and συμπλοκή.

II

The precise point of time at which the συμπλοκή began to show

12. Clearly to press the resemblances too far would be absurd. One obvious difference is that the shuttle goes *boustrophedon*, whereas the historians' path is a cyclical one, completing all the theatres of activity for one Olympiad year, and then starting afresh with Italy in the next.

13. 3. 32. 2; this passage implies that forty books were planned, but not necessarily that they had already been published; see the note in my *A Historical Commentary on Polybius* (2 vols., Oxford 1957, 1967) on 3. 1–5.

14. κατὰ μίτον means 'thread by thread, in due order, continuously', and the sense here is that Polybius' forty books lie side by side, like the threads of a warp, which are woven (ἐξυφασμένας) into a single fabric by means of the weft. See my note *ad loc.* in my *Commentary*.

15. Cf. Ephorus, *Die Fragmente der griechischen Historiker*, 70 F 31 (b); for a similar meaning on a *tabula defixionis* from Egypt see P. Collart, *Rev. Phil.* 56 (1930), 250 (quoted in *LSJ* s.v. σωματοειδής).

16. See Lorenz, *Untersuchungen* (n. 7), p. 87, n. 92; p. 99, n. 227, and my *Commentary* on 1. 3. 4. Paton in the Loeb edition mistranslates σωματοειδής as 'lifelike' both in 1. 3. 4 and in 14. 12. 5; in both passages it means 'a unified whole'.

17. See above, n. 14.

itself in the history of Rome is indicated in an important chapter in Book 4,[18] where Polybius explains that Ol. 140 opened with separate events in Italy, Greece and Asia, and with wars breaking out in those areas quite independently of each other, but that towards the end of the Olympiad these wars had conclusions 'common to all' (τὰς συντελείας κοινάς) and at that point events became interconnected (συνεπλάκησαν) and began to tend towards a single end (πρὸς ἕν τέλος ἤρξαντο τὴν ἀναφορὰν ἔχειν).[19] This development in historical events finds its appropriate reflection in Polybius' procedure as a historian; for by giving a separate account of the various wars down to the moment of combination he is able (so he says) to make the beginnings clearer and the συμπλοκή itself plain, and so to show 'when and how and for what reasons it came about'. That done, and the point of interconnection having been reached, he will proceed to compose a common history about all three areas,[20] in which he will deal with events all together 'following their chronology'.[21] But up to that point (which is defined more precisely as occurring in the third year of the 140th Olympiad, i.e. 217 B.C.)[22] he proposes to treat each theatre separately, merely using synchronisms with the events of the Hannibalic War (which he has already related in Book 3).[23] This will render his narrative easy to follow and more likely to create an impression on his readers (εὐπαρακολούθητος... καὶ καταπληκτική).[24] Polybius' concern to stimulate his readers' interest is a subject to which I shall revert below.[25]

Polybius is not content to date the beginning of the universal

---

18. 4. 28. 3–4; cf. 5. 31. 4–5.

19. Cf. 1. 3. 4 (quoted above, p. 198).

20. 4. 28. 4, κοινὴν ποιήσασθαι περὶ πάντων τὴν ἱστορίαν; Paton translates περὶ πάντων 'about all three wars', i.e. the Social War, the Hannibalic War and the Fourth Syrian War. But this is nonsense, since the συμπλοκή came in 217 at a time when two of these wars came to an end. περὶ πάντων means 'about all the events in Italy, Greece and Asia'.

21. 4. 28. 5, τοῖς καιροῖς ἀκολουθοῦντες. Polybius means that he will treat events year by year, and within each year area by area; see below, pp. 203–4 and 5. 31. 5.

22. 4. 28. 5.

23. I have discussed these synchronisms in *Polis and Imperium: Studies in honour of Edward Togo Salmon* (Toronto 1974), pp. 59–80.

24. Cf. 5. 31. 4–5, εὐπαρακολούθητον καὶ σαφῆ; cf. 5. 31. 7 for his stress on clarity.

25. See below, n. 47.

συμπλοκή to the year 217; in a passage in the fifth book[26] he tells us that it was at the conference called to Naupactus by Philip V to bring to an end the war between the Aetolian League and the Hellenic Alliance that the affairs of Greece, Italy and Africa were first linked together (τὰς... πράξεις... τοῦτο τὸ διαβούλιον συνέπλεξε πρῶτον). Attributing such ecumenical importance to this somewhat parochial peace conference involves Polybius in some slight difficulty; for previously (in 1. 3. 4 and 4. 28. 4)[27] he has defined the συμπλοκή as linking the affairs of Italy and Africa with those of Greece and Asia, but it is rather hard to find any connection with Asia in the Peace of Naupactus. However, he continues with the assertion that speedily (ταχέως) the same thing happened to the islanders and the people of Asia;[28] 'for those with grievances against Philip and some of Attalus' adversaries no longer turned to the south and east, to Antiochus and Ptolemy, but henceforth looked to the west, some sending embassies to Carthage and others to Rome'.

As we shall see,[29] this emphasis on the sending of embassies is important; but in its general terms Polybius' statement here is much exaggerated.[30] There is no evidence for any appeal to Rome by the islanders or the Greeks of Asia Minor for many years after 217. During the First Macedonian War neutral embassies were sent from Egypt, Rhodes, Chios, Mytilene and Byzantium, to endeavour to persuade the belligerents to make peace – but they did not visit Rome or the Roman forces. We have no knowledge of any islanders or Asian Greeks opposed to Attalus sending an embassy to Carthage;[31] and the earliest Roman embassy to cross the Aegean was dispatched in 200.

There were, it is true, good reasons why the eastern Greeks might no longer have felt able to appeal to Ptolemy or Antiochus. Despite his victory over Antiochus at Raphia, the effect of this battle (which was probably fought about the same time as

26. 5. 105. 4.
27. See above, nn. 5 and 20.
28. 5. 105. 6–7.
29. See below, pp. 207–8.
30. On this see my *Commentary*, *ad loc.* and Walbank, *Polybius*, pp. 68–70.
31. Pédech, *La Méthode de Polybe*, p. 506, interprets 5. 105. 4–10 to mean that Philip's enemies sent envoys to Rome and the enemies of Attalus approached Carthage; though not specifically stated, this seems likely.

Trasimene)[32] was to weaken Ptolemy IV, since in the course of his preparations he had armed the Egyptian μάχιμοι, and this step led to the national revolt which went on into the reign of his successor.[33] As for Antiochus III, he was soon involved in a campaign against the pretender Achaeus,[34] which lasted until Achaeus' capture and death at Sardes in 213,[35] and after that undertook his eastern *anabasis*, which was to occupy him from 212 until 205.[36] However, the fact that both kings were to some extent out of the picture is not by itself evidence that anyone in the Aegean area or in Asia Minor saw the Romans as an alternative.

It has been argued by Pédech,[37] following Siegfried,[38] that although there were still no contacts with Asia, Naupactus in fact marks a historical turning point, since what matter to Polybius are not so much actual military and diplomatic contacts as men's thoughts; and from now on by his plan against Rome Philip precipitated the συμπλοκή. This may well be a fair account of how Polybius saw the situation; but it does not really explain how the Greeks of Asia came to be involved in the συμπλοκή from 217 onward, for the acceptance of Siegfried's assertion that for Polybius thoughts as well as actions count as πράξεις[39] does not dispose of the historian's palpably false statement that embassies now began to go backward and forward between Asia Minor and Rome or Carthage.[40] Nor can Polybius' remark be taken as a reference to

32. The news of Trasimene led Philip to seek a peace with Aetolia (5. 101. 6–8). The evidence of the Pithom *stele* suggests that Raphia was fought on 22 June, while Ovid, *Fasti* 6. 767–8 dates Trasimene to 21 June; but uncertainty about intercalation in the Roman calendar means that the Julian equivalent of the latter date could very well be two or three weeks different either way (cf. R. M. Errington, *Latomus* 29 (1970), 55).

33. Cf. 5. 107. 1–3.

34. 5. 107. 4.

35. 7. 15–18; 8. 15–21.

36. 8. 23; 10. 27. 1–31. 15; 10. 48. 1–49. 15; 11. 34; 13. 9.

37. *La Méthode de Polybe*, p. 507.

38. W. Siegfried, *Studien zur geschichtlichen Anschauung des Polybios* (Berlin 1928), p. 46.

39. Cf. 5. 105. 4 for πράξεις.

40. Pédech, *La Méthode de Polybe*, p. 507, further asserts that Polybius' formulation, which makes 217 the decisive year for the συμπλοκή, is based on a Greek point of view 'which considers the fate of Greece and takes no account of the concept of Roman expansion, which imposes itself upon us today'. This is hard to believe, if one considers the fact that Roman expansion is the main subject of Polybius' *Histories*.

exchanges which began from the end of the century, since by that time Antiochus was back in the west and fully active in both war and diplomacy.

III

Thus Polybius' picture of a process of universal συμπλοκή beginning in 217 is not without difficulties when measured against the historical facts known to us. But I want to consider now the structural framework which Polybius set up so as to convey the nature of this συμπλοκή to his readers. Events had to be arranged according to both time and place, when they happened and where they happened, and, as I have already mentioned,[41] this was done by dividing up the continuous process of history into Olympiad years (a device borrowed from Timaeus),[42] and within each year treating the happenings in the various regions in a fixed sequence which was only rarely broken: this sequence[43] related the events of Italy, Sicily, Spain, Africa, Greece and Macedonia, Asia and Egypt in that order.[44] Now any such system is to some extent a compromise for, as Diodorus (probably echoing Duris of Samos)[45] points out, in reality (ἀλήθεια) events occur simultaneously in different places, whereas history (ἱστορία) is forced to divide them up unnaturally and relate them one after another; it is this, in Duris' opinion, that renders written history an inadequate μίμησις of the real events and causes it to fall short of them in πάθος.[46]

Now this difficulty is one inherent in any process of setting down an account of historical events in narrative form, and the combination of Olympiad years and 'theatres of action' goes some way towards overcoming it. But Polybius' problem (after Ol. 140) was

41. See above, n. 21.

42. See Walbank, *Polybius*, p. 101.

43. 32. 11. 2, τὴν εἰθισμένην τάξιν, ᾗ χρώμεθα παρ' ὅλην τὴν πραγματείαν; cf. 15. 25. 19.

44. See Walbank, *Polybius*, pp. 103–4, for discussion of this device.

45. Diod. 20. 43. 7; cf. H. Strasburger, 'Die Wesensbestimmung der Geschichte durch die antiken Geschichtsschreiber' (*Sitzungsberichte der wissenschaftlichen Gesellschaft an der Johann Wolfgang Goethe-Universität*, Frankfurt/Main, 5 (1966), n. 3), 47 n. 4.

46. For Duris' emphasis on μίμησις in history see *F. gr. Hist.* 76 F 1 = Photius, *Bibliotheca*, p. 121 a 41.

not merely one of narrating in succession events which in reality
occurred simultaneously, but also of bringing out the relationship
between separate sets of events which, by definition, were becoming causally more and more integrated, as the συμπλοκή grew.
This had to be done, moreover, in such a manner as not only to
reflect the true character of the συμπλοκή, but also to rivet his
readers' attention – for, as we saw, history should ideally be both
easy to follow and arresting (εὐπαρακολούθητος... καὶ καταπληκτική).[47] To achieve this aim was not entirely simple, and not every
historian accepted Polybius' solution. Appian, for example, who
elected to write a continuous history of each area separately, was
to complain that those historians of Rome who included material
from all over the world in a single narrative 'frequently took me
from Carthage to Spain, and from Spain to Sicily or Macedonia,
or to some embassies sent to other peoples or alliances made with
them; and they brought me back again to Carthage or Sicily as if
I were wandering in exile, then they took me off again without
finishing the matter'.[48] This is a serious criticism and one to which
Polybius is obviously open; his discussion of it and his attempt to
answer it will be our next concern.

IV

Polybius' reply to this charge (which had clearly been made by
others before Appian) comes in two chapters in Book 38,[49] which
have recently been the subject of a study by Klaus Meister.[50] In
these chapters Polybius defends his method of dividing up his
material so as to treat the events of the various areas under each
year, against the charge that this makes his narrative incomplete
and disconnected;[51] his method, he claims, follows the example of
Nature herself, by providing a proper variety, which is lacking in
a treatment κατὰ γένος. Moreover it is preferable to that of 'the
wisest among the ancient writers' – almost certainly he is referring

47. In 4. 28. 6 these criteria are applied to his account of events of Ol. 140
before the συμπλοκή began; see above, n. 24.

48. Appian, *Hist.* praef. 12.

49. 38. 5–6.

50. 'Die synchronistische Darstellung des Polybios im Gegensatz zur
Disposition des Ephoros und Theopompos', *Hermes*, 99 (1971), 506–8.

51. 38. 5. 1, ἀτελῆ καὶ διερριμμένην (the last word is uncertain in the
defective MS).

to Theopompus[52] – who set out to achieve this end in an unorganized way (ἀτάκτως) by the insertion of a series of mythological and anecdotal digressions in their narratives; whereas he himself by his regular switch from theatre to theatre (τεταγμένως) ensures that the necessary variety is as it were built into his history. Now this disagreement with Theopompus over the best method of attaining variety is a comparatively small matter. A much more fundamental quarrel is that with the advocates of a treatment κατὰ γένος in contrast to one based on a year-by-year system. The arguments which he is here attacking are clearly part of the stock-in-trade of Hellenistic literary controversy. I have already quoted Appian's comments;[53] and Dionysius has a similar criticism of Thucydides:[54] 'since in the same summer or the same winter many events occur, in all likelihood, in a variety of places, he (i.e. Thucydides) leaves his first subject incomplete and goes on to the next' – a procedure which, Dionysius claims, makes him 'obscure and hard to follow'.[55] But it has for some time been suspected,[56] and Meister has now confirmed,[57] that Polybius' polemic in 38. 5 is directed against Ephorus, who employed the κατὰ γένος method of composition. Incidentally, although Polybius rejects Ephorus' views on this matter, there is reason to believe that he felt them to possess some force, for in one or two places he abandons the Olympiad arrangement in order to achieve clarity and importance for his material. For example, Book 14 contained a single unified account, now lost, of the reign of Ptolemy IV from Raphia onwards;[58] and in Book 32[59] he included the whole story of the

52. Cf. Ed. Meyer, *Theopomps Hellenika* (Halle 1909), p. 137; Jacoby on *F. gr. Hist.* 115 F 28; K. Ziegler, *RE*, 'Polybios', col. 1546; G. Avenarius, *Lukians Schrift zur Geschichtsschreibung* (Diss. Frankfurt/Main, 1954), p. 126, n. 55. On digressions see also A. E. Wardman, *Historia* 9 (1960), 406.

53. See above, p. 204, n. 48.

54. Dion. Hal. *ad Pomp.* 2. 237. 10ff.; cf. *de Thucyd.* 9.

55. ἀσαφὴς καὶ δυσπαρακολούθητος.

56. Cf. Avenarius, *Lukians Schrift*, p. 126, 'dürfen wir annehmen, dass er hier sinngemäss wiederholt, was schon Ephoros selbst gegen das synchronistische Prinzip vorgetragen hat'.

57. *Hermes*, 99 (1971), 507–8, comparing Ephorus' views as expressed in Diod. 5. 1. 4 (= *F. gr. Hist.* 70 T 11) and 16. 1. 1–2.

58. 14. 12. 1–5; according to a note in the manuscript it occupied forty-eigh sheets.

59. 32. 11. 1–6.

relations between Oropus and Athens, 'partly reverting to the past (he says) and partly anticipating the future, so that the separate details being in themselves insignificant, I may not by relating them under different dates produce a narrative that is both trivial and obscure'.

Meister has pointed out a curious omission from Polybius' defence of his literary method against Ephorus and Theopompus: he says nothing about its suitability for securing a proper representation of the συμπλοκή of events throughout the *oecumene*, although, as I have indicated, this was one of the main reasons for adopting it.[60] This omission may suggest that it was not on these grounds that his method had been challenged, and that whereas his critics charged him with being incomplete, disconnected, trivial and obscure, they did not argue that his procedure failed to do justice to the growing interconnection of political events throughout the Mediterranean area. The point may, of course, have been simply ignored. On the other hand, an examination of the organization of the *Histories* in relation to the question of συμπλοκή furnishes some support for the claims which Polybius makes on behalf of the method which he adopted.

V

The first and most obvious advantage of that method – that is, the treatment of the separate theatres in a fixed order, Olympiad year by Olympiad year – is that it allows him, so to speak, to keep several balls in the air at once. But, more particularly, the *order* in which he chose to arrange the various theatres was especially well adapted to dealing with the events which he had to describe. The effect of the συμπλοκή was to intensify the links between Rome and the rest of the Mediterranean world;[61] and these links took the form both of peaceful contacts, which expressed themselves (as Polybius says)[62] in the exchange of embassies between the various states and Rome, and of warlike activities involving the dispatch

60. See above, pp. 200ff.

61. 5. 105. 4, discussed above, pp. 201ff.

62. *Ibid.* Polybius' readers are hardly likely to ignore the importance of these embassies in view of the fact that (thanks partly to the chances of manuscript survival) so many of our fragments of Polybius from the Constantinian excerpts are concerned with these.

on various occasions of Roman armies to Africa, Greece, the Balkan peninsula and Asia Minor. I leave aside Roman campaigns in other areas such as northern Italy and Spain because, if the surviving fragments of his *Histories* are anything to go by, Polybius was less interested in these; no doubt they seemed less relevant to his main theme.

The normal procedure at Rome was to hear foreign embassies at the beginning of the new consul year;[63] even important missions usually had to await the entry into office of the new consuls. Similarly, Roman embassies to foreign states were normally dispatched about the same time. Now Polybius nominally divided up his history into Olympiad years; but in practice these were usually extended to include events up to the end of the current campaigning season.[64] Consequently the dispatch of envoys from the east at any time down to late autumn of any Julian year would be recorded among events occurring in the appropriate geographical area – Greece, Macedonia, Asia, etc. – during the Olympiad year which nominally ended in the August of that year; and since Italy came first in the list of such geographical areas in Polybius' scheme, the hearing of such envoys at Rome would be described at the beginning of the next Olympiad year, not too many pages after the account of their dispatch. Likewise the sending of Roman *legati* would normally be recorded early in a given Olympiad year under *res Italiae*, and their arrival at their destination would be described when Polybius reached the *res Graeciae*, or wherever it might be, of the same Olympiad year.

Of course, events did not always occur in this convenient way. In the late winter or early spring of 170/69 the Rhodians sent envoys to Rome to defend the city against charges arising out of their policy during the Third Macedonian War, and the Senate, contrary to its usual practice, gave these envoys a special hearing when they arrived in Rome late in the summer of 169.[65] Thus both the sending of the envoys and their reception at Rome took place in the same Olympiad year, Ol. 152. 3 = 170/69, and in describing their dispatch under the affairs of Rhodes in 28. 16, Polybius,

63. On this see G. De Sanctis, *Storia dei Romani*, vol. IV. 1 (Turin 1923), p. 387, giving examples of delays in the hearing of foreign embassies.
64. See my *Commentary*, 1. 35–6.
65. 28. 2. 1, ἤδη τῆς θερείας ληγούσης.

after observing that their kindly reception by the Senate has already been related in 28. 2, continues:

> 'as regards this, it is useful to remind my readers frequently, as indeed I try to do, that I am often obliged to report the hearing and proceedings of embassies before describing their appointment and dispatch; for, since in narrating in their proper order the events of each year I try to bring together in a single section the events that happened in each country in that year, it is clear that this must sometimes happen in my work.'[66]

Such occasional dislocations were more likely to occur, however, in the account of embassies moving not between Rome and the east but between two eastern theatres. For example, the negotiations between Ptolemy the son of Sosibius and Philip V of Macedon in 203/2 had to be related before the account of Ptolemy's dispatch from Alexandria, because Macedonia came before Egypt in Polybius' list of theatres of action;[67] and there must have been many other similar cases since Polybius speaks of having to mention the problem frequently (πλεονάκις).[68] Evidently he felt that to tamper with the order in which he had elected to deal with the various countries would be liable to create more difficulties than it solved; and certainly it would have made it more difficult to find one's way around in the *Histories*. In support of this rigid treatment is the fact that, as I have pointed out, both generally and as a device for describing the relations between Rome and the Hellenistic states, the order he had adopted was the one best suited to his purpose. However, he was, very occasionally, prepared to modify his strict scheme. His use in one or two places of Ephorus' division κατὰ γένος has already been mentioned;[69] but in addition we also find him in one place changing the conventional order in which the various regions were treated. After recounting the

66. For similar comments see 15. 24a, 25. 19; the first of these two passages should stand after the second (see Walbank, *Commentary*, 2. 23 (discussing the points made by P. Maas, *AIPhO* (1949), 443–6) and Walbank, *Polybius*, p. 111, n. 75 (defending Maas against the criticisms of K. Abel, *Hermes* 95 (1967), 81–4)).

67. 15. 25. 19; see the previous note.

68. 28. 16. 10.

69. See above, pp. 205–6.

restoration of Ariarathes of Cappadocia under the Olympiad year
155. 3 = 158/7, he remarks:[70]

> 'Having given a brief account of Ariarathes' restoration, I
> shall resume the regular course of my narrative, which I follow
> throughout the whole of this work. For in the present instance,
> passing over the affairs of Greece, I took out of turn (προελά-
> βομεν) those matters in Asia relating to Cappadocia, because
> I could find no justifiable means of separating the departure of
> Ariarathes from Italy from his return to power. I will there-
> fore now go back to the events that happened in Greece at
> the same date.'[71]

In this year then some at least of the *res Asiae* preceded *res Graeciae*.

As Polybius approached the period which in his original plan
marked the culmination of the συμπλοκή and the unification of the
oecumene under Rome, that is the period dominated by the Third
Macedonian War, it looks as if he became increasingly conscious
of the hampering effect of his geographical divisions. At any rate,
for the years 172/68, dealt with in Books 17–29, he may have
adopted the war with Perseus as a single subdivision into which
events from both Europe and Asia might be introduced. For
example, the order of events in Livy 42. 43–6, based directly on
Polybius, shows that the visit of Roman envoys to Rhodes (in 171),
which Polybius records in 27. 3. 1–5, is unlikely to have formed
part of his *res Asiae* for 172/1, since in Livy the narrative reverts
immediately afterwards to events occurring the same year in
Greece.[72] Similarly in Book 29, the passage 19. 1–11 (corresponding to Livy 45. 3. 3–8), though describing the reception of Rhodian
envoys at Rome, must form part of the account of the war with
Perseus during Ol. 152. 4 = 169/8, since in the excerpts *de leg.
gent.*, from which it is taken, it is preceded by passages dealing with
events at Rhodes (29. 10. 1–7 and 11. 1–6) and followed by the
arrival of an Egyptian embassy in Achaea, all from the same

70. 32. 11. 2–3.
71. The Greek events to which he refers are those of Oropus, on which see
above, n. 59; thus Book 32 contained a double breach of his normal procedure
at this point – an inversion of the order of theatres of action and a modification
of the principle of recounting events under their appropriate Olympiad year.
72. Cf. Livy, 42. 43–4 (= Polyb. 37. 1. 1–2. 12: events of Boeotia); 45. 1–8
(= Polyb. 37. 3. 1–5: Roman envoys in Asia); 46. 1ff. (affairs in Greece).

Olympiad year. In the same way Polybius may have adopted a single geographical theatre of action to embrace all the events of the war between Antiochus and Egypt in Books 28 and 29 (Ol. 152. 3–4 = 170/69 and 169/8) – though this is less certain.[73] Thus the concept of a single war extending into several geographical areas was in some degree permitted to supersede the rigid division into separate theatres, and thus to become a further expression of the growing συμπλοκή of events. But this extension was limited in scope and rigidly controlled, and in general the regional treatment was maintained down to the end of the *Histories*.

As we have seen, it generally suited the account of diplomatic exchanges; but it also suited the description of military campaigning, since there again, in the major wars with which Polybius was primarily concerned, the war decision usually followed the entry of the new consuls into office,[74] and could therefore be recorded in the *res Italiae* of any Olympiad year, to be followed in due course by a description of the arrival of the general and his legions in the war-area later in the *res Graeciae* or *res Asiae* etc. of the same year.

VI

Thus Polybius' arrangement of his material under separate theatres within the successive Olympiad years served him very well as a means of describing the growing συμπλοκή of events throughout the civilized world. Of this συμπλοκή Pédech sees an important expression in the way in which one major historical event leads to another.[75] In a passage in Book 3 Polybius notes

73. Two fragments dealing with the Egyptian appeal to Achaea in 169/8, 29. 23. 1–24. 16 and 25. 1–7, may form part of the *res Graeciae* of that year, in which case they will have to be transposed to stand between 21. 1–9 and 22. 1–5; but it is equally possible that they should go after 22. 1–5 (where Büttner-Wobst puts them) to form part of a composite section *bellum Antiochi et Ptolomaei*, embracing both Egypt and Asia.

74. This point is not easy to illustrate from the extant fragments where the only major war-decision within the period 216/146 to be recorded is that against Carthage in 36. 3. 9 (150/49). Livy's records of the war-decisions against Philip in 200, Antiochus and Perseus all occur in annalistic passages (Livy, 31. 5–8; 36. 1. 1–6; 42. 30. 8–11). But the sending out of armies at the beginning of a campaigning season (200 is an exception) imposes some such time-table.

75. Pédech, *La Méthode de Polybe*, p. 508.

how 'the war with Antiochus derived its origins from that with Philip, the latter from that with Hannibal and the Hannibalic War from that about Sicily (i.e. the First Punic War)'.[76] It is true that this nexus of cause and effect is one of the features contributing to the συμπλοκή, if only because as a process it was not confined to one area, but spread its influence over the three continents. But I doubt if Polybius had it prominently in mind in this context, since it is not something peculiar to the period 217/167, as the reference to the First Punic War makes clear. I suspect that he is thinking rather of the kind of thing that happened in 168, when the Roman victory over Perseus at Pydna permitted the sending of Popillius to Egypt, and so settled the conflict between Ptolemy and Antiochus at a stroke.[77] This, rather than the causal nexus between one war and the next, perhaps better illustrates what Polybius meant by συμπλοκή.

Polybius nowhere states clearly whether he believes the συμπλοκή to continue to operate once Rome has become mistress of the world in 168/7. In a passage in Book 3 he claims a unity for the whole of his *Histories*,[78] which, he says, are easy to acquire and read, since they consist of forty books, 'all, as it were, woven together in an unbroken series'; thus readers can clearly follow events in Italy, Sicily and Africa from the time of Pyrrhus down to the capture of Carthage and those in the rest of the world from the flight of Cleomenes of Sparta down to the battle of the Romans and the Achaeans at the Isthmus. However, this passage, though it employs the metaphor of weaving, is not concerned only with the period of συμπλοκή. It occurs in a context in which the author is pleading the cause of universal history against the special monograph, and the reference to the time of Pyrrhus as well as to the events of 146 shows that he is not thinking only of the fifty-three years from 220 to 168/7.

Since in fact the συμπλοκή began at a specific moment – the Conference of Naupactus in 217[79] – it would seem reasonable to

76. 3. 32. 7; the process is worked out in detail by Pédech, *La Méthode de Polybe*, pp. 507–8, who adds that in the same way the war with Perseus is seen as growing out of the war with Antiochus, since it was Philip's discontent at his inadequate rewards after that war that led to his conceiving the plan for the Third Macedonian War – which Perseus fought; cf. Livy, 39. 23. 5–13.

77. 29. 27. 11–13 for the close connection.

78. 3. 32. 2–3; see above, p. 199.   79. See above, n. 26.

assume that with the completion of Roman control over the *oecumene*, the συμπλοκή, as the process which brought that about, was also complete; and Pédech has argued plausibly for this view.[80] After 167 Rome was mistress of the world; henceforth the *oecumene* was under her control and events responded more than ever to her decisions. From that point of view the συμπλοκή was now something in the past. Moreover, the Celtiberian War, the Third Punic War, the rivalries of Asian dynasts, the revolt of Andriscus and that of the Achaean League are not described as events in any way linked together; they were separate in their origins, like the wars of the Olympiad period 220/16, and many were the outcome of decisions (on the part of the opponents of Rome) which seemed to Polybius to show evidence of crazy infatuation. Because this was a time of disjointed and to some extent irrational events, Polybius characterizes it as ταραχὴ καὶ κίνησις and in relating its history feels himself to be virtually starting on a new work.[81] I have argued elsewhere[82] that Polybius added this later period to his *Histories* primarily because it covered events from about 152 onwards in which he had himself played a striking part, and that this decision carried with it the corollary that he must also relate the events of the years between 167 and 152, concerning which in any case he had assembled a mass of useful material during his enforced stay at Rome.

This material, covering more than twenty years, took up another ten books; and Polybius continued to use the same organization under theatres of action and Olympiad years as he had used for the earlier parts. He had indeed no good reason to stop doing so. But the whole character of this later section (167/46), both in its conception and in its alleged purpose inside the *Histories*,[83] is such that it is no longer concerned with the συμπλοκή which had been so essential an ingredient of the period down to Pydna.

80. *La Méthode de Polybe*, p. 508.
81. 3. 4. 13, οἷον ἀρχὴν ποιησάμενος ἄλλην γράφειν. See on this Walbank, *Polybius*, pp. 182–3; Pédech, *La Méthode de Polybe*, p. 16.
82. Walbank, *Polybius*, pp. 182–3.
83. On Polybius' alleged reason for his extension, viz. to enable readers to pass judgment on Rome, see 3. 4. 1–13 with Walbank, *Commentary, ad loc.* and *Polybius*, pp. 181–3.

Plutarch and the Megarian decree

CHARLES FORNARA

THE MEGARIAN DECREE, with its context of associated events, the violation of the *hiera orgas*, Anthemocritus' embassy and the decree of Charinus, has prompted considerable discussion in recent years.[1] The possibility of reconciling the evidence of our three main witnesses, Thucydides, Aristophanes and Plutarch, would be difficult even if it were not compounded by difficulties in the interpretation of each of them. Thus the mere determination of the date of the central decree – that banning the Megarians from the Athenian *agora* and the harbors of the allied cities – cannot be disentangled from the literary and philosophical problem of judging Thucydides' version of the causes or occasions of the Peloponnesian War. Brunt could argue, for example, that Thucydides' failure to inform us when or why the Megarian decree was passed is presumptive evidence that it was not a preliminary of the War and that it therefore must have been voted substantially before 433 or 432.[2] Ignoring for the present the possibility that Thucydides did not know that he did not tell us its date, Brunt's judgment is clearly based upon his general assessment of Thucydides' mode of operation. Working from a different assessment, Meiggs could as reasonably conclude that the reason Thucydides makes so little of the decree is that others had made so much of it.[3] He did not tell us simply because he refused to count it among the αἰτίαι and διαφοραί and, as Jacoby would say, was being stiff-necked about the whole matter.[4]

Difficulties of another sort arise with Aristophanes. We possess his virtually contemporaneous comments in the *Acharnians* of 425

1. See, for an excellent bibliography, G. E. M. de Ste Croix, *The Origins of the Peloponnesian War* (London 1972), Appendix xxxv, pp. 381–3, to which now add R. Meiggs, *The Athenian Empire* (Oxford 1972), p. 430.
2. *AJP* 72 (1951), 270ff.
3. *Athenian Empire*, p. 431.
4. *Die Fragmente der griechischen Historiker*, IIIB (Suppl.), 1, p. 490.

and the *Peace* of 421; and no one would accuse him of expressing himself ambiguously or, as to the main fact, with lack of consistency. In both plays the Megarian decree caused the war though Pericles is motivated differently in the *Acharnians* from in the *Peace*. But it is always possible to disdain putative historical material when retailed by the comic poet, whether in iamb or in anapaest. Thus Brunt wrote that 'it is doubtful how far sober history can ever be reconstructed from the jests of comedy';[5] and de Ste Croix, in his recent study, *The Origins of the Peloponnesian War*, certainly did not attempt to do so.[6] Instead he devoted considerable space to the demonstration that because it is not sound historical method to pick and choose between Aristophanic items when some are exaggerative or false, it is legitimate to exclude them as evidence.[7] Such blanket skepticism seems unreasonably harsh: it is not a question, after all, of constructing history from comic jests, but from a comedy presupposing actual historical events. Nevertheless, uncertainty remains.

No such comparatively philosophical issue has been raised against Plutarch. His discussion of the Megarian decree in the *Pericles* c. 30 is merely stigmatized point-blank as being hopelessly muddled and chronologically confused.[8] Plutarch has been accused by one scholar of being so far from having a clear idea about his subject that it is uncertain at any given time which of his medley of decrees he is referring to.[9] Perhaps no treatment accorded him was quite so contemptuous as Jacoby's, who in his commentary to Philochorus F. 121 ignored Plutarch in that part of his discussion devoted to the Megarian decree.[10] One consequence which has followed from the general opinion is far-reaching. Some scholars have concluded that the tradition was in turmoil by the time Plutarch consulted it and have consequently felt no compunction in rearranging it. Indeed, as Plutarch currently is interpreted, ample justification exists for violent measures. For he is supposed

5. *AJP* 72 (1951), 273.

6. *Athenian Empire*, especially pp. 236–44.

7. See below, pp. 222–6.

8. W. R. Connor, *AJP* 83 (1962), 225–46; de Ste Croix, *Origins*, pp. 230 ('the vital passage, *Per.* 29. 4–32, is in a state of hopeless chronological confusion', p. 230), 249.

9. Connor, *AJP* 83 (1962), 226ff.

10. *F. gr. Hist.* IIIB (Suppl.), 1, p. 489 with n. 29.

to list, in chronological order, first, the main decree of exclusion, then the mild and benevolent protest carried by the envoy Anthemocritus who was dispatched to complain about Megarian violation of the *hiera orgas*, and, finally, Charinus' decree, ordering the generals to invade the Megarid twice yearly and providing for the burial of Anthemocritus, allegedly murdered by the Megarians. This sequence makes no historical sense: the notion of Pericles' having sent Anthemocritus to Megara and to Sparta with a justification of the Megarian decree by way of a counter-complaint, gently couched, is absurd, and Charinus' decree can hardly have been passed before March 431, when conditions of war began,[11] so that its relation to the Megarian decree seems exiguous. Plutarch's supposed sequence has accordingly been amended variously by different scholars. Cawkwell modified Plutarch's account by supposing that Anthemocritus' role in the dispute was as a herald sent by the Athenians in the spring of 431 to deny the Megarians access to the Eleusinian Mysteries.[12] Connor suggested that the entire episode involving Anthemocritus and Charinus belongs in the middle of the fourth century.[13] Kagan theorized that the legislation of Charinus could have been contemplated but failed of passage.[14] De Ste Croix altered the order of events, making the embassy of Anthemocritus first in the sequence, the exclusionary decree following on its heels.[15] Any of these views could perhaps be correct; but I would maintain that such speculation is as unnecessary as it is without probative value, for it is possible to interpret Plutarch in such a way that his discussion becomes not muddled but coherent and, in virtue of that, worthy of being taken seriously.

Plutarch's sketch of the Megarian affair in c. 30 does not seem to have been regarded in the light of its surrounding context. It has been understood as if it were an account of the Megarian decree as a cause of the war and a narration of the events leading from the time of Pericles' refusal to cancel the decree to the war's outbreak. Yet the chapter is part of a larger whole, extending from

11. Busolt's discussion in *Griechische Geschichte*, III. 2, p. 814, n. 4 remains standard.

12. G. L. Cawkwell, *REG* 82 (1969), 332ff.

13. *AJP* 83 (1962), 225–46; *REG* 83 (1970), 305–8.

14. *The Outbreak of the Peloponnesian War* (Cornell 1969), p. 261.

15. *Origins*, p. 249.

29. 4 through 32, and the entire section is concerned not with the historical events but with Pericles' motive – as Plutarch viewed it – for wanting war. It is a good example of the different emphases of biography and history, and his summation, in 32. 6, puts it clearly. After having mentioned the attacks made against Pheidias, Aspasia and Anaxagoras in the context of the charge that Pericles wanted war because he was under personal attack, he ends as follows: 'These are the causes, then, on account of which it is alleged that he did not allow the People to yield to the Lacedaemonians. But as to the truth of them, it is unclear' – αἱ μὲν οὖν αἰτίαι, δι' ἃς οὐκ εἴασεν ἐνδοῦναι Λακεδαιμονίοις τὸν δῆμον, αὗται λέγονται· τὸ δ' ἀληθὲς ἄδηλον. The operative words are 'he did not allow the People to yield': 'yield', obviously, in the matter of the Megarian decree. And just as the whole discussion is devoted to possible reasons for Pericles' adamancy, so is that part of it which is chapter 30. Yet students of the question have viewed it in isolation as if it were a narration of the events leading to the war. How crucial the difference is can be seen from the implications of one interpretation, Cawkwell's, of 30. 4, where 'the Megarians denied the murder of Anthemocritus and turned the blame on Aspasia and Pericles': Μεγαρεῖς δὲ τὸν 'Ανθεμοκρίτου φόνον ἀπαρνούμενοι, τὰς αἰτίας εἰς 'Ασπασίαν καὶ Περικλέα τρέπουσι. Cawkwell began his discussion with the automatic assumption that τὰς αἰτίας here refers to the causes of the war.[16] I think it can be shown, however, that it must refer to the causes of Pericles' enactment of the Megarian decree, and if so, a totally different chronology begins to unfold, for it follows that Plutarch himself believed that Anthemocritus' embassy was prior to Pericles' exclusionary decree.

The disposition of this chapter is compatible with the assumption that Plutarch studied Pericles' refusal to rescind the decree in the light of motives which prompted him to pass it. It is this problem, or *aporia*, which is Plutarch's main interest, and he pursues it with the same procedure he uses in the next chapter, 31, where he considers the possible relevance of the trial of Pheidias. The sequence in c. 30 is psychological and allusive, of a type frequently found in the *Lives*. There is a sort of parallel in the *Pericles* c. 24, where Pericles' expedition against Samos is dis-

16. *REG* 82 (1969), 327.

cussed. The question of Aspasia's role in that decision launches him into a discussion about her – her background, prowess in oratory, relationship with Pericles. Finally, by a circuitous route, bringing us all the way to the name of the younger Cyrus' favorite mistress, he returns in 25. 1 to the Samian war with the remark that Pericles is accused of having begun it because of Aspasia's connection with Miletus. Plutarch's concern is with motives and he enlarged upon the tradition to shed light upon them regardless of chronological sequence.

The same preoccupation is observable in 29. 4–31. 1. In 29. 4–6 Plutarch mentions the complaints of the Corinthians, the Megarians, the Aeginetans, and the issue of Potidaea, all in that order:

> χαλεπαίνουσι δὲ τοῖς Κορινθίοις καὶ κατηγοροῦσι τῶν Ἀθηναίων ἐν Λακεδαίμονι προσεγένοντο Μεγαρεῖς, αἰτιώμενοι πάσης μὲν ἀγορᾶς, ἁπάντων δὲ λιμένων ὧν Ἀθηναῖοι κρατοῦσιν εἴργεσθαι καὶ ἀπελαύνεσθαι παρὰ τὰ κοινὰ δίκαια καὶ τοὺς γεγενημένους ὅρκους τοῖς Ἕλλησιν· (5) Αἰγινῆται δὲ κακοῦσθαι δοκοῦντες καὶ βίαια πάσχειν, ἐποτνιῶντο κρύφα πρὸς τοὺς Λακεδαιμονίους, φανερῶς ἐγκαλεῖν τοῖς Ἀθηναίοις οὐ θαρροῦντες. (6) ἐν δὲ τούτῳ καὶ Ποτίδαια, πόλις ὑπήκοος Ἀθηναίων, ἄποικος δὲ Κορινθίων, ἀποστᾶσα καὶ πολιορκουμένη μᾶλλον ἐπετάχυνε τὸν πόλεμον.

His role here is that of the historian listing the various causes of the war. There is a shift, however, in 29. 7, when he returns to the Megarian question and expresses the conviction that the war could have been averted if Pericles had been willing to rescind the exclusionary decree against the Megarians:

> οὐ μὴν ἀλλὰ καὶ πρεσβειῶν πεμπομένων Ἀθήναζε, καὶ τοῦ βασιλέως τῶν Λακεδαιμονίων Ἀρχιδάμου τὰ πολλὰ τῶν ἐγκλημάτων εἰς διαλύσεις ἄγοντος καὶ τοὺς συμμάχους πραΰνοντος, οὐκ ἂν δοκεῖ συμπεσεῖν ὑπό γε τῶν ἄλλων αἰτίων ὁ πόλεμος τοῖς Ἀθηναίοις, εἰ τὸ ψήφισμα καθελεῖν τὸ Μεγαρικὸν ἐπείσθησαν καὶ διαλλαγῆναι πρὸς αὐτούς.

To Plutarch, Pericles' obstinacy was a puzzle requiring explanation. For that he was obstinate is the point of the anecdote he relates in 30. 1, where Pericles will not be moved by the good-natured cajolery of a Spartan envoy.[17] But although the anecdote indeed presupposes the enactment of the decree, we should not conclude that Plutarch is beginning another chronological list as in the chapter before. He has already given us the list and is now going back to one item in it to explore the psychology of it. His inference in 30. 2 that there must have been more to the matter than met the eye addresses that issue. For by a natural progression Plutarch proceeded to ask what moved Pericles to pass the decree in the first place since his refusal to cancel it was presumably explicable by the motives prompting him to enact it. The motives, secret and public, are then passed in review. The proleptic assumption of a secret hostility seemed required because the 'public complaint', the ostensible cause for Pericles' hatred of Megara as exemplified by his passage of the decree and his refusal to rescind it seemed relatively too trival to cause a war which otherwise could have been stopped. 'Apparently', Plutarch said, 'he had a secret and private animosity against the Megarians, but he made as his open and public grievance against them, that the *hiera orgas* was being appropriated by them': ὑπῆν μὲν οὖν τις ὡς ἔοικεν αὐτῷ καὶ ἰδία πρὸς τοὺς Μεγαρεῖς ἀπέχθεια, κοινὴν δὲ καὶ φανερὰν ποιησάμενος αἰτίαν κατ' αὐτῶν ἀποτέμνεσθαι τὴν ἱερὰν ὀργάδα κτλ. Plutarch then mentions the embassy of Anthemocritus, whose message was conciliatory and humane – εὐγνώμονος καὶ φιλανθρώπου δικαιολογίας ἐχόμενον – his death and Charinus' decree.

It would be reasonable to suppose that Plutarch believed that the embassy took place before the enactment of the Megarian decree (his proper subject through chapter 32) if only because not even his worst enemy should accuse him, when it is unnecessary, of pursuing a psychologically absurd train of thought.[18] Here

17. λέγουσι δὲ πρεσβείας ᾿Αθήναζε περὶ τούτων ἐκ Λακεδαίμονος ἀφιγμένης, καὶ τοῦ Περικλέους νόμον τινὰ προβαλομένου κωλύοντα καθελεῖν τὸ πινάκιον ἐν ᾧ τὸ ψήφισμα γεγραμμένον ἐτύγχανεν, εἰπεῖν Πολυάλκη τῶν πρέσβεών τινα· 'σὺ δὲ μὴ καθέλῃς, ἀλλὰ στρέψον εἴσω τὸ πινάκιον· οὐ γὰρ ἔστι νόμος ὁ τοῦτο κωλύων.' κομψοῦ δὲ τοῦ λόγου φανέντος, οὐδέν τι μᾶλλον ὁ Περικλῆς ἐνέδωκεν. The anecdote may be authentic insofar as a clause (not Plutarch's 'law') could have been inserted in the decree barring reconsideration of its terms. Cf. *IG* I², 92. 17–19 (Meiggs–Lewis, no. 58 B), *IG* II², 43. 51ff. (Tod, no. 123).

18. Indeed, Plutarch is more insistent than moderns on verisimilitude and a 'rational' emotional progression. Cf., for example, Gomme's discussion (*A Historical Commentary on Thucydides*, vol. 1 (Oxford 1959), pp. 62f.) of Plutarch's

Plutarch is speaking of a conciliatory and humane embassy Pericles sent both to Sparta and to Megara, and he has just finished his anecdote about Pericles' remorseless attitude to a Spartan envoy to Athens, and in the last sentence of 29 has characterized his attitude as the opposite of benevolent or pacific.[19] The usual view condemns Plutarch not only for historical confusion, always possible, but for a mystifying *nonsequitus* on the psychological plane. This is the weakness of such rescue-attempts as that made by Cawkwell, which seeks to find a context for Anthemocritus in 431. It fails to acquit Plutarch of the psychological absurdity. In any case, the proof that Plutarch's *aporia* in c. 30 is the enactment of the decree, not why Pericles refused to abrogate it, comes in 30. 4. Plutarch states that the Megarians denied the murder of Anthemocritus and instead fixed the blame on Pericles and Aspasia: Μεγαρεῖς δὲ τὸν ᾿Ανθεμοκρίτου φόνον ἀπαρνούμενοι, τὰς αἰτίας εἰς ᾿Ασπασίαν καὶ Περικλέα τρέπουσι. The blame, *tas aitias*, for what? For the murder of Anthemocritus, for Charinus' decree, for the outbreak of war? The lines from the *Acharnians* which the Megarians quote show that what they denied was that the murder of Anthemocritus was the cause of the enactment of the Megarian decree:

πόρνην δὲ Σιμαίθαν ἰόντες Μέγαράδε
νεανίαι κλέπτουσι μεθυσοκότταβοι·
κᾆθ᾿ οἱ Μεγαρῆς ὀδύναις πεφυσιγγωμένοι
ἀντεξέκλεψαν ᾿Ασπασίας πόρνας δύο.

For the lines immediately following the point at which Plutarch breaks off are of course those making the Olympian thunder and lighten and pass a law written like a drinking-song, namely, the Megarian decree. Of the utmost importance is the distinction we must make (but which seems not to have been made) between Aristophanes' explanation of the Megarian decree as the cause of

general treatment of Aristeides. Had Plutarch believed that the predictable progression of emotion had been disrupted (i.e. that Anthemocritus' mild and reasonable embassy followed the Megarian decree), the anomaly would have drawn his comment, just as Pericles' apparently curious behavior regarding the Megarian decree in fact has done.

19. διὸ καὶ μάλιστα πρὸς τοῦτο Περικλῆς ἐναντιωθεὶς καὶ παροξύνας τὸν δῆμον ἐμμεῖναι τῇ πρὸς τοὺς Μεγαρεῖς φιλονικίᾳ, μόνος ἔσχε τοῦ πολέμου τὴν αἰτίαν.

the Peloponnesian War and Aristophanes' explanation of Pericles' motives for enacting the Megarian decree. And the Megarians here are cited as putting forward Aristophanes' comic explanation of Pericles' motives for its enactment. Can we seriously suppose Plutarch ignorant even of this or that the Megarians were as confused as we have made Plutarch, so that they are made to counter an accusation about a murdered herald by reference to an event – the rape of wanton women – everybody in the world[20] knew allegedly incited Pericles to pass the Megarian decree?

The manifest absurdity of the 'Megarian explanation' as an historically authentic claim does not in the least affect the conclusion that Plutarch has been talking about the reasons for the enactment of the Megarian decree.[21] The allegedly confused[22] first sentence of 31 is therefore sensible and not the helpless assertion of an author who does not know what decree he is talking about. He is speaking of the Megarian decree, and the sentence is resumptive. 'Thus its origin is not easy to know' i.e. the Athenians and Megarians differ as to the reason for its enactment) 'but everybody is united in blaming Pericles for not cancelling the psephism': τὴν μὲν οὖν ἀρχὴν ὅπως ἔσχεν οὐ ῥᾴδιον γνῶναι, τοῦ δὲ μὴ λυθῆναι τὸ ψήφισμα πάντες ὡσαύτως τὴν αἰτίαν ἐπιφέρουσι τῷ Περικλεῖ.

Plutarch's account can therefore be understood as internally consistent and historically sensible. The only difficulty, perhaps, concerns the decree of Charinus. The question arises that if Plutarch thought that Anthemocritus' embassy and the dispute about the *hiera orgas* preceded the Megarian decree, did he not also believe that Charinus' decree preceded it? There seems to be no compelling reason to suppose so. Such an assumption is based on the ruling view of c. 30 – that Plutarch was hopelessly confused – and it can be rejected if we suppose that he was not. For it is plausible to infer that Plutarch simply was finishing up the story of Anthemocritus and the Megarian question, and Charinus' decree is part of the story. For although one scholar conveys the impres-

20. Hence Plutarch's characterization of the verses as 'notorious and hackneyed': περιβοήτοις καὶ δημώδεσι.
21. I therefore see no reason to suppose, with K. J. Dover, *AJP* 87 (1966), 203ff., that the explanation derives from Megarian historians.
22. Connor, *AJP* 83 (1962), 227f.

sion that Anthemocritus' embassy and death is a footnote to the central fact of Charinus' decree,[23] the priorities were reversed for Plutarch. Charinus' decree is a footnote to Anthemocritus, for it dictated his burial at the Dipylon gate[24] and signals the last stage of the hostility. For artistic considerations, it was the appropriate point at which to bring it in; and if Plutarch were clear in his chronology and supposed that it was self-evident to his readers, he could hardly anticipate that it would become a chronological problem for us. The point needs emphasis that there is no hint in the ancient literature of the slightest chronological problem involving the Megarian decree, though it has been assumed in support of one thesis or another or in order to constrain the passage of Plutarch here under discussion. The dispute, for example, about the date of the trial of Pheidias[25] is purely modern, just as is the question of the date of the Megarian decree itself. These may be legitimate questions, but there is no evidence of polemic, disagreement or uncertainty among the ancients.[26] The reason for Plutarch's nonchalance in c. 30, if that is what it is, therefore derives from the conviction that the events he mentioned were too well-known to make difficulties for anyone. To him and, he presumed, to his reader, Pericles' enactment of the decree and his refusal to rescind it were merely two sides of the same coin.

One may therefore believe that there is ancient authority for a sequence of events, already inferred by de Ste Croix,[27] beginning with the dispute about the *hiera orgas*, leading to Anthemocritus' embassy, his death and the passage of the exclusionary decree. One consequence of this is that certain adventurous assumptions which have been made about possible dislocation of the tradition on the basis of the supposed confusion of Plutarch or his sources

---

23. *Ibid.*, pp. 226f.

24. Cf. Harpocration, s.v. Anthemokritos.

25. See Jacoby's entire commentary on Philochorus F. 121.

26. As to Pheidias, there was, of course, a dual tradition as to where he died – in Athens or in Olympia – but I am speaking of the date of his trial; see note 55 for the likely date in Philochorus of the Megarian decree. Nor does the error of the scholiast to *Peace* 246, who attributes Pericles' exclusionary decree to Charinus, suggest more than his own confusion – assuming that the scholium (already corrupt) has not been so abbreviated as to report his words incorrectly. (I see no indication in schol. *Acharnians* 527 and *Peace* 609 of confusion between Pericles' and Charinus' decree (de Ste Croix, *Origins*, p. 392).)

27. Pp. 249f.

can be discarded.[28] Plutarch's account is unproblematic and presumably historical. There is no compelling reason for ejecting Anthemocritus from the historical record, for such an embassy is at least compatible with Thucydides' narrative, and no one will wonder at Thucydides' having ignored the role of the herald who considers how little Thucydides makes of the entire question.[29] As to Aristophanes, Anthemocritus' embassy, if historical, was not a proper subject for amusement in 425 or 421.

But although the tradition about the order of events can be made to yield an acceptable pattern, the question that tantalized Plutarch remains as troublesome as ever and has affected our views of the decree's importance and even its date. Why was Pericles so unyielding, and how could Thucydides not give predominance to an issue which to Aristophanes was the cause of the war? Beloch's assumption,[30] that Pericles wanted war, inevitable in any case, to break out in order to secure his position against internal attack, has been distasteful to most scholars[31] – though Thuc. 2. 65. 8 is hardly a refutation of it, as many suppose.[32] But one may well believe that if Pericles' position actually was parlous, any move to bring war on would only have compounded it. To Brunt,[33] who considered the decree important but who respected Thucydides' decision not to class it among the *aitiai* of the war, the hypothesis was suggested that the decree long had antedated the complaints of the Megarians. On a different tack, de Ste Croix, in his recent and provocative study, accepts the usual date and supposes that the decree was quite as trivial as Thucydides implied.[34] Far from being an economic embargo, the decree was not even necessarily 'belligerent'; its purpose was to humiliate the Megarians, not destroy them, the reason being that they were accursed because they had appropriated a portion of the *hiera orgas*. Hence they were excluded from the Athenian agora (but not from Athens) and from the harbors of the allied cities (but not necessarily from their markets).[35]

---

28. See above, p. 215.
29. 1. 67. 4; 139. 1–2, 4; 140. 3–5; 144. 2.
30. *G.G.* ii². 1, pp. 292ff.
31. See, e.g., de Ste Croix, *Origins*, p. 237.
32. *Ibid.*   33. *AJP* 72 (1951), 269–82.
34. *Origins*, pp. 225ff.
35. See, especially, pp. 252ff.

The novelty of the study, and its implications for our assessment of the tradition, make the work important. But the difficulties are formidable, for this hypothesis has not so much been developed from the implications of the evidence as it has been tailored to conform with them. On purely general grounds, the conjunction in Thucydides of the words harbors and agora[36] – in that order and not the reverse – irresistibly suggests that trade is at issue and that Thucydides must have phrased it differently if it were not.[37] De Ste Croix' argument that an exclusionary trade embargo would have been tantamount to a breach of the peace[38] will not embarrass those who have been uncomfortable about Thucydides' treatment of the decree for precisely that reason and who note that the Megarians made the complaint 'that they were excluded from the harbors of the cities in the Athenian empire and from the agora of Attica contrary to the treaty' (1. 67. 4). Again, the traditional assumption of exclusion from trade in the territory of a particular state in time of peace may be otherwise unknown,[39] but it remains more attractive than de Ste Croix's alternative,[40] that a state would have banned the Megarians from the use of all the harbors of the allies in answer to a religious infraction, and not to penalize them economically, and that when the Athenians spoke of harbors they meant areas with that formal designation and not any point at which a trading vessel could put to shore. This is equally unparalleled and rather more eccentric. Nor is a list of hypothetical ways in which the Athenians could have inflicted heavier economic damage on Megara[41] evidence that the Megarian decree was therefore not intended to inflict economic damage.

36. 1. 67. 4; 139. 1. The order is reversed in 144. 2.

37. The prominent mention of temples in the decree might also reasonably be expected.

38. P. 256; this argument depends entirely on de Ste Croix's belief that 'the Athenians did not want war'; and even if that were true, it would not follow that they were unwilling to risk it.

39. Perdikkas, however, utilized this technique against Methone (*IG* I², 57. 18ff. = Meiggs–Lewis, no. 65); the Thasians, late in the fifth century, could interdict trade from their Peraea (*IG* xii Suppl. 347, ii, 8–10 = H. W. Plecket, *Epigraphica* i, no. 2); and pseudo-Xenophon 2. 11 expresses the concept as a generality.

40. Especially pp. 284ff.

41. Pp. 259–61.

De Ste Croix's hypothesis, in fact, only compounds the dilemma which provoked Plutarch's mystification, Beloch's idiosyncratic view, and Brunt's theory of an earlier date for the Megarian decree. For how do we then explain the importance attached to the Megarian decree by Aristophanes and the implication he seems to make that the decree was a trade embargo? The attempt by de Ste Croix to show that of the two main passages, *Peace* 605ff. is pure invention[42] and *Acharnians* 795ff. finds its explanation in events after 431[43] is therefore central to his case.

Peace 605–9 may be translated as follows: 'First of all Pheidias started it by faring badly. / Then Pericles, afraid of sharing his fate, / fearing your natures and your ferocious temper, / before he himself suffered something dreadful, fired the city / by casting into it the tiny spark of the Megarian decree.'[44] Trygaios in 615 states that he formerly had heard nothing of these simple facts and the chorus agrees. Now since Pheidias probably was tried in 438/7, 'we can safely ignore', according to de Ste Croix, 'the attempt to connect Pheidias with the Megarian decree'.[45] This shows 'that there is *no truth whatever* in Hermes' allegations against Pericles in the *Peace*; the whole thing is not mere exaggeration but pure invention by Aristophanes'.[46] The condemnation is a little sweeping. Pheidias did fare badly; Pericles did pass the Megarian decree; and so the whole thing is not demonstrably an invention and the Megarian decree therefore a triviality. One can insist that Aristophanes' jest fails to justify Beloch's hypothesis and even that Aristophanes unknowingly telescoped the fate of Pheidias and Pericles' enactment of the decree – though that is neither necessary nor likely, whatever the scholiast may have thought.[47] But Aristophanes' invention does not undermine the assumption that for him and his audience the decree was the cause of the war. For his invention simply consists in the connection made between Pheidias' trial and Pericles' motive for causing war. What is presupposed, and is not part of that invention, and what de Ste

42. P. 236.
43. Pp. 237ff.
44. πρῶτα μὲν γὰρ †αὐτῆς ἦρξεν† Φειδίας πράξας κακῶς· / εἶτα Περικλέης φοβηθεὶς μὴ μετάσχοι τῆς τύχης, / τὰς φύσεις ὑμῶν δεδοικὼς καὶ τὸν αὐτοδὰξ τρόπον, / πρὶν παθεῖν τι δεινὸν αὐτός, ἐξέφλεξε τὴν πόλιν / ἐμβαλὼν σπινθῆρα μικρὸν Μεγαρικοῦ ψηφίσματος.
45. P. 236.   46. *Ibid.*   47. At 605.

Croix's analysis does not even speak to, is that the Megarian decree was of cardinal importance.

De Ste Croix's consideration of the chief passage in the *Acharnians* is more fruitful. Many scholars have been too ready to read into the play proof of the decree's adverse effects upon the Megarian economy.[48] Consistent with his belief that the enactment did not intend the infliction of economic damage against Megara, the unanswerable argument is advanced that the double invasion of the Megarid sufficiently explains the hunger of the Megarians mocked in the play. But this proper criticism of some modern exegesis does not affect the main issue. An economic boycott in 432 cannot be disproven by the fact that conditions drastically deteriorated from 431;[49] and the argument is not relevant to Aristophanes' belief that the Megarian decree caused the war. For after mentioning Pericles' motives in passing it (the Megarian kidnap of two of Aspasia's females), Aristophanes thus continues in lines 530–43:

> 'Then Pericles the Olympian in his wrath / thundered, lightened, threw Hellas into confusion, / passed laws that were written like drinking songs / (decreeing) that the Megarians shall not be on our land, in our market, / on the sea or on the continent.[50] // Then the Megarians, since they were starving little by little, / begged the Lacedaemonians to have the decree / arising from the three strumpets withdrawn. / But we were unwilling, though they asked us many times. / Then came the clash of the shields. / Someone will say it was not right. But say, then, what was. / Come, if a Lacedaemonian sailed out in a boat / and denounced and confiscated a Seriphian puppy, / would you have sat still?'[51]

The claim that the crucial line, that the Megarians actually were

48. P. 237. 49. P. 238.
50. 'In heaven': Bentley. See de Ste Croix, *Origins*, p. 392.
51. ἐντεῦθεν ὀργῇ Περικλέης οὐλύμπιος / ἤστραπτ' ἐβρόντα ξυνεκύκα τὴν Ἑλλάδα, / ἐτίθει νόμους ὥσπερ σκόλια γεγραμμένους, / ὡς χρὴ Μεγαρέας μήτε γῇ μήτ' ἐν ἀγορᾷ / μήτ' ἐν θαλάττῃ μήτ' ἐν ἠπείρῳ μένειν. / ἐντεῦθεν οἱ Μεγαρῆς, ὅτε δὴ 'πείνων βάδην, / Λακεδαιμονίων ἐδέοντο τὸ ψήφισμ' ὅπως / μεταστραφείη τὸ διὰ τὰς λαικαστρίας· / κοὐκ ἠθέλομεν ἡμεῖς δεομένων πολλάκις. / κἀντεῦθεν ἤδη πάταγος ἦν τῶν ἀσπίδων. / ἐρεῖ τις, οὐ χρῆν· ἀλλὰ τί ἐχρῆν, εἴπατε. / φέρ' εἰ Λακεδαιμονίων τις ἐκπλεύσας σκάφει / ἀπέδοτο φήνας κυνίδιον Σεριφίων, / καθῆσθ' ἂν ἐν δόμοισιν;

starving (535), 'is not to be taken seriously'[52] because in fact they would not yet have come to that pass, does not weaken the conclusion that this line shows Aristophanes' association of the decree with the economic condition of Megara. That it is an exaggeration or even an impossibility is less important than the connection in Aristophanes' mind between the two. Precisely the same connection is involved in the jest about the Seriphian puppy. For Aristophanes' claim that the Athenians would not sit by idly if the Spartans were to sail out and confiscate the puppy pinpoints the economic grievance even if the jest is absurd.[53]

In brief, the basic objection to de Ste Croix's interpretation of Aristophanes' evidence is that the method he has applied wrenches the play out of the real world and Aristophanes' humor out of contact with the reality it needs in order to be funny. The difficulty of determining whether there is any truth to an Aristophanic jest makes it legitimate to be skeptical about one alleged fact or another. But it does not thereby follow that it is legitimate to reverse things and infer that the occasion for jesting is also a jest. Aristophanes attests the importance of the Megarian decree because he builds on it humorously by motivating Pericles by way of Aspasia and Pheidias. He mocks the language of the decree, the reasons for its enactment, and its effects on the Megarians. These comic inventions do not cancel the decree's importance but presuppose it, and nothing in the world suggests that Aristophanes invented his own raw material.

The alternative view of Brunt, that the Megarian decree, if important, was early, perhaps around 440, has been noted by most scholars mainly to be rejected.[54] Aristophanes brings the decree's enactment into close causal conjunction with the beginning of the war; and it seems ingenuity misspent to argue Aristophanes into a position counter to the impression he gives, especially since that

52. P. 241.
53. The same inference follows from verses 820f., where the Megarian is about to have his piglet-daughters confiscated by the sycophant. His remark – τοῦτ' ἐκεῖν', ἵκει πάλιν / ὅθενπερ ἀρχὰ τῶν κακῶν ἁμῖν ἔφυ – is clearly a reference to the Megarian decree (*pace* de Ste Croix, *Origins*, p. 386). The beginning of the Megarians' difficulties is the war, or rather the cause of it; verses 520–2, with which de Ste Croix instead connects them, merely form a prologue to the Aristophanic cause of lines 523ff.
54. See, e.g., Kagan, *Ovtbreak* pp. 257ff.

impression is easily compatible with Thucydides and Philochorus.[55] Indeed, it is more than merely compatible, for if the interval separating the enactment of the Megarian decree and their complaints about it were considerable, Thucydides' silence would be utterly irresponsible. It would have concealed a fact essential to the reader's estimate of the validity of the Megarians' complaint and the Spartan ultimatum since in that case it was actually a diplomatic ploy used by the Spartans in order to make a crisis (precisely as de Ste Croix inferred).[56]

The main problem, however, which has incited speculation about the Megarian decree remains. Why Thucydides makes comparatively little of the Megarian decree is a question which will be answered by each of us according to our own predilections and prejudices. My own opinion is that the question is not nearly as important as it has been made to appear. Even without Aristophanes, purely on the basis of Thucydides' remarks, we would know that this enactment turned into the supreme diplomatic issue, and so there is no real disharmony as to fact. Pericles believed that the war was inevitable; evidently he had been preparing for it from the time of the Corcyrean alliance.[57] To other Athenians, those, for example, who voted against that alliance and, in general, those who were anti-war, especially those who did not live in the city, the Megarian decree and Pericles' refusal to yield were decisive. But Thucydides did not write his

55. Far more emphasis has been placed on the fact that Philochorus (*F. gr. Hist.* 328 F 121) provides a date for Megarian complaints and not for the Megarian decree itself than that it is natural to assume that Thucydides and Philochorus closely connected in time the decree and complaints about it. The likely reason that no date is given explicitly in relative terms by Thucydides and in absolute terms by Philochorus is that it occurred to neither one that an effort would be made to drive a wedge between the adoption of the decree and Megarian protests. The detail, in any case, given by Philochorus – that the decree was carried by Pericles – suggests that he discussed the decree nowhere else; and this inference is confirmed by the fact that the scholiast, who turned to Philochorus for information about the Megarian decree and not the Megarian protest, found the relevant material at the year 432/1. Alternatively, Philochorus may not have dated the decree because it was undateable, i.e. lacked an archon's name. Even so, he does not seem to have viewed it as a problem.

56. P. 257.

57. Even before it, if the Callias decrees are properly dated to 434/3: see Meiggs, *Athenian Empire*, p. 601 (against Fornara, *GRBS* 11 (1970), 185–96).

history to reflect their views. And since he shared Pericles' perspective, the enactment of this psephism did not seem to him to alter the course of history. In that case, he would have been misleading if he gave it greater prominence, or unnecessarily polemical if he argued against what he considered a mistaken view, and, above all, untrue to his vision if he had written differently from the way he did about the question.[58]

58. This paper was read to a meeting of ancient historians at Chapel Hill, 5 May 1973, and I am grateful for the criticism it engendered.

Herodian and Elagabalus

G. W. BOWERSOCK

THE LATE ADAM PARRY, whom this volume commemorates, was a perceptive reader of Thucydides. The subsequent influence of the great historian of the Peloponnesian War was well known to Parry, and it may therefore be appropriate to dedicate to his memory the following inquiry. In the middle of the third century A.D. Herodian set for himself Thucydides' lofty aims of sound judgment and of accuracy, and he expressed them in Thucydidean language.[1] Modern assessments of Herodian's success have varied, but at the present time there is almost a consensus in the condemnation of this historian. It is not merely that he failed to reach the standard of his classical predecessor: most believe that he did not even make the effort. Frank Kolb, the latest scholar to publish a work on Herodian, labels the history a *Geschichtsroman*.[2] In the same vein Geza Alföldy declares that it is 'mehr eine Art historischen Romans als ein Geschichtswerk'.[3] T. D. Barnes refers to Herodian's 'ubiquitous distaste for facts',[4] and Sir Ronald Syme calls him 'fluent and superficial'.[5] The denigration has acquired the strength and majesty of a chorus, and it has encouraged scholars to dismiss the testimony of Herodian with minimal reflection.[6] Kolb's

1. Note Herod. 1. 1. 1–3, with the phrases ὡς εἴ τι καὶ μυθῶδες λέγοιεν and τὸ δ' ἀκριβὲς τῆς ἐξετάσεως as well as the pointed juxtaposition of ἔργα and λόγοι (so crucial to an understanding of Thucydides: it was the subject of Parry's Harvard doctoral dissertation). On the relation of Herodian to Thucydides, see F. J. Stein, *Dexippus et Herodianus rerum scriptores quatenus Thucydidem secuti sint* (Bonn 1957). For the time at which Herodian wrote his History, see C. R. Whittaker, *Herodian*, Loeb Library, vol. 1 (1969), pp. xvff. (ca. 248), and G. Alföldy, *Ancient Society* 2 (1971), 209ff. (251/3).
2. F. Kolb, *Literarische Beziehungen zwischen Cassius Dio, Herodian und der Historia Augusta* (Bonn 1972), p. 161.
3. G. Alföldy, *Hermes* 99 (1971), 431.
4. T. D. Barnes, *Bonner Historia-Augusta-Colloquium 1970* (1972), 62.
5. R. Syme, *Phoenix* 26 (1972), 275.
6. A few scholars have gone to the other extreme and over-valued Herodian: e.g. F. Altheim, *Literatur and Gesellschaft im ausgehenden Altertum* (Halle 1948),

dissertation has even reached the conclusion that Herodian simply
added dramatic and rhetorical embellishment to the narrative of
Cassius Dio.[7] Yet Herodian, though falling far short of Thucydides'
goals (so did Thucydides) and obviously a creature of his own
sophistic age, states that he is writing of events which he saw and
heard (εἶδόν τε καὶ ἤκουσα).[8] Are we justified in thinking him a
barefaced liar, like the postulated author of the *Historia Augusta*?

No reasonable person, on the evidence now available, will argue
that Herodian is a historian of any great merit, nor will it be
denied that in general Dio's narrative, where it overlaps with
Herodian's, is the more trustworthy. But the two sources do not
maintain a constant level of quality, and generalizations which
apply to their accounts of one stretch of history are not necessarily
applicable to their accounts of others. Herodian's merits, such as
they are, become conspicuous in his narrative of a period which
source critics have tended to avoid: the reign of Elagabalus. Kolb
does not discuss it. Dio's treatment of the period is not one of the
better portions of his work and has accordingly been neglected.
Barnes calls Dio's account 'a violent and hysterical diatribe',[9] and

pp. 165ff.; F. Cassola, *Atti dell'Accad. Pontaniana* n.s. 6 (1956–7), 195ff.;
F. Grosso, *La lotta politica al tempo di Commodo* (Turin 1964). G. Alföldy chides
C. R. Whittaker, whose Loeb Herodian is very valuable in the absence of a full
commentary: 'Selbst C. R. Whittaker hat in seinem ausführlichen Kommentar
zahlreichen Fälschungen Herodians Glauben geschenkt' (*Hermes* 99 (1971),
431, n. 3). A series of articles on Herodian by G. Alföldy takes a strong negative
position and presupposes the conclusions of Kolb, whose work was available to
him before publication. Notable among Alföldy's papers, in addition to the one
in *Hermes* already cited ('Zeitgeschichte und Krisenempfindung bei Herodian'),
are 'Cassius Dio und Herodian über die Anfänge des neupersischen Reiches'
in *Rh. Mus.* 114 (1971), 360ff.; 'Herodians Person' in *Ancient Society* 2 (1971),
204ff.; and 'Der Sturz des Kaisers Geta und die antike Geschichtsschreibung'
in *Bonner Historia-Augusta-Colloquium 1970* (1972), 19ff.

7. Cf. Kolb, *Literarische Beziehungen*, pp. 160–1: 'Die wohl wichtigste Quelle
für die Historien Herodians war die "Römische Geschichte" des Cassius Dio.
Bei deren Verwertung hat sich Herodian über die Prinzipien einer wahr-
heitsgetreuen historischen Darstellung, zu denen er sich zu Beginn seines
Werkes grossartig bekennt, nicht weniger leicht hinweggesetzt als die HA,
freilich aus anderen Motiven. Das Hauptkennzeichen seines rhetorisch
aufgeblähten, an Fakten überaus armen Werkes, ist das Streben nach farbiger
und dramatischer Darstellung.'

8. Herod. 1. 2. 5.

9. T. D. Barnes, *Bonner Historia-Augusta-Colloquium 1968/9* (1970), 31. Cf.
R. Syme, *Phoenix* 26 (1972), 277: 'Excellent in so many ways, Dio's account
of the reign is confused and marred by defects of structure.'

Millar dismissed it curtly with the words 'Little of this calls for comment'.[10] It is true that Dio admits he was in Asia during Elagabalus' reign,[11] but nevertheless in contrasting him with Herodian we have the good fortune of having Dio's original text, instead of epitomators' excerpts, for part of the reign. No doubt the inevitably indelicate subject matter has deterred many historians from taking a close look at the sources for Elagabalus. In an article of major importance Barnes has shown how to do it by examining the life of the emperor in the *Historia Augusta*.[12] He has demonstrated that this *vita*, far from being a 'farrago of cheap pornography',[13] exhibits a high degree of accuracy in factual reporting, unlike both the *vita Macrini* and the *vita Diadumeni*. It may still be open to question whether Barnes is right in explaining the relatively high quality of the life of Elagabalus as due to the use of Marius Maximus, but his re-evaluation of the life is definitive.

The reputation of Herodian stands to gain somewhat from a consideration of his treatment of Elagabalus. While rhetorical and highly colored, it is still superior to Dio's treatment and at least comparable to that of the *Historia Augusta*. It is, moreover, independent of the former and not the source of the latter. In these respects it seriously undermines Kolb's hypotheses about Herodian's general reliance on Dio and the *Historia Augusta*'s use of Dio and Herodian.

A series of distinctive items in Herodian calls for attention.

I. The names of Elagabalus and Alexander (Herod. 5. 3. 3)

Herodian says that Soaemias' son was named Bassianus and Mamaea's son Alexianus. These are the emperors Elagabalus and

---

10. F. Millar, *A Study of Cassius Dio* (Oxford 1964), p. 169.

11. Dio 80. 7. 4.

12. Barnes, *Bonner Historia-Augusta-Colloquium 1970* (1972), 53 ('Ultimus Antoninorum'), elaborating his own view advanced in *Bonner Historia-Augusta-Colloquium 1968/9* (1970), 30ff. See also R. Syme, *Emperors and Biography: Studies in the Historia Augusta* (Oxford 1971), pp. 118ff. The superior quality of part of the Elagabalus *vita* (13. 1–17. 7) had been observed long before: O. F. Butler, *Studies in the Life of Heliogabalus*, Univ. Michigan Studies 4 (1910), pp. 140ff.; K. Hönn, *Quellenuntersuchungen zu den Viten des Heliogabalus und des Severus Alexander* (Leipzig 1910 [*sic*] and 1911), pp. 30ff.

13. R. Syme, *Bonner Historia-Augusta-Colloquium 1964/5* (1966), 258.

Severus Alexander respectively. Dio, on the other hand, calls
Soaemias' son Avitus, and he mentions the *nomen* of the father,
Varius. Mamaea's son he calls Bassianus, and again he gives the
father's *nomen*, this time Gessius.[14] The two historians are in open
contradiction, and the variation in Herodian can scarcely be
described as dramatic or rhetorical. It is generally assumed that
Dio, the better historian, is correct. Yet that assumption is perhaps
hasty and ill considered. No text apart from Dio gives the names
as he does. The *Epitome de Caesaribus* presupposes that Elagabalus
was named Bassianus, for it reports the emperor's command that
his name be altered to Bassiana: *cupiditatem stupri, quam assequi
naturae defectu nondum poterat, in se convertens muliebri nomine Bassianam
se pro Bassiano iusserat appellari.*[15] The name Bassiana looks like part
of the story of Elagabalus as the 'bride' of Zoticus: observe the
HA's words *nubsit et coit* together with Dio's quotation of the
emperor's plea, μή με λέγε κύριον· ἐγὼ γὰρ κυρία εἰμί.[16] Barnes
has shown that the *HA* version of this matter is different from
Dio's and may possibly derive from Marius Maximus.[17] *Bassiana*
in the *Epitome* is likewise independent of Dio and may also
derive from Maximus.[18] The Zoticus story does not occur in
Herodian.

The life of Elagabalus in the *HA* incorporates Varius as
Elagabalus' *nomen*, but there is no hint of Avitus.[19] That *cognomen*
belonged to the husband of Julia Maesa.[20] Furthermore, the
attribution of the name Bassianus to Elagabalus and Alexianus to
Alexander makes the greater sense on four counts: (1) Elagabalus'

14. Dio 79. 30. 2–3. The fathers are Sex. Varius Marcellus (*ILS* 478) and
Gessius Marcianus (*PIR²*, G 171). See the stemma at the end of Barnes, *Bonner
Historia-Augusta-Colloquium 1970* (1972). The Arval brother in 214, M. Julius
Gessius Bassianus (*PIR²*, J 342), is obviously not Alexander (born ca. 209)
though he must be a close relative.

15. *Epit. de Caes.* 23. 3.

16. *HA* Elag. 10. 5; Dio 80. 16. 4. Cf. Dio 80. 14. 4, γυνή τε καὶ δέσποινα
βασιλίς τε ὠνομάζετο, and the marriage to Zoticus' rival, Hierocles (Dio 80. 15.
1–4).

17. Barnes, *Bonner Historia-Augusta-Colloquium 1970* (1972), 60.

18. On the epitomator's use of Maximus, cf. Barnes, *ibid.*, p. 73.

19. *HA* Elag. 1–2. The mention of Bassianus as one of Elagabalus' names at
HA Macr. 8. 4 has no significance in this discussion since the *Macrinus* is heavily
indebted to Herodian (unlike the *Elagabalus*): cf. Barnes, *Bonner Historia-
Augusta-Colloquium 1970* (1972), 58.

20. C. Julius Avitus: *PIR²*, J 190.

claim to the purple was based on the promulgation of the story that he was Caracalla's illegitimate child, and Caracalla was called Bassianus after his maternal grandfather;[21] (2) Soaemias herself had the name Bassiana, whence it could naturally pass to her son;[22] (3) Alexianus was a name in the family of Maesa, as can be seen from the suffect consul of 208 C. Julius Avitus Alexianus:[23] Herodian is the only literary source to mention such a *cognomen*; (4) the romantic change of name to Alexander is more easily explained if the future emperor already had the suggestive name of Alexianus.[24] This last point could not stand alone, but it acquires cogency in the light of those preceding. Perhaps, therefore, Herodian is right, whereas Dio transmits garbled information which percolated to the province of Asia. If indeed Herodian is right, we may assume (since he was certainly not an assiduous researcher) that he was so placed as to have ready access to this information.

In regard to names, it is worth pointing out that neither Dio nor Herodian ever calls Elagabalus by that name or by the Hellenized form Heliogabalus. The emperor is simply and correctly Antoninus to Herodian, while to the outraged Dio he is Pseudantoninus, Sardanapallus, the Assyrian, Tiberinus. Elagabalus (Heliogabalus) was for these writers only the name of the emperor's god, and it is in fact a god's name – 'the god of the mountain'.[25] In addition, no coin or inscription refers to Elagabalus the emperor by that name. There is accordingly no evidence that any contemporary referred to him by the name of his god. It is not impossible, however, that Marius Maximus, on the model of Suetonius in the case of Caligula, recorded a vulgar usage and provided the foundation for the universal appellation from the fourth century to the present. Whatever the truth of that idea, the source of the life in the *HA*

21. The grandfather: *PIR²*, J 202. For Caracalla as Bassianus, cf., e.g., Dio 79. 9. 3 (Βασσιανὸν τὸ ἀρχαῖον ὄνομα), *ILS* 8914.

22. Julia Soaemias Bassiana: *PIR²*, J 704.

23. *PIR²*, J 192. Herodian calls Alexianus τὸ παππῷον ὄνομα, the ancestral name (5. 7. 3).

24. On the change of name: Dio 80. 17. 3; cf. Herod. 5. 7. 3. The *Epit. de Caes.* 23. 4 asserts that Alexander's name had been Marcellus, which is the cognomen of Elagabalus' father. It is hard to believe that this misinformation derives from Marius Maximus.

25. Cf. K. Gross, 'Elagabalus', *Reallexikon für Antike und Christentum*, vol. IV, p. 992.

(Marius Maximus or not) must have called the emperor by his god's name.

II. The black stone of Emesa (Herod. 5. 3. 5)

Herodian is the only source to give a description of the stone. It was rounded at the base and came to a point on top – conical and black, with small projecting bits. No one has questioned the accuracy of Herodian's description. The stone was apparently some kind of meteorite (cf. Herodians' διοπετῆ) not unlike the stone in the Ka'aba at Mecca.[26] Manifestly this information does not derive from Dio. The source used by the *HA* may have been aware of it,[27] but the *HA* does not depend on Herodian here. It is difficult not to believe that Herodian is describing an object which he actually saw.

III. The picture of the emperor (Herod. 5. 5. 6)

An enormous painting of Elagabalus and his god was sent to Rome in anticipation of his arrival there. This detail is nowhere else attested; it would be hard to explain as a dramatic or rhetorical invention. An ἔκφρασις is out of the question since the painting is not described in any detail at all. Herodian had seen it or heard about it. His imperfect knowledge of its resting place in the senate[28] was due to the fact that he was not a senator and had not seen it in that place.

IV. The removal of the Palladium (Herod. 5. 6. 3)

Elagabalus' first choice of a bride for his god in a sacred union was Pallas. Herodian records the removal of the Palladium for this purpose. Elagabalus later decided to bring over Urania from Carthage instead. The importation of Urania is known to Dio as it is to Herodian,[29] but it appears – though, to be sure, we are

26. The parallel was noted by Barnes, *Bonner Historia-Augusta-Colloquium 1970* (1972), 61.
27. Barnes, *ibid.*, p. 61: 'The HA is therefore entirely accurate when it describes the God as the equivalent of Jupiter or Sol.'
28. Cf. Kolb, *Literarische Beziehungen*, p. 11, n. 76.
29. Dio 80. 12. 1.

dealing with the *excerpta* here – that Dio altogether omitted to mention the earlier plan which included the removal of the Palladium. This plan does, however, occur in the well-informed *vita* of Elagabalus in the *HA*, as Barnes points out.[30] The *HA* does not depend upon Herodian, who errs in his report of the place to which the Palladium was taken. But Herodian reports the move, and that is something. It is no rhetorical invention.

Here then are four items in which Herodian appears both superior to Dio and unrelated to him. By contrast, apart from circumstantial details not treated by Herodian, Dio's narrative is better in only one notable point: he knows, like the author of the *HA vita* of Elagabalus, that Diadumenianus was proclaimed Augustus at Apamea during Macrinus' war against Elagabalus. Herodian does not.[31] But Herodian, while eschewing details and diverging from Dio in his account of where Macrinus died, at least knows that Diadumenianus was a παῖς when he died. In the Elagabalus *vita* the child is presented as a grown man.[32]

Errors such as the foregoing do not diminish the force of Barnes' argument for the overall value of the *HA vita*. They do cause concern if Marius Maximus is thought to be the source of these errors as well as of what is accurate. To cite another example: it is stated that Alexander was saluted as Caesar immediately after Macrinus' death in June 218. Barnes proposes that this egregious mistake 'might derive ultimately from Marius Maximus and be a deliberate, contemporary invention from the reign of Severus Alexander'.[33] But it is hard to believe that Maximus would have misreported by three years a major event of recent history, or that anyone could have expected such a misrepresentation to be credited. It might be simpler to assume that a reliable source, which may indeed be Maximus, has been alloyed in the source actually used by the *HA*. And that source may perhaps be Enmann's *Kaisergeschichte*, one of the hardiest plants in the whole

30. *HA* Elag. 6. 8–9; cf. Barnes, *Bonner Historia-Augusta-Colloquium 1970* (1972), 68.

31. Dio 79. 34. 2, 37. 6; *HA* Elag. 1. 4. Cf. Herod. 5. 4. 12; also Barnes, *Bonner Historia-Augusta-Colloquium 1970* (1972), 64.

32. Herod. 5. 4. 12. Cf. Syme, *Phoenix* 26 (1972), 285ff.

33. *HA* Elag. 5. 1; cf. Barnes, *Bonner Historia-Augusta-Colloquium 1970* (1972), 67.

enchanted garden of the *Historia Augusta*.[34] If this notion be countenanced, we shall be relieved of the need to postulate that Maximus, contrary to the usage of both Dio and Herodian, called the last of the Antonines by the name of the god of Emesa. That development can be comfortably placed later.

This trial investigation into certain aspects of the reign of Elagabalus in Herodian indicates that the neglect of the period by many students of later Greek historiography has permitted some insubstantial hypotheses to look stronger than they are. Herodian, while generally inferior to Dio as a source, can at times be an independent, reliable witness in matters of which he happens to have personal knowledge. In the case of Elagabalus he is indepenpent of Dio, and the *HA* is independent of them both. Herodian, and the *HA* are more useful for this reign than they are for many others. It is agreeable to speculate about Herodian's knowledge of names at Emesa or of the black stone. Perhaps the βασιλικαὶ ὑπηρεσίαι to which he so obliquely refers in 1. 2. 5 were in the service of Elagabalus; perhaps he was in Emesa at the time of Elagabalus' elevation and saw the young priest whose appearance in 218 he describes so fully (5. 3. 6–8).[35]

34. On this subject, for which there is a vast bibliography, see Barnes, *Bonner Historia-Augusta-Colloquium 1968/9* (1970), 13ff. ('The Lost Kaisergeschichte and the Latin Historical Tradition'). Syme, *Emperors and Biography*, p. 120 rejects the KG as the source of the *Elagabalus* because 'there is no sign that the KG carried any narrative so extensive'.

35. It is futile to wonder whether these details show Herodian's origins. On this frustrating subject, see Alföldy's article, 'Herodians Person' (cited in n. 6), especially pp. 219ff. It may be noted that Herodian's one explicit reference to Emesa by name (5. 3. 2) employs, as editors agree, a rare form of the name (ἀπὸ 'Εμέσου instead of ἀπὸ 'Εμέσης).